MONOLOGUES FROM LITERATURE

A Sourcebook for Actors

EDITED BY

MARISA SMITH

AND

KRISTIN GRAHAM

Fawcett Columbine
NEW YORK

A Fawcett Columbine Book
Published by Ballantine Books

Library of Congress Catalog Card Number: 89-90913

ISBN: 0-449-90535-7

Cover design by James R. Harris
Text design by Holly Johnson

Manufactured in the United States of America

First Edition: October 1990
20 19 18 17 16 15 14 13

ACKNOWLEDGMENTS

Unqualified gratitude to Jocelyn Beard, writer/researcher extraordinaire, and to Elizabeth Lerner, an editor's editor.

CONTENTS

FOREWORD

Eureka! This collection of monologues, *the first from literature*, is an essential addition to any actor's library. At last an anthology that will shorten the actor's often futile search for unique audition material. When does an actor need a monologue? An actor needs a monologue when an actor needs a job, or to become a member of a workshop or to apply to a school/college or to show to an agent. Producers and directors and agents hear hundreds of monologues, most of which are taken from plays. How many times does an actor have to choose something from a classic and something from a contemporary work? Innumerable. Why does it have to be a play? It doesn't. There are regional auditions held annually for summer jobs in the theatre. Last year a list of at least a dozen plays was circulated with the plea to spare the auditioners these too-often-heard monologues.

Your material does have to present *you*, your ability to interpret, to access your emotional and physical qualities and present them larger than life. If you are twenty years old, please do not bring in a character who is fifty years older. If you are seventy please. . . . I did see a wonderful young actress do Romeo with great freedom and very convincingly. In this instance the exception to the rule worked very well. There also have been productions using a female to play Hamlet. Shakespeare wrote for all male companies. That was in the sixteenth century. Why not adapt his plays to reflect today?

Herein is a tremendous range of centuries and styles, dialects and characters. It is a veritable treasure trove of literary gems. The synopses of the novels, poems, and short stories are miraculously concise. It is strongly recommended that an actor become familiar with the whole body of work for which a monologue is delivered. What a good excuse to re-read *Treasure Island*, *The Odyssey*, *The Last of the Mohicans* and *Jane Eyre*. Remember life without TV?

Is it a regional part you're after? Among others this beautiful book includes the Southernisms of Eudora Welty and William Faulkner, the "roadisms" of Jack Kerouac, and the Los Angeles localisms of Bret

Easton Ellis. Could you use a monologue to exhibit your aptitude with accents? Within these covers you will find *Sophie's Choice* and *Rosamund's Vision*. The latter gives you French, Greek, English, and New Jersey! You also have surprises: satire by Poe, prose by Rimbaud, mystery by Alcott, and other revelations—many others.

You don't have to be an actor to utilize and enjoy *Monologues From Literature*.

—Lee Richardson

INTRODUCTION

The best advice I can offer about the audition process is: never seek advice about auditions. Each one is uniquely different. Even if you've auditioned many times—even a few times for the same director or casting agent—the last experience will have little bearing on the current one. The time of day, the weather, the collective mood of everyone involved, the audition material, the play for which the actors are being sought . . . these are just a few of the variables that will make today's audition different from all others.

So now I'm giving advice: drop your expectations, leave them outside the audition space, stay calm, and decide that you're going to enjoy the variables and learn from what happens. Stay in the moment. Enjoy the process of the audition, don't seek a job. Especially if you really need one.

I've been on both sides of the process. As an actor, I've found it most useful to say to myself, "Alright. I have a chance to study and explore a piece of material and present it to people I (perhaps) admire or wish to meet. I'll work on it as I would work on a role in a rehearsal process, after rehearsal's over, without the director present. I'll do my homework. This could be fun."

A number of years ago, I read for film director Arthur Penn. I'd admired *Bonnie and Clyde* as well as his other pictures, and as the audition approached, I became extremely anxious about it. Then I thought, "Wait a minute. I may not get the job, but at least I'll get a chance to meet Arthur Penn." The director was gracious, the reading went well, and though I didn't get the role, I spent twenty fascinating minutes with an artist whose work I admire. An actor's day could be a lot less interesting.

As a director at auditions, I say to myself, "Keep open. The auditioning actor is capable of showing me something I couldn't possibly understand about the play because I can't see it from his or her angle. As I watch each actor, I'll be able to see more of the play emerge. Perhaps some of my conclusions about the play will be changed. This could be extremely useful and interesting—especially if the actor is reading for a role I don't yet understand as well as I hope to." This has proved true a number of times. When I was auditioning actors for Lincoln Center's *Measure For Measure*, Campbell Scott, with whom I'd worked on another production, was due to read for Isabella's younger brother Claudio. After we exchanged greetings, he launched (to my surprise) into *Angelo*'s great first monologue. I hadn't thought of casting the part with a young actor, but his reading was superb, and by the time Campbell left the room he'd not only won the role but altered significantly my conception of the Isabella-Claudio-Angelo-Duke axis in the production.

As an actor in the audition situation, I have to remind myself that I am not in control of the *social* situation. Then I have to let that be O.K. for myself and actually enjoy it, because I will be in control of the *entire* situation once I begin to read for the part. After all, they need me. No matter who's directing, no matter who's written the play, the actor is the prism through which the script will come to light.

As a director I look for confidence, affability, and a sense of purpose in the auditioning actor. The audition is a process, it is part of the work. Because so much is conditional, because so much judgment is being exercised, a healthy dollop of grace is required from all participants: actor, director, casting director. There's nothing wrong with social grace. After all, the rehearsal process will be an ensemble effort involving collaboration among many people. Everyone will be working together, actors with other actors, as well as designers, company managers, costumiers, dressers, props people, etc. An audition process is really the formation of a family. Or the entrance into one.

As a director, I have little patience with actors who find it their duty to share with me criticisms of the play for which they are auditioning. I'm probably pretty well aware of many of the play's pitfalls and problems. I also love the play, otherwise I wouldn't be doing it in the first place. If you hate the play, why are you auditioning for it? If the answer to that question is, "I need the job," or "My agent thought it would be a good idea for you to see me even though I'm not available or interested in the production," then you shouldn't be in the room. You're breaking the agreement and wasting the time of the director, as well as that of all the other actors waiting to get a chance to audition.

When an auditioning actor enters the stage or room, he is coming into an alien space, one in which he does not have the control a production gives him. He may sense an atmosphere warmed by hope, or charged with despair; it may feel soggy with boredom and frustration or riddled with waves of giddiness. What the previous actor has done can change the reactions and feelings of those who are watching. As an actor, it is up to you to change the energy of that space. Check it out, sense it, then, as you begin to read, make it completely yours. Rather: allow it to be rightfully yours.

Every director is different, of course, but when actors audition for me, they practically have the job as soon as they enter the space. The audition process is really a process of determining whether the actor will continue to keep the job or lose it along the way. It's like a rodeo rider. When he comes out of the gate, he's on the horse. If he can stay on the horse, he wins. It's like an audience's perspective as they watch an actor enter the play. Always, at the beginning of the actor's performance, or as the curtain rises, hopes and expectations are at their highest.

The Watchers—casting directors, directors, assistants, etc.— must look interested. Must actually *be* interested. If the actor does not at first interest you, you must try harder. It's entirely possible that you could be missing someone wonderful just because you think you're not interested. Directors should use days of auditions to hone their ability to concentrate. Even a bad actor or an actor who is not at all "right" for a role will teach you something of interest. Perhaps the actor is going to flower more effectively in another role. Perhaps you never thought of the role being played by an actor like the one you're watching. Could he or she make the role work? Might that actor's interpretation be far more challenging and interesting than the one you'd imagined while studying the play on your own? Think twice. The greatest acting performances have often been the nontraditional ones.

Sometimes actors will ask to read for roles other than the one for which they've been called in to audition. Sometimes, when I've agreed to their requests, I've been surprised and gratified. Occasionally, I've even cast them in those roles. However, I've noticed that the more mature actors, who have come to know their mechanisms and hone their abilities over many years, can be trusted in such situations more consistantly than younger actors. But of course . . . you never know.

Which is the most interesting thing about auditions.

I think this book is a good idea. It can free the actor from working on the same old pieces. It can release him or her into thinking about auditioning in a new way. It may also serve as an introduction to books not yet discovered and return the inveterate reader to forgotten favorites. Just as it's useful for everyone in the performing arts to visualize anything—even so-called "nondramatic literature"—as an act of theater, so it's necessary to contemplate and enjoy and appreciate and understand great literature, good modern writing. As the performing arts of our age succumb to the purely visual, it is necessary to hone our skills with the written word and notice how it can breathe, live, and create visualizations.

—Mark Lamos
Artistic Director
Hartford Stage Company

HOW TO USE THIS BOOK

Fresh audition and rehearsal material is something every actor searches for. We hope you'll be inspired and excited by the richness and variety of the monologues in this collection, which makes use of classic literary works from Homer and Hemingway to popular fiction of today such as *Presumed Innocent* and *Slaves of New York*.

The collection of monologues is arranged chronologically, according to publication. But to get the most out of this book, please refer to the monologue chart beginning on page 299. The chart divides the monologues into sex and age groups, i.e., Young Men/Men/Older Men and Young Women/Women/Older Women. The chart is then further broken down into type of role: dramatic, seriocomic, and comedic; setting; a brief description of the character; and the age range. For example, an actress in search of a monologue that will enable her to showcase her comedic talent would turn to the section of the chart labeled "Young Women" and scan the "Type of Role" column for those marked "Comedy."

The monologues in this book have been selected for their spoken appeal; each one captures a dramatic moment, turning point, emotional transition, or private realization. The length of a monologue varies from a paragraph or two to a page or two of text, and, of course, can be modified as needed. A brief introduction to each monologue gives the actor a sense of the book, but a bibliography at the end provides publishing information including the paperback edition (when available) for actors who want to expand on the monologues here, or to get a larger sense of the work and character.

Many monologues have been "lifted" directly from the text, others have been "created" from a few pages of text. In a few cases ellipses have been used to indicate where the text is not contiguous.

MONOLOGUES
FROM
LITERATURE

THE ODYSSEY

by Homer

c. 700 B.C.

4 MONOLOGUES
Calypso
Odysseus
Agamemnon
Penelope

SETTING: ancient Greece

In this classic epic poem, Homer tells the tale of Odysseus, the hero's hero. Odysseus, the young king of Ithaca, travels to Troy, where he fights for ten years, then spends the next ten years of his life trying to get home. He wanders from adventure to adventure while his wife, the faithful Penelope, staves off the many suitors who desire her hand in marriage and the leadership of Ithaca. Protected by the goddess Athene, Odysseus finally returns home. He strings his famous bow and defeats the suitors before presenting himself to the woman he loves, his journeying done.

CALYPSO

Athene, daughter of Zeus, complains to her father that the nymph Calypso keeps Odysseus captive upon her island. Zeus then sends Hermes to instruct Calypso to release the king from her enchantment. In this monologue, the sea nymph bids farewell to her former captive.

Listen, unhappy man; no need to stay here lamenting longer, no need to let your life be wasted; I am willing now, quite willing, to let you

3

go. Come then; take tools of bronze, cut long beams and fashion them into a wide raft; then build half-decks on it, well above, so that the craft may carry you over the misty ocean. I myself will put food in it, with water and with red wine as well, things that will stave off hunger and please the taste. I will give you clothes to wear and will send a fair wind behind you to let you reach your own land unharmed—all this if it please the gods whose home is wide heaven itself, because they are better able than I both to plan and to achieve.

. . . So be it then—let earth be witness to me in this, and the arching heaven above, and the downward water of the Styx—most solemn and most fearsome of oaths with the blessed gods—that I will plot against you no new mischief to your ruin. No; I have in mind— I will ponder now—the very plans I would shape for myself if ever need pressed as hard on me. My whole bent is to honest dealing; in this breast of mine there is no heart of iron; I have compassion.

Son of Laertes, subtle Odysseus—so then, your mind is firmly set on returning now without delay to your home and country? Go then, and joy go with you, in spite of all. Yet if you knew—if you fully knew—what miseries are fated to fill your cup before you attain your own land, you would choose to stay here, to join with me in calm possession of this domain, to be beyond reach of death—this despite all your zeal to see once more the wife that you yearn for day by day. And yet I doubt if I fall behind her in form and feature—for indeed it would be unbecoming that mortal women should vie in form and face with immortal goddesses.

ODYSSEUS

The hero is befriended by King Akinous, who asks to hear his tale. Here, Odysseus introduces himself and begins his fantastic story.

I am Odysseus, son of Laertes; among all mankind I am known for subtleties, and the fame of me goes up to heaven. The place I live in is far-seen Ithaca; on it stands out Mount Neriton, quivering with leafy coppices; round it are clustered other islands—Dulichium, Same, forested Zacynthus. Ithaca itself is low-lying, farthest out in the sea westwards, and the other islands lie away from it, towards the rising sun. My land is rugged, but knows how to breed brave sons. A man can see no country more lovable than his own, and so it is with myself and Ithaca. There was a time when divine Calypso kept me within her arching caverns and would have had me to be her husband, and another time when subtle Aeaean Circe confined me in her palace and would have had me for husband also. Yet neither of them could win the heart within me; so true it is that nothing is sweeter to a man than his own country and his own parents, even though he were given a sumptuous dwelling-place elsewhere, in a strange land and far from his parents.

Enough; I must speak now of the fearful journeying that Zeus enforced on me when I left Troy and made for home.

AGAMEMNON

Odysseus summons the spirits of those comrades now dead to learn of their fates. Here, King Agamemnon tells of his wife Clytemnestra's treachery and his death at her hands.

Son of Laertes, subtle Odysseus, Poseidon roused no hideous blast of contrary winds to destroy me among the ships that went with me, nor did hostile men strike me down on land. It was Aegisthus and my accursed wife who plotted death and destruction for me; he invited me to his house and gave me a feast and killed me as a man kills an ox at stall. Thus I died the most pitiful of deaths, and my comrades too were killed around me mercilessly like white-tusked boars in the house of some rich and powerful man, at a wedding or feast or sumptuous banquet. You have seen in your time many men meet death, in single combat or violent battle, but much more then would compassion have pierced your heart, had you seen how we lay there in the hall by the mixing-bowl and the laden tables, while the whole floor seethed with blood. But most pitiful of all was the cry I heard from Priam's daughter Cassandra as treacherous Clytemnestra slaughtered her over me; and as I died with the sword thrust through me I raised my hands and beat them upon the ground; but that shameless one turned away from me and even as I went down to Hades' house would not stretch out her hand to close my eyes and mouth. Truly nothing is deadlier and loathsomer than a woman when she sets her mind on deeds like these. Thus did my wife devise this abomination, contriving murder against her own wedded husband, when I had been thinking all the while how children and household would bid me welcome home. By her utter wickedness of will she has poured dishonour both on herself and on every woman that lives hereafter, even on one whose deeds are virtuous.

PENELOPE

Odysseus' wife greets her long-lost king. She blames the gods for their misery and then offers her heart to her husband.

Odysseus, do not be angry with me now; you were always the most understanding of mankind. It was the gods who sent us misery, grudging us a life with each other, grudging us the happiness of our prime and the passage thence to the threshold of old age. But do not hold it against me now, do not nurse your anger, if I did not lovingly welcome you as soon as I had set eyes upon you. Deep in my heart I always have had misgivings that some strange man might come and beguile me with his words; schemers of dark designs are many. There was Argive Helen, child of Zeus; never would she have lain with a foreign lover if she had but known that the warrior sons of the Achaeans were to carry her back again to her own land. But the god impelled her to do the shameless deed; not till then did her mind conceive that fatal folly that was the beginning of distress not only for her but for us also. But now—you have told me beyond all contradiction the secrets of how our bed was built, though no one ever set eyes upon it but you and I and that one maid, Actoris, whom my father gave me when first I came here and who kept the door of that strong-built room. Now indeed you have won my stubborn heart at last.

DON QUIXOTE

by Miguel de Cervantes

1605, 1615

2 MONOLOGUES
Don Quixote
Sancho Panza

SETTING: Spain, sixteenth century

Don Quixote is the story of a wealthy Spanish landowner who becomes obsessed with reading popular novels of chivalry and derring-do. He assumes the identity of a bold knight and sets forth upon his old horse, Rozinante, to perform deeds of valor for Dulcinea, the name he gives a local peasant girl whom he sees as his lady fair. He appoints Sancho Panza, a roly-poly peasant, as his squire, promising the little man an island kingdom in return for his service. Although Sancho happily leaves his nagging wife behind to accompany Quixote on his mad adventures, he never fails to point out the discrepancies between his master's fantasies and what he believes to be real.

DON QUIXOTE

In one of their early adventures, Quixote, with Sancho at his side, spots a group of three windmills. He believes that they are evil giants and prepares to attack them.

Fortune is guiding our affairs better than we ourselves could have wished. Do you see over yonder, friend Sancho, thirty or forty hulking giants? I intend to do battle with them and slay them. With their

7

spoils we shall begin to be rich, for this is a righteous war and the removal of so foul a brood from off the face of the earth is a service God will bless.

Those you see over there, with their long arms; some of them have them well-nigh two leagues in length.

It is clear that you are not experienced in adventures. Those are giants, and if you are afraid, turn aside and pray whilst I enter into fierce and unequal battle with them.

Fly not, cowards and vile caitiffs; one knight alone attacks you! Although you flourish more arms than the giant Briareus, you shall pay for it!

SANCHO PANZA

At the end of Part II, Don Quixote has been forced by his concerned family to give up chivalry. Returned to his family home, he soon becomes ill. As he lies dying, his old friend Sancho pleads with him to live and to lead them on to greater glory. It is too late, however, for the old don passes away with dreams of his former valor shining in his eyes.

Woe is me! Don't die on me; but take my advice and live on for many a year; the maddest trick a man can play in his life is to yield up the ghost without more ado, and without being knocked on the head or stabbed through the belly to mope away and die of the doldrums. Shame on you, master; don't let the grass grow under your feet. Up with you this instant, out of your bed, and let us put on our shepherd's clothing and off with us to the fields as we had resolved a while back. Who knows but we may find Lady Dulcinea behind a hedge, disenchanted and as fresh as a daisy. If it's your defeat that is tearing your heart, lay the blame on me and say that it was my fault in not tightening Rozinante's girths enough, and that was why you were unhorsed. You must remember, too, sir, from your books on knight-errantry how common it was for knights to jostle one another out of the saddle, and he who's lying low today may be crowning his victory tomorrow.

CANDIDE

by Voltaire

Translated by Lowell Blair

1759

4 MONOLOGUES
Dr. Pangloss
Cunegonde
Old Woman
Cacambo

SETTING: Europe, early eighteenth century

Candide by Voltaire (François-Marie Arouet) is a biting satire on philosophical optimism. The story follows the trials and tribulations of Candide, a naive young man; his beloved Cunegonde; and their tutor, Dr. Pangloss, a "doctrinaire optimist" who claims that everything is for the best in this best of all possible worlds.

During the course of the story, the three are attacked by Bulgars, torn from their home in Thunder-ten-tronckh, and separated—each character enduring tortures worse than the other. Cunegonde is raped, stabbed, kidnapped, and forced to be the mistress of both a wealthy Jew and the Grand Inquisitor. Candide is shanghaied, beaten, and left for dead. Dr. Pangloss contracts syphilis, is stabbed, and hanged in an auto-da-fé.

Through it all, they steadfastly believe that "all is for the best." After many sea voyages, scrapes with cannibals, the Inquisition, pirates, and deaths, they finally retire to a little farm where each puts their skills to work as Candide tends his garden.

DR. PANGLOSS

After a period of separation, Candide discovers his mentor begging along the roadside. The good doctor has contracted syphilis and is gravely ill, yet he clings to his optimism.

Alas, it was love: love, the consoler of the human race, the preserver of the universe, the soul of all sensitive beings, tender love.

My dear Candide, you knew Paquette, our noble baroness's pretty maid; in her arms I tasted the delights of paradise, and they produced these torments of hell with which you see me devoured: she was infected with them, and by now she may have died of them. It was a present given to her by a learned Franciscan friar who had derived it from the point of origin, for it was given to him by an old countess, who received it from a cavalry captain, who owed it to a marquise, who got it from a page, who was given it by a Jesuit who, while still a novice, had received it in a direct line from a shipmate of Christopher Columbus. As for me, I won't give it to anyone, because I'm dying.

It was an indispensable element in the best of worlds, a necessary ingredient, because if Columbus, on an American island, hadn't caught that disease which poisons the source of generation, which often even prevents generation, and which is obviously opposed to the great goal of nature, we would now have neither chocolate nor cochineal. It must also be noted that so far, on our continent, this disease is peculiar to us, like religious controversy. The Turks, Indians, Persians, Chinese, Siamese and Japanese are still unacquainted with it; but there's a sufficient reason for their also coming to know it within a few centuries. Meanwhile, it's made amazing progress among us, especially in those great armies, composed of honest and well-bred mercenaries, which decide the fate of nations: it can safely be said that whenever thirty thousand men fight a pitched battle against an equal number of enemy troops, there are about twenty thousand syphilitics on each side.

CUNEGONDE

Candide's true love describes how she came to be attacked by Bulgars and sold into slavery.

I was in my bed, sleeping soundly, when it pleased heaven to send the Bulgars to our beautiful castle of Thunder-ten-tronckh. They butchered my father and brother, and cut my mother to pieces. A big, six-foot Bulgar saw that I'd fainted at the sight and began raping me. That brought me back to my senses; I screamed, struggled, bit, clawed and tried to scratch his eyes out, not knowing that everything happening in my father's castle was quite customary. The brute stabbed me on the left side; I still have the scar.

A Bulgar captain came in and saw the blood streaming from me. The soldier paid no attention to him. The brute's lack of respect for him made the captain angry, so he killed him while he was still on me. Then he had my wounds dressed and took me to his quarters as a prisoner of war. I washed the few shirts he had, and did his cooking. I must confess that he found me very pretty, and I won't deny that he was a handsome, well-built man with soft, white skin. But he had little intelligence and knew little about philosophy. . . . Three months later, he'd lost all his money and become tired of me, so he sold me to Don Issachar, a Jew who traded in Holland and Portugal and was passionately fond of women. Don Issachar took a great liking to my person, but he was unable to triumph over it: I resisted him better than I had the Bulgar soldier. A lady of honor may be raped once, but it strengthens her virtue. . . .

One day the Grand Inquisitor noticed me at mass. He stared at me for a long time and sent word to me that he had some secret matters to discuss with me. I was taken to his palace. I told him of my birth, and he pointed out to me how degrading it was for a lady of my rank to belong to an Israelite. It was then suggested to Don Issachar that he should cede me to His Eminence. Don Issachar, who's the court banker and a man of influence, flatly refused. The Inquisitor threatened him with an auto-da-fé. Finally Don Issachar, intimidated, made a bargain whereby the house and I belong to both of them in common: to him on Mondays, Wednesdays and the Sabbath, and to the Inquisitor on the other days of the week. The agreement has been in effect for six months now, but not without quarrels, because it's often been undecided whether the night between Saturday and Sunday belongs to the old law or the new. For my part, I've resisted them both so far, and I think that's why I've always been loved.

OLD WOMAN

Cunegonde's servant tells the story of her girlhood as a princess and how she came to be kidnapped by pirates and taken to North Africa.

My eyes haven't always been bloodshot and red-rimmed, my nose hasn't always touched my chin, and I haven't always been a servant. I am the daughter of Pope Urban X and the Princess of Palestrina. Until the age of fourteen I was brought up in a palace so magnificent that all the castles of your German barons couldn't have served as its stable, and one of my dresses was worth more than all the splendor in Westphalia. I grew in beauty, grace and talent, amid pleasures, respects and hopes. I had already begun to inspire love. My breasts were forming, and what breasts! They were white and firm, and as shapely as those of the Venus de' Medici. And what eyes I had! What eyelids! What black eyebrows! What fire shone from my two pupils, dimming the glitter of the stars, as the local poets used to tell me! . . .

I was betrothed to a sovereign prince of Massa-Carrara. What a prince! . . . I loved him as we always love the first time: with idolatry and wild passion. . . . I was about to reach the peak of my happiness when an old marchesa who'd once been my prince's mistress invited him to her house for chocolate. He died in less than two hours, with horrible convulsions. But that's only a trifle. My mother, in despair, though less deeply afflicted than I, decided to leave the tragic scene for a while. She had a beautiful estate near Gaeta. We set out in a galley that was gilded like the altar of St. Peter's in Rome. Suddenly a Barbary pirate ship bore down on us and boarded us. Our soldiers defended themselves like soldiers of the pope: they all knelt, threw down their arms and asked the pirates for absolution *in articulo mortis*. . . .

I won't tell you how painful it is for a young princess to be taken off to Morocco as a slave with her mother. You can easily imagine everything we had to suffer on board the pirate ship. My mother was still quite beautiful; our ladies-in-waiting and even our ordinary maids had more charms than can be found in all of Africa. As for me, I was exquisitely lovely; I was beauty and grace personified, and I was a virgin. Not for long, though.

. . . I've grown old in poverty and shame, with only half a behind, always remembering that I'm a pope's daughter. I've wanted to kill myself a hundred times, but I still love life. That ridiculous weakness is perhaps one of our most pernicious inclinations. What could be more stupid than to persist in carrying a burden that we constantly want to cast off, to hold our existence in horror, yet cling to it nonetheless, to fondle the serpent that devours us, until it has eaten our heart?

CACAMBO

Candide's valet successfully reasons with ferocious cannibals who are about to consume his master and him.

Gentlemen, you expect to eat a Jesuit today; that's perfectly all right: nothing could be more just than to treat your enemies that way, for natural law teaches us to kill our neighbor, and that's how people behave all over the world. If we don't exercise the right to eat him, it's because we have other things to make a good meal of. But you don't have the same resources as we do, and it's certainly better to eat your enemies than abandon the fruit of your victory to crows and ravens. However, gentlemen, you wouldn't want to eat your friends. You think you're about to put a Jesuit on the spit, but you're actually about to roast your defender, the enemy of your enemies. I myself was

born in your country, and this gentleman is my master. Far from being
a Jesuit, he's just killed a Jesuit and is wearing his clothes: that's the
cause of your mistake. To verify what I'm saying, take his robe, bring
it to the nearest border post of the Fathers' kingdom, and find out
whether or not my master has killed a Jesuit officer. It won't take
long, and you can still eat us if you find out I've lied to you. But if
I've told the truth, you're too well acquainted with the principles of
international law, morality and justice not to spare our lives.

LES LIAISONS DANGEREUSES (DANGEROUS LIAISONS)

by Pierre Choderlos de Laclos

Translated by Lowell Blair

1782

3 MONOLOGUES
Valmont 1
The Marquise
Valmont 2

SETTING: France, late eighteenth century

This brilliant novel first appeared in 1782 and proceeded to shock and scandalize the French aristocracy with its frighteningly perceptive depictions of their jaded lifestyles. Pierre Choderlos de Laclos, a career military officer, tells the story of the wicked Vicomte de Valmont, his partner in crime, the Machiavellian Marquise de Merteuil, and their infernal plottings against their peers in society.

Valmont wishes to seduce the lovely and pious Madame de Tourvel for the sole pleasure of watching her renounce all that she holds dear. He wishes to insinuate lust between this poor woman, her wedding vows, and her belief in God.

The icy Marquise's plans are far more sinister. Having been spurned by a man who is now engaged to marry a lovely young virgin, the Marquise seeks to have the virgin seduced by Valmont as revenge.

What ensues is a tale so complex and titillating, it is no wonder that it continues to shock present-day readers.

VALMONT 1

The evil Vicomte writes to the Marquise of his desire to seduce the innocent Madame de Tourvel.

Your orders are charming and your way of giving them is more charming still; you would make despotism attractive. As you know, this is not the first time I have been sorry that I am no longer your slave, and although you now call me a monster, I never recall without pleasure the days when you used to honor me with sweeter names. Often I wish to deserve them again, and to end by giving the world an example of constancy with you. But we are called to greater things; our destiny is to conquer, and we must follow it. . . .

Do not be angry; and listen to me. You already share all the secrets of my heart, and I am now going to confide to you the greatest project I have ever conceived. . . .

You know Madame de Tourvel, her piety, her conjugal love and her stern principles. That is what I am attacking, that is the foe worthy of me, that is the goal I intend to achieve. . . .

I must also tell you that her husband, the magistrate, is in Burgundy because of an important lawsuit. . . . His inconsolable wife is to remain here for the entire period of her painful temporary widowhood. A Mass every day, a few visits to the poor of the district, prayers morning and evening, solitary walks, pious conversations with my old aunt, and sometimes a dreary game of whist: such were to be her only diversions; but I am preparing more efficacious ones for her. . . . Fortunately it takes four to play whist, and since there is no one here but the local priest, my eternal aunt urged me to sacrifice a few days to her. You may be sure I consented. You cannot imagine how she has been flattering me since then, and especially how edified she has been to see me regularly at prayer and at Mass with her. She does not suspect which divinity I am worshiping.

And so for the past four days I have been in the grip of a powerful passion. You know how keenly I desire and devour obstacles; but what you do not know is how much solitude adds to the ardor of desire. . . . I must have this woman, to save myself from the ridiculousness of being in love with her. . . . How fortunate we are that women defend themselves so badly! Otherwise we would be only their timid slaves. I now have a feeling of gratitude to women of easy virtue which naturally brings me to your feet. I prostrate myself before you to obtain forgiveness, and I now end this long letter. Good-by, my lovely friend—without rancor.

THE MARQUISE

Here, the Marquise reviles Valmont for his efforts with Madame de Tourvel and continues to tell of her life's struggle to raise herself above other women.

How I pity you for your fears! How clearly they show my superiority over you! And you want to teach me, to guide me? Ah, my poor Valmont, what a great distance there still is between you and me! No, all the pride of your sex would not be enough to bridge the gap that separates us. Because you could not carry out my plans, you judge them to be impossible! It well befits you, you proud, weak creature, to try to measure my means and judge my resources! Really, Vicomte, your advice has put me in a bad temper, and I cannot conceal it from you. . . .

What have you done that I have not surpassed a thousand times? You have seduced, even ruined, many women; but what difficulties did you have to overcome, what obstacles did you have to surmount? Where was there any merit that was truly yours? . . .

Believe me, Vicomte, one seldom acquires qualities one can do without. Fighting without risk, you necessarily act without caution. For you mean, defeats are only so many fewer victories. In that unequal battle, our good fortune is not to lose, and your misfortune is not to win. . . .

Ah, keep your advice and your fears for those delirious women who claim to be "women of feeling"; whose feverish imagination would make one think nature had placed their senses in their heads; who, never having reflected, constantly confuse love with a lover; who, in their foolish illusions, believe that the man with whom they have sought pleasure is the sole depository of it; and who, being truly superstitious, give the priest the respect and faith which ought to be given only to the divinity.

Fear also for those women who, more vain than prudent, do not know how to consent to being abandoned when necessary.

Tremble above all for those women, active in their idleness, whom you call "sensitive," and of whom love takes possession so easily and so powerfully. . . .

But what have I in common with those rash women? When have you ever seen me depart from the rules I have laid down for myself, and violate my principles? I call them my principles and I do so deliberately, for they are not, like those of other women, given at random, received without examination and followed from habit; they are the fruit of my profound reflections; I have created them, and I can say that I am my own work. . . .

Can you suppose that after having made so many efforts I shall not enjoy the fruits of them? That after having raised myself above other women I shall consent to crawl like them between rashness and timidity? That I could ever be so afraid of a man as to see safety only in flight? No, Vicomte, never. I must conquer or perish. As for Prévan, I want to have him and I shall have him; he wants to tell it and he will not tell it: that, in a few words, is our whole story. Good-by.

VALMONT 2

The Vicomte sends this gloating letter to the Marquise in which he describes his victory over the defenseless Madame de Tourvel, comparing his efforts to those of a military officer waging a campaign.

She is vanquished, that haughty woman who had dared to think she could resist me! Yes, my friend, she is mine, entirely mine; since yesterday she has had nothing more to grant me.

I am still too full of my happiness to be able to appreciate it, but I am amazed at the unknown charm I felt. Could it be true that virtue increases a woman's value even at the very time of her weakness? But

let us relegate that puerile idea to the category of old wives' tales. . . .
Yet it was not the charm of love, for while it is true that occasionally,
with that astonishing woman, I had moments of weakness which re-
sembled that abject passion, I was always able to overcome them and
return to my principles. . . . I confess, in fact, that yielding to it would
give me rather sweet pleasure, if it did not cause me a certain anxiety.
At my age, shall I be overwhelmed like a schoolboy by an involuntary
and unknown feeling? No: before everything else, I must combat it
and fathom it. . . .

It was six o'clock in the evening when I arrived at the house of
my fair recluse. . . . She tried to stand up when I was announced,
but her trembling knees made it impossible and she immediately sat
down again. . . . At last we were left alone and I began my attack. . . .

"I desire your happiness," she said.

The sound of her voice was beginning to indicate rather strong
emotion, so I threw myself at her feet and cried out in the dramatic
tone with which you are familiar. "Ah, cruel woman, can there be
any happiness for me which you do not share? Where could I find
happiness away from you? No, never, never!" I confess that in this
outburst I had counted heavily on the aid of tears, but whether because
I was unfavorably disposed or merely because of the close attention I
was constantly giving to everything, I was unable to weep.

Fortunately I recalled that all methods of subjugating a woman
are equally good, and that the shock of any strong emotion is enough
to make a deep and favorable impression on her. I therefore made up
by terror for the sensibility I found lacking: remaining in the same
position and changing only the inflection of my voice, I said, "Yes,
I swear to you at your feet that I shall either possess you or die." . . .
I added in a low, sinister tone, but loudly enough for her to hear, "So
be it, then: death!" . . .

At this point I took her in my arms; she made no resistance whatever. . . .

While I was speaking, I felt her heart palpitating violently; I observed the discomposure of her face; I saw that tears were choking
her, yet flowing only seldom and with difficulty. It was only then that

I decided to pretend to go away. She held me by force and said quickly, "No, listen to me!"

"Let me go," I replied.

"You will listen to me, I insist on it."

"I must leave you, I must!"

"No!" she cried.

At this last word she threw herself, or rather fell, unconscious into my arms. Since I still doubted such a stroke of good fortune, I pretended to be greatly alarmed; but at the same time I led her, or carried her, to the place I had previously chosen as the field of my glory; and indeed she did not regain consciousness until she had been entirely subjugated to the will of her happy conqueror.

. . . I forced the enemy to fight when she wanted to avoid action; by skillful maneuvers I gave myself the choice of terrain and disposition; I inspired her with confidence, so that I could overtake her more easily in her retreat; I made confidence give way to terror before joining battle; I left nothing to chance, except from consideration of a great advantage in case of victory, and the certainty of resources in case of defeat; finally, I did not join battle until I had an assured retreat by which I could cover and hold everything I had previously conquered. I think this is all one can do. But now I am afraid I may have become softened like Hannibal in Capua.

EMMA

by Jane Austen

1816

4 MONOLOGUES
Frank Churchill
George Knightly 1
Emma
George Knightly 2

SETTING: the village of Highbury, England, in the nineteenth century

Emma is a delightful comedy of manners that gently pokes fun at the mores of the English gentry. Emma Woodhouse is a strong-willed young woman who does not know her own heart. She indulges in matchmaking, much to the consternation of the family friend George Knightly, who counsels her not to interfere in other people's lives. The story follows Emma's efforts to match her friends with one another. Nothing works the way she planned, and she soon finds herself admitting her love for George, who happily returns her feelings. In the end, Emma's father finally approves of George, and everyone else has found someone they truly love.

FRANK CHURCHILL

At a picnic, Frank asks Emma to find him a wife to tease Jane, with whom he has recently quarreled.

It is only by seeing women in their own homes, among their own set,

just as they always are, that you can form any just judgment. Short
of that, it is all guess and luck—and will generally be ill-luck. How
many a man has committed himself on a short acquaintance, and rued
it all the rest of his life! . . .

Well, I have so little confidence in my own judgment, that whenever I marry, I hope somebody will choose my wife for me. Will you?
I am sure I should like anybody fixed on by you. . . . Find somebody
for me. I am in no hurry. Adopt her; educate her. . . .

She must be very lively and have hazel eyes. I care for nothing
else. I shall go abroad for a couple of years—and when I return, I
shall come to you for my wife. Remember.

GEORGE KNIGHTLY 1

*During the picnic, Emma has challenged each of her friends to say "one
thing very clever . . . or two things moderately clever . . . or three things
very dull indeed." When Emma suggests that Miss Bates, an old maid, will
have great difficulty in keeping it to only three dull things, George chastises
her for her lack of sensitivity.*

How could you be so unfeeling to Miss Bates? How could you be so
insolent in your wit to a woman of her character, age, and situation?
Emma, I had not thought it possible. . . . She felt your full meaning.
She has talked of it since. . . . I wish you could have heard her hon-
ouring your forbearance, in being able to pay her such attentions, as
she was forever receiving from yourself and your father, when her
society must be so irksome. . . . Were she your equal in situation—
but, Emma, consider how far this is from being the case. She is poor;
she has sunk from the comforts she was born to; and if she live to old
age must probably sink more. Her situation should secure your compassion. . . . This is not pleasant to you, Emma—and it is very far
from pleasant to me; but I must, I will . . . tell you truths while I
can; satisfied with proving myself your friend by very faithful counsel
and trusting that you will some time or other do me greater justice
than you can do now.

EMMA

George tells Emma of the betrothal of Frank Churchill to Jane Fairfax, fearing the news will upset her as she has always claimed to be attracted to Frank. To his surprise, Emma claims that she has never loved Frank.

Mr. Knightly, I am in a very extraordinary situation. I cannot let you continue in your error; and yet, perhaps, since my manners gave such an impression, I have as much reason to be ashamed of confessing that I never have been at all attached to the person we are speaking of, as it might be natural for a woman to feel in confessing exactly the reverse. But I never have. . . . I have very little to say for my own conduct. I was tempted by his attentions, and allowed myself to appear pleased. . . . Many circumstances assisted the temptation. . . . My vanity was flattered, and I allowed his attentions. . . . He has imposed on me, but he has not injured me. I have never been attached to him. . . . He never wished to attach me. It was merely a blind to conceal his real situation with another. It was his object to blind all about him; and no one, I am sure, could be more effectually blinded than myself—except that I was *not* blinded—that it was my good fortune—that, in short, I was somehow or other safe from him.

GEORGE KNIGHTLY 2

Emma has opened the door to George to admit his feelings toward her. Thus encouraged, he reveals that he has loved Emma for a long time.

My dearest Emma, for dearest you will always be, whatever the event of this hour's conversation, my dearest, most beloved Emma—tell me at once. Say 'No,' if it is to be said. You are silent, absolutely silent! At present I ask no more. . . . If I loved you less, I might be able to talk about it more. But you know what I am. You hear nothing but truth from me. I have blamed you, and lectured you, and you have borne it as no other woman in England would have borne it. Bear with the truths I would tell you now, dearest Emma, as well as you have borne with them. The manner, perhaps, may have as little to recommend them. God knows, I have been a very indifferent lover. But you understand me. Yes, you see, you understand my feelings—and will return them if you can. At present, I ask only to hear—once to hear your voice.

FRANKENSTEIN

by Mary Shelley

1818

3 MONOLOGUES
Victor Frankenstein
The Monster 1
The Monster 2

SETTING: Europe, early nineteenth century

Subtitled "The Modern Prometheus," *Frankenstein* is the dark tale of a man obsessed with death, which he hopes to conquer by learning the secrets of creation. Victor Frankenstein's experiments with the reanimation of dead tissue eventually lead to the creation of his "monster," a pitiful creature whom the doctor soon vows to destroy. Reviled and hunted, the monster vows to ruin his creator by destroying everything that Victor holds dear. But the monster is denied a confrontation with his creator, for Victor dies aboard a ship bound for the North Pole. The monster manages to cross the ice and reach the ship just after Victor has died. He is discovered in Frankenstein's cabin by Robert Walton, the tale's narrator. The monster pledges to destroy himself. He then leaps from the cabin window onto his ice raft and disappears into the darkness.

VICTOR FRANKENSTEIN

The doctor confronts his creation with rage and hatred. The monster has murdered his younger brother, William, and Victor seeks revenge.

Devil, do you dare approach me? And do not you fear the fierce vengeance of my arm wreaked on your miserable head? Begone, vile insect! Or rather, stay, that I may trample you to dust! And, oh! That I could with the extinction of your miserable existence, restore those victims whom you have so diabolically murdered!

Abhorred monster! Fiend that thou art! The tortures of hell are too mild a vengeance for thy crimes. Wretched devil! You reproach me with your creation; come on, then, that I may extinguish the spark which I so negligently bestowed.

Why do you call to my remembrance circumstances of which I shudder to reflect, that I have been the miserable origin and author? Cursed be the day, abhorred devil, in which you first saw light! Cursed be the hands that formed you! You have made me wretched beyond expression. You have left me no power to consider whether I am just to you or not. Begone! Relieve me from the sight of your detested form.

THE MONSTER 1

In the same scene, the monster calls upon his creator to do his duty. He blames Frankenstein for his misery and asks that the doctor listen to his story before condemning him.

How can I move thee? Will no entreaties cause thee to turn a favourable eye upon thy creature, who implores thy goodness and compassion? Believe me, Frankenstein, I was benevolent; my soul glowed with love and humanity; but am I not alone, miserably alone? You, my creator, abhor me; what hope can I gather from your fellow creatures, who owe me nothing? They spurn and hate me. The desert mountains and dreary glaciers are my refuge. I have wandered here many days; the caves of ice, which I only do not fear, are a dwelling to me, and the only one which man does not grudge. These bleak skies I hail, for they are kinder to me than your fellow beings. If the multitude of mankind knew of my existence, they would do as you do, and arm themselves for my destruction. Shall I not then hate them who abhor me? I will keep no terms with my enemies. I am miserable, and they shall share my wretchedness. . . . Let your compassion be moved, and do not disdain me. Listen to my tale; when you have heard that, abandon or commiserate me, as you shall judge that I deserve. But hear me. The guilty are allowed, by human laws, bloody as they are, to speak in their own defence before they are condemned. Listen to me, Frankenstein. You accuse me of murder, and yet you would, with a satisfied conscience, destroy your own creature. Oh, praise the eternal justice of man! Yet I ask you not to spare me; listen to me, and then, if you can, and if you will, destroy the work of your hands.

THE MONSTER 2

Robert Walton faces the monster over the dead body of Victor Frankenstein. The monster tells Walton of his wretchedness and of his plan to end his life.

Farewell! I leave you, and in you the last of humankind whom these eyes will ever behold. Farewell, Frankenstein! If thou wert yet alive and yet cherished a desire of revenge against me, it would be better satiated in my life than in my destruction. But it was not so; thou didst seek my extinction, that I might not cause greater wretchedness; and if yet, in some mode unknown to me, thou hadst not ceased to think and feel, thou wouldst not desire against me a vengeance greater than that which I feel. Blasted as thou wert, my agony was still superior to thine, for the bitter sting of remorse will not cease to rankle in my wounds until death shall close them forever.

But soon I shall die, and what I now feel be no longer felt. Soon these burning miseries will be extinct. I shall ascend my funeral pile triumphantly and exult in the agony of the torturing flames. The light of that conflagration will fade away; my ashes will be swept into the sea by the winds. My spirit will sleep in peace, or if it thinks, it will not surely think thus. Farewell.

IVANHOE

by Sir Walter Scott

1820

1 MONOLOGUE
Rebecca

SETTING: England during the reign of Richard Lion-Heart

This is the story of Ivanhoe, a Saxon knight in love with the beautiful Lady Rowena. Severely wounded in a tournament, Ivanhoe is taken to Lady Rowena's castle to rest and heal. The castle is then stormed by Normans, led by the evil Prince John. All within are captured except Ivanhoe, who is left to die. He is discovered, near death, by Isaac, a Jew, and his daughter Rebecca, who return an old favor and take him to their home to hide him from Prince John.

REBECCA

The beautiful young Jewess has fallen in love with Ivanhoe. Although she knows their love can never be, she confesses her deep feelings to him as he lies sleeping.

He sleeps, nature exhausted by sufferance and the waste of spirits, his wearied frame embraces the first moment of temporary relaxation to sink into slumber. Alas! is it a crime that I should look upon him, when it may be for the last time? When yet but a short space, and those fair features will be no longer animated by the bold and buoyant spirit which forsakes them not even in sleep! When the nostril shall be distended, the mouth agape, the eyes fixed and bloodshot; and when the proud and noble knight may be trodden on by the lowest caitiff of this accursed castle, yet stir not when the heel is lifted up against him! And my father!—oh, my father! evil is it with his daughter, when his grey hairs are not remembered because of the golden locks of youth! What know I but that these evils are the messengers of Jehovah's wrath to the unnatural child who thinks of a stranger's captivity before a parent's? who forgets the desolation of Judah, and looks upon the comeliness of a Gentile and a stranger? But I will tear this folly from my heart, though every fibre bleed as I rend it away!

THE EMPRESS CATHERINE AND PRINCESS DASHKOF

by Walter Savage Landor

1824

1 MONOLOGUE
Empress Catherine

SETTING: Russia, nineteenth century

From *Imaginary Conversations*, this short story presents a fictional dialogue between the empress of Russia and a close friend. Together they listen to the assassination of Peter, Catherine's husband. The empress has ordered the assassination because she detests Peter's tyrannical ways. The empress and the princess discuss how Catherine will rule Russia and the shallow nature of men.

EMPRESS CATHERINE

The empress tells her friend to catch her when she "faints" upon hearing of Peter's death. They must appear inconsolable.

I am heated and thirsty: I cannot imagine how. I think we have not yet taken our coffee—was it so strong? What am I dreaming of? I could eat only a slice of melon at breakfast; my duty urged me *then*; and dinner is yet to come. Remember, I am to faint at the midst of it when the intelligence comes in, or rather when, in despite of every effort to conceal it from me, the awful truth has flashed upon my mind. Remember, too, you are to catch me, and to cry for help, and to tear those fine flaxen hairs which we laid up together on the toilet; and we are both to be as inconsolable as we can be for the life of us. . . . I wish all things of this sort could be done and be over in a day. They are mightily disagreeable when by nature one is not cruel. People little know my character. I have the tenderest heart upon earth: I am courageous, but I am full of weaknesses. I possess in perfection the higher part of man, and—to a friend I may say it—the most amiable part of woman. Ho, ho! at last you smile!

THE LAST OF THE MOHICANS

by James Fenimore Cooper

1826

1 MONOLOGUE
Indian

SETTING: The early American frontier, 1757

The Last of the Mohicans is part of a group of novels called "The Leatherstocking Tales," named for the series' hero, Natty Bumppo, nicknamed Leatherstocking. Bumppo is variously called "The Deerslayer," "The Pioneer," and in this novel, "Hawkeye." This is a vivid portrait of frontier life, depicting the character of both Indian and Pioneer. The series of five novels introduces Natty as a young man and follows him through his entire life up until his death. The stories contrast the lives of Natty and his noble Indian friends, who exist in harmony with nature, with the lives of the settlers who brought "social order" and "civilization" to the frontier, along with their self-centered lack of respect for the wilderness.

INDIAN

In this scene, a Mohawk Indian tells Hawkeye of the way life used to be before the arrival of the white settlers.

A pine grew then where this chestnut now stands. The first palefaces who came among us spoke no English. They came in a large canoe, when my fathers had buried the tomahawk with the red men around them. Then, Hawkeye, then, Hawkeye, we were one people, and we

were happy. The Salt Lake gave us its fish, the wood its deer, and
the air its birds. We took wives who bore us children; we worshipped
the Great Spirit; and we kept the Maquas beyond the sound of our
songs of triumph!

My tribe is the grandfather of nations, but I am an unmixed man.
The blood of chiefs is in my veins, where it must stay forever. The
Dutch landed, and gave my people the firewater; they drank until the
heavens and the earth seemed to meet, and they foolishly thought
they had found the Great Spirit. Then they parted with their land.
Foot by foot, they were driven back from the shores, until I, that am
a chief and a Sagamore, have never seen the sun shine but through
the trees, and have never visited the graves of my fathers!

COMEDIES AND SATIRES

by Edgar Allan Poe

1833–1840

4 MONOLOGUES
Breathless Man
Signora Psyche Zenobia
Mr. Blackwood
The Business Man

SETTING: America, nineteenth century

The following monologues are taken from three short stories written by America's master of the macabre, Edgar Allan Poe. "Loss of Breath," "How to Write a *Blackwood* Article," and "The Business Man" are three humorous tales that show the lighter side of Poe, whose chilling tales of the supernatural have haunted generation after generation. Poe was, in fact, an expert satirist whose comedic stories delightfully lampoon society and its stereotypes. "Loss of Breath" is the tale of a man who loses his breath while yelling at his bride on the day following their wedding. "How to Write a *Blackwood* Article" introduces us to Signora Psyche Zenobia, a pompous young woman who desires to write a titillating article for a true-story magazine. "The Business Man" is a gentleman who despises geniuses, claiming instead that they are all asses.

BREATHLESS MAN

A man who rails against his young bride loses his breath in the midst of a tirade. Here he recounts his strange tale.

34

'Thou wretch!—thou vixen!—thou shrew!' said I to my wife on the morning after our wedding, 'thou witch!—thou hag!—thou whipper-snapper!—thou sink of iniquity!—thou fiery-faced quintessence of all that is abominable!—thou—thou—' here standing upon tiptoe, seizing her by the throat, and placing my mouth close to her ear, I was preparing to launch forth a new and more decided epithet of opprobrium, which should not fail, if ejaculated, to convince her of her insignificance, when, to my extreme horror and astonishment, I discovered that *I had lost my breath*.

The phrases 'I am out of breath', 'I have lost my breath', etc., are often enough repeated in common conversation; but it had never occurred to me that the terrible accident of which I speak could *bona fide* and actually happen! Imagine—that is if you have a fanciful turn—imagine, I say, my wonder, my consternation, my despair! . . .

Although I could not at first precisely ascertain to what degree the occurrence had affected me, I determined at all events to conceal the matter from my wife, until further experience should discover to me the extent of this my unheard of calamity. Altering my countenance, therefore, in a moment, from its bepuffed and distorted appearance to an expression of arch and coquettish benignity, I gave my lady a pat on the cheek, and a kiss on the other, and without saying one syllable (Furies! I could not), left her astonished at my drollery, as I pirouetted out of the room in a *pas de zéphyr*.

Yes! breathless. I am serious in asserting that my breath was entirely gone. . . . Hard fate! . . .

Throwing myself upon a chair, I remained for some time absorbed in meditation. . . . A thousand vague and lachrymatory fancies took possession of my soul, and even the idea of suicide flitted across my brain; but it is a trait in the perversity of human nature to reject the obvious and the ready for the far-distant and equivocal. Thus I shuddered at self-murder as the most decided of atrocities, while the tabby cat purred strenuously upon the rug, and the very water-dog wheezed assiduously under the table; each taking to itself much merit for the strength of its lungs, and all obviously done in derision of my own pulmonary incapacity.

SIGNORA PSYCHE ZENOBIA

A Philadelphia socialite introduces herself and tells of her ladies' club and their efforts to improve their thinking and writing.

I presume everybody has heard of me. My name is the Signora Psyche Zenobia. This I know to be a fact. Nobody but my enemies ever calls me Suky Snobbs. I have been assured that Suky is but a vulgar corruption of Psyche, which is good Greek, and means 'the soul' (that's me, I'm *all* soul), and sometimes 'a butterfly', which latter meaning undoubtedly alludes to my appearance in my new crimson satin dress, with the sky-blue Arabian *mantelet*, and the trimmings of green *agraffas*, and the seven flounces of orange-colored *auriculas*. As for Snobbs—any person who should look at me would be instantly aware that my name wasn't Snobbs. Miss Tabitha Turnip propagated that report through sheer envy. Tabitha Turnip indeed! Oh, the little wretch! But what can we expect from a turnip? Wonder if she remembers the old adage about 'blood out of a turnip, etc.?' . . . Where was I? Ah! I have been assured that Snobbs is a mere corruption of Zenobia, and that Zenobia was a queen (so am I. Dr Moneypenny always calls me the Queen of Hearts), and that Zenobia, as well as Psyche, is good Greek, and that my father was 'a Greek', and that consequently I have a right to our patronymic, which is Zenobia, and not by any means Snobbs. Nobody but Tabitha Turnip calls me Suky Snobbs. I am the Signora Psyche Zenobia.

As I said before, everybody has heard of me. I am that very Signora Psyche Zenobia so justly celebrated as corresponding secretary to the 'Philadelphia, Regular, Exchange, Tea, Total, Young, Belles, Lettres, Universal, Experimental, Bibliographical, Association, To, Civilize, Humanity'. Dr Moneypenny made the title for us, and says he chose it because it sounded big, like an empty rum-puncheon. . . . At any rate we always add to our names the initials P.R.E.T.T.Y.B.L.U.E.B.A.T.C.H.—that is to say, Philadelphia, Regular, Exchange, Tea, Total, Young, Belles, Lettres, Universal, Experimental, Bibliographical, Association, To, Civilize, Humanity—one letter for each word. Dr Moneypenny will have it that our initials give our true character, but for my life I can't see what he means. . . .

When I joined the Society it was my endeavor to introduce a better style of thinking and writing, and all the world knows how well I have succeeded. We get up as good papers now in the P.R.E.T.T.Y.B.L.U.E.B.A.T.C.H. as any to be found even in *Blackwood*. I say *Blackwood*, because I have been assured that the finest writing, upon every subject, is to be discovered in the pages of that justly celebrated magazine.

MR. BLACKWOOD

Signora Zenobia pays a call on Mr. Blackwood and the magazine editor tells her the elements that make a good Blackwood *article.*

Sensations are the great things, after all. Should you ever be drowned or hung, be sure and make a note of your sensations; they will be worth ten guineas a sheet. If you wish to write forcibly, Miss Zenobia, pay minute attention to the sensations.

I see you are a pupil after my own heart. But I must put you *au fait* to the details necessary in composing what may be denominated a genuine *Blackwood* article of the sensation stamp, the kind which you will understand me to say I consider the best for all purposes.

The first thing requisite is to get yourself into such a scrape as no one ever got into before. The oven, for instance,—that was a good hit. But if you have no oven or big bell at hand, and if you cannot conveniently tumble out of a balloon, or be swallowed up in an earthquake, or get stuck fast in a chimney, you will have to be contented with simply imagining some similar misadventure. I should prefer, however, that you have the actual fact to bear you out.

Take a dose of Brandreth's pills, and then give us your sensations. However, my instructions will apply equally well to any variety of misadventure, and in your way home you may easily get knocked in the head, or run over by an omnibus, or bitten by a mad dog, or drowned in a gutter. But to proceed.

Having determined upon your subject, you must next consider the tone, or manner, of your narration. There is the tone didactic, the tone enthusiastic, the tone natural—all commonplace enough. But then there is the tone laconic, or curt, which has lately come much into use. It consists in short sentences. Somehow thus: Can't be too brief. Can't be too snappish. Always a full stop. And never a paragraph.

Then there is the tone elevated, diffusive, and interjectional. Some of our best novelists patronize this tone. The words must be all in a whirl, like a humming-top, and make a noise very similar, which answers remarkably well instead of meaning. This is the best of all possible styles where the writer is in too great a hurry to think.

THE BUSINESS MAN

A lover of logic and method here denounces geniuses as being "arrant asses."

I am a business man. I am a methodical man. Method is *the* thing, after all. But there are no people I more heartily despise than your eccentric fools who prate about method without understanding it; attending strictly to its letter, and violating its spirit. . . .

If there is anything on earth I hate, it is a genius. Your geniuses are all arrant asses—the greater the genius the greater the ass—and to this rule there is no exception whatever. Especially, you cannot make a man of business out of a genius, any more than . . . the best nutmegs out of pine-knots. The creatures are always going off at a tangent into some fantastic employment, or ridiculous speculation, entirely at variance with the 'fitness of things', and having no business whatever to be considered as a business at all. Thus you may tell these characters immediately by the nature of their occupations. If you ever perceive a man setting up as a merchant or a manufacturer; or going into the cotton or tobacco trade, or any of those eccentric pursuits;

or getting to be a dry-goods dealer, or soap-boiler, or something of that kind; or pretending to be a lawyer, or a blacksmith, or a physician—anything out of the usual way—you may set him down at once as a genius, and then, according to the rule-of-three, he's an ass.

ETHAN BRAND

by Nathaniel Hawthorne

1837

1 MONOLOGUE
Ethan Brand

SETTING: New England, early nineteenth century

"Ethan Brand" is the story of a lime burner who, after many years of staring into the flames of the lime fire, has gone in search of the one unpardonable sin. After eighteen years of debauchery, he returns with his discovery: it is the sin of self-gratification at the expense of one's fellow man. Brand's quest for knowledge was purely selfish and was not conducted to benefit his brothers. When he walks into the lime fire, what is left of him the next morning is a skeleton with a heart of marble.

ETHAN BRAND

Here, Brand tells Bartram, another lime burner, and his young son that he has found the one unpardonable sin.

Man, what need have I of the Devil? I have left him behind me, on my track. It is with such halfway sinners as you that he busies himself. Fear not because I open the door. I do but act by old custom, and am going to trim your fire, like a lime-burner, as I was once.

I have looked into many a human heart that was seven times hotter with sinful passions than yonder furnace is with fire. But I found not there what I sought. No, not the Unpardonable Sin! It is a sin that grew within my own breast. A sin that grew nowhere else! The sin of an intellect that triumphed over the sense of brotherhood with man and reverence for God, and sacrificed everything to its own mighty claims! The only sin that deserves a recompense of immortal agony! Freely, were it to do again, would I incur the guilt. Unshrinkingly I accept the retribution!

OLIVER TWIST

by Charles Dickens

1838

2 MONOLOGUES
Nancy 1
Nancy 2

SETTING: London, nineteenth century

Oliver Twist is an indictment of the harsh conditions of English work-houses. Oliver is a child of unknown parentage who lives in a work-house under the tyranny of Mr. Bumble, who relentlessly beats and starves the children placed in his care. Oliver runs away to London, where he falls in with a gang of pickpockets headed by the old thief Fagin. Oliver is then forced to join Bill Sikes, an exceptionally cruel man, on a burglary in which he is wounded and left for dead. Oliver is found and nursed back to health by Mrs. Maylie and her protégée, Rose.

Bill's mistress, Nancy, risks her life out of fondness for Oliver and warns Rose that Oliver is in danger. Nancy's duplicity is discovered and she is brutally murdered by Sikes. When her body is discovered, there is an outcry, and Bill is chased through the streets of London by an angry crowd. Trying to escape over the rooftops, Sikes acci-dentally hangs himself. The rest of Fagin's gang is captured, and their leader is executed. It is discovered that Rose is Oliver's maternal aunt and Oliver is then adopted by Mr. Brownlow, a kindly gentleman who loves him. With his newfound family, Oliver lives happily at last.

NANCY 1

Knowing that Oliver is in grave danger, Nancy endeavors to help him. It is a testimony to her bravery and kindness that she risks her own life to help the young orphan.

Hush! You can't help yourself. I have tried hard for you, but all to no purpose. You are hedged round and round; and if ever you are to get loose from here, this is not the time.

I have saved you from being ill-used once: and I will again: and I do now, for those who would have fetched you, if I had not, would have been far more rough than me. I have promised for your being quiet and silent: if you are not, you will only do harm to yourself and me too: and perhaps be my death. See here! I have borne all this for you already, as true as God sees me show it.

Remember this! And don't let me suffer more for you, just now. If I could help you, I would; but I have not the power. They don't mean to harm you; and whatever they make you do, is no fault of yours. Hush! every word from you is a blow for me. . . . Give me your hand. Make haste! Your hand!

NANCY 2

Arriving at the fashionable home of Mrs. Maylie, Nancy begs Rose to have pity on her.

I am about to put my life, and the lives of others in your hands. I am the girl that dragged little Oliver back to old Fagin's on the night he went out from the house in Pentonville.

I am the infamous creature you have heard of, that lives among the thieves, and that never from the first moment I can recollect my eyes and senses opening on London streets have known any better life, or kinder words than they have given me, so help me God! Do not mind shrinking openly from me, lady. I am younger than you

would think, to look at me, but I am well used to it. The poorest
women fall back, as I make my way along the crowded pavement.

Thank Heaven upon your knees, dear lady, that you had friends
to care for and keep you in your childhood, and that you were never
in the midst of cold and hunger, and riot and drunkenness, and—
and something worse than all—as I have been from my cradle; I may
use the word, for the alley and the gutter were mine, as they will be
my death-bed.

JANE EYRE

by *Charlotte Brontë*

1847

5 MONOLOGUES
Mr. Brocklehurst
Helen Burns
Jane Eyre
Rochester 1
Rochester 2
SETTING: England, early nineteenth century

First published in 1847, *Jane Eyre* was an instant success. This heroine, so brilliantly crafted by Charlotte Brontë, was the first of her kind. Neither beautiful nor wealthy, Jane Eyre triumphs over her lack of conventional feminine attributes by sheer force of will. From the loneliness and privation suffered at Lowood, a school for orphans, to her passion for a married man, Jane is able to rise above the complications of her life by resisting them—a novel concept for the day.

Plain, "Quakerlike" Jane survives an unhappy childhood to become a governess at Thornfield Hall, residence of the darkly passionate Lord Rochester, with whom Jane falls in love. Rochester is harboring a secret. When he was a younger man, he married a woman in the West Indies, only to discover that her insatiable sexual appetites would take her from his bed and lead to her destruction. Totally insane, she lives an animalistic existence in a secret wing at Thornfield. A purifying fire destroys both Thornfield and Rochester's mad wife. Rochester also loses his vision in the blaze. Jane is now free to choose to marry him, which she does, and in doing so becomes the precursor of the modern heroine, a woman in charge of her own destiny.

MR. BROCKLEHURST

The fundamentalist head of the Lowood school displays his aptitude for harsh discipline in this scene when he punishes Jane for lying.

Ladies, Miss Temple, teachers, and children, you all see this girl? You see she is yet young; you observe she possesses the ordinary form of childhood; God has graciously given her the shape that He has given to all of us; no single deformity points her out as a marked character. Who would think that the Evil One has already found a servant and agent in her? Yet such, I grieve to say, is the case.

My dear children, this is a sad, melancholy occasion; for it becomes my duty to warn you that this girl, who might be one of God's own lambs, is a little castaway—not a member of the true flock, but evidently an interloper and an alien. You must be on your guard against her; you must shun her example—if necessary, avoid her company, exclude her from your sports, and shut her out from your converse. Teachers, you must watch her; keep your eyes on her movements, weigh well her words, scrutinize her actions, punish her body to save her soul—if, indeed, such salvation be possible, for . . . this girl, this child, the native of a Christian land, worse than many a little heathen who says its prayers to Brahma and kneels before Juggernaut—this girl is—a liar!

This I learned from her benefactress—from the pious and charitable lady who adopted her in her orphan state, reared her as her own daughter, and whose kindness, whose generosity the unhappy girl repaid by an ingratitude so bad, so dreadful, that at last her excellent patroness was obliged to separate her from her own young ones, fearful lest her vicious example should contaminate their purity. She has sent her here to be healed, even as the Jews of old sent their diseased to the troubled pool of Bethesda; and, teachers, superintendent, I beg of you not to allow the waters to stagnate round her.

Let her stand half an hour longer on that stool, and let no one speak to her during the remainder of the day.

HELEN BURNS

Jane's one friend at Lowood admonishes her for speaking out against Mr. Brocklehurst after he has punished her. Helen points out that greater glory awaits in the next life.

Hush, Jane! you think too much of the love of human beings; you are too impulsive, too vehement: the sovereign Hand that created your frame, and put life into it, has provided you with other resources than your feeble self, or than creatures feeble as you. Besides this earth, and besides the race of men, there is an invisible world and a kingdom of spirits: that world is round us, for it is everywhere; and those spirits watch us, for they are commissioned to guard us; and if we were dying in pain and shame, if scorn smote us on all sides, and hatred crushed us, angels see our tortures, recognize our innocence, . . . and God waits only a separation of spirit from flesh to crown us with a full reward. Why, then, should we ever sink overwhelmed with distress, when life is so soon over, and death is so certain an entrance to happiness—to glory?

JANE EYRE

Jane mistakenly believes that Rochester is going to propose to Miss Ingram. She can no longer live under the same roof with this man whom she loves so fiercely if he is wed to another and tells him so in this passionate monologue.

I tell you I must go! Do you think I can stay to become nothing to you? Do you think I am an automaton?—a machine without feelings? and can bear to have my morsel of bread snatched from my lips, and my drop of living water dashed from my cup? Do you think, because I am poor, obscure, plain, and little, I am soulless and heartless? You think wrong!—I have as much soul as you—and full as much heart! And if God had gifted me with some beauty and much wealth, I should have made it as hard for you to leave me, as it is now for me to leave you. I am not talking to you now through the medium of custom, conventionalities, nor even of mortal flesh: it is my spirit that addresses your spirit; just as if both had passed through the grave, and we stood at God's feet, equal—as we are!

ROCHESTER 1

The lord of the manor tells Jane the truth about his secret wife, refusing her offer of pity and dwelling upon the hell he has been living since the madness began.

Jane, I will not trouble you with abominable details; some strong words shall express what I have to say. I lived with that woman upstairs four years, and before that time she had tried me indeed: her character ripened and developed with frightened rapidity; her vices sprang up fast and rank: they were so strong, only cruelty could check them, and I would not use cruelty. Bertha Mason, the true daughter of an infamous mother, dragged me through all the hideous and degrading agonies which much attend a man bound to a wife at once intemperate and unchaste.

Jane, I approached the verge of despair; a remnant of self-respect was all that intervened between me and the gulf. In the eyes of the world, I was doubtless covered with grimy dishonour; but I resolved to be clean in my own sight—and to the last I repudiated the con-tamination of her crimes, and wrenched myself from connection with her mental defects. . . .

One night I had been awakened by her yells—. . . it was a fiery West Indian night; one of the description that frequently precede the hurricanes of those climates. The air was like sulphur-streams—I could find no refreshment anywhere. Mosquitoes came buzzing in ·and hummed sullenly round the room; the sea, which I could hear from thence, rumbled dull like an earthquake—black clouds were casting up over it; the moon was setting in the waves, broad and red, like a hot cannon-ball—she threw her last bloody glance over a world quiver-ing with the ferment of tempest. I was physically influenced by the atmosphere and scene, and my ears were filled with the curses the maniac still shrieked out: wherein she momentarily mingled my name with such a tone of demon-hate, with such language!—no professed harlot ever had a fouler vocabulary than she: though two rooms off, I heard every word—the thin partitions of the West Indian house opposing but slight obstruction to her wolfish cries.

'This life,' said I at last, 'is hell: this is the air—those are the sounds of the bottomless pit! I have a right to deliver myself from it if I can. The sufferings of this mortal state will leave me with the heavy flesh that now cumbers my soul. Of the fanatic's burning eternity I have no fear: there is not a future state worse than this present one— let me break away, and go home to God!'

ROCHESTER 2

Here, Rochester declares his passion for Jane. He has come to realize that it is her indomitable spirit that he cherishes and not her "brittle frame."

Never, never was anything at once so frail and so indomitable. A mere reed she feels in my hand! I could bend her with my finger and thumb: and what good would it do if I bent, if I uptore, if I crushed her? Consider that eye: consider the resolute, wild, free thing looking out of it, defying me, with more than courage—with a stern triumph. Whatever I do with its cage, I cannot get at it—the savage, beautiful creature! If I tear, if I rend the slight prison, my outrage will only let the captive loose. Conquerer I might be of the house; but the inmate would escape to heaven before I could call myself possessor of its clay dwelling-place. And it is you, spirit—with will and energy, and virtue and purity—that I want: not alone your brittle frame. Of yourself you could come with soft flight and nestle against my heart, if you would: seized against your will, you will elude the grasp like an essence—you will vanish ere I inhale your fragrance. Oh! come, Jane, come!

WUTHERING HEIGHTS

by Emily Brontë

1847

3 MONOLOGUES
Catherine 1
Catherine 2
Heathcliff

SETTING: England, nineteenth century

This dark romance tells the story of Catherine Earnshaw and her passion for Heathcliff, a young man adopted by her father. The two grow up on the wild moors that surround their home and form a bond that can never be broken—not even by death.

When Mr. Earnshaw dies, Catherine's brother, Hindley, inherits the farm and takes the opportunity to demean and humiliate Heathcliff at every turn. As a result, Heathcliff grows brooding and resentful. Edgar Linton, a young gentleman of a neighboring estate, courts Catherine and proposes. Catherine decides to marry Linton, hoping that she will thus spare Heathcliff further degradation. When Heathcliff hears of Catherine's decision to marry Linton, he mistakenly believes that she no longer loves him. He leaves Wuthering Heights in a rage, and Catherine follows, searching the moors for him until she collapses with pneumonia. When she recovers, she marries Edgar.

Three years later, Heathcliff returns to Wuthering Heights. He has made his fortune and seeks to avenge himself. He courts and marries Edgar's sister, Isabella, knowing the anguish it will cause Catherine. He then turns against Hindley, now an alcoholic with great debts, and buys Wuthering Heights.

Catherine is tortured by Heathcliff's return. She loves him desperately and cannot understand what has made him turn against her. She becomes pregnant with Edgar's child and dies in childbirth. Heathcliff is driven to madness by Catherine's death and after years of inflicting further revenge upon the next generation of Lintons and Earnshaws, he, too, dies, free at last to join his beloved Catherine.

CATHERINE 1

In this scene, Catherine confides to Nelly Dean her reasons for marrying Edgar, even though she loves Heathcliff more than her own life.

I've no more business to marry Edgar Linton than I have to be in heaven; and if the wicked man in there had not brought Heathcliff so low, I shouldn't have thought of it. It would degrade me to marry Heathcliff now; so he shall never know how I love him: and that, not because he's handsome, Nelly, but because he's more myself than I am. Whatever our souls are made of, his and mine are the same; and Linton's is as different as a moonbeam from lightning, or frost from fire. . . .

I cannot express it; but surely you and everybody have a notion that there is or should be an existence of yours beyond you. What were the use of my creation, if I were entirely contained here? My great miseries in this world have been Heathcliff's miseries, and I watched and felt each from the beginning: my great thought in living is himself. If all else perished, and *he* remained, I should still continue to be; and if all else remained, and he were annihilated, the universe would turn to a mighty stranger: I should not seem a part of it. . . . I *am* Heathcliff! He's always, always in my mind: not as a pleasure, any more than I am always a pleasure to myself, but as my own being.

CATHERINE 2

Confined to bed at the Linton estate, Catherine is dying from complications with her pregnancy. Heathcliff is at her bedside, and she both condemns and forgives him for breaking her heart.

You and Edgar have broken my heart, Heathcliff! And you both come to bewail the deed to me, as if you were the people to be pitied! I shall not pity you, not I. You have killed me—and thriven on it, I think. How strong you are! How many years do you mean to live after I am gone?

I wish I could hold you till we were both dead! I shouldn't care what you suffered. I care nothing for your sufferings. Why shouldn't you suffer? I do! Will you forget me? Will you be happy when I am in the earth? . . .

I'm not wishing you greater torment than I have, Heathcliff. I only wish us never to be parted: and should a word of mine distress you hereafter, think I feel the same distress underground, and for my own sake, forgive me! . . . I'm tired, tired of being enclosed here. I'm wearying to escape into that glorious world, and to be always there: not seeing it dimly through the tears, and yearning for it through the walls of an aching heart; but really with it, and in it.

HEATHCLIFF

Grief stricken, Heathcliff tells a dying Catherine of the anguish he suffered when she married Edgar.

You teach me now how cruel you've been—cruel and false. Why did you despise me? Why did you betray your own heart, Cathy? I have not one word of comfort. You deserve this. You have killed yourself. Yes, you may kiss me, and cry; and wring out my kisses and tears: they'll blight you—they'll damn you. You loved me—then what *right* had you to leave me? What right—answer me—for the poor fancy you felt for Linton? Because misery, and degradation, and death, and nothing that God or satan could inflict would have parted us, *you*, of your own will, did it. I have not broken your heart—*you* have broken it; and in breaking it, you have broken mine. So much the worse for me, that I am strong. Do I want to live? What kind of living will it be when you—oh, God! would *you* like to live with your soul in the grave? Kiss me again; and don't let me see your eyes! I forgive what you have done to me. I love *my* murderer—but *yours*! How can I?

MADAME BOVARY

by Gustave Flaubert

1857

3 MONOLOGUES
The Chemist
Rodolphe
Emma Bovary

SETTING: France, late nineteenth century

Upon publication of *Madame Bovary* in 1857, Gustave Flaubert was arrested and held on charges of "irreligion" and immorality. His acquittal assured the success of both book and author.

Emma Bovary is a selfish woman married to Charles, a dull yet devoted man whose occupation as a country doctor keeps Emma isolated from society and the stimulation she desires. She escapes the boredom of country life through romantic fantasies in which she dreams of an exciting man who will sweep her off her feet and provide her with the passion she craves.

Emma believes that she has found such a man when she meets the darkly handsome Rodolphe, who easily seduces the doctor's wife. Unfortunately, Rodolphe regards Emma as a pretty diversion and nothing more. When Emma finally sees Rodolphe for the cad that he is, she finds that she can no longer bear life. She wills herself into a state of consumption from which she eventually dies, as Charles watches helplessly: a fitting end for such an absurdly pitiable heroine.

THE CHEMIST

The village chemist expounds upon his progressive philosophy of religion and his contempt for the clergy.

I have plenty of respect for religion, for my own religion, that is, and a good deal more than they have with their tricks and their mummery! I worship God! I believe in the Supreme Being, in a Creator—of what nature I do not inquire—who has put us into this world to fulfil our duties as citizens and fathers. But I don't feel called upon to go kissing silver dishes in church, or to pay good money in order to fatten a lot of play-actors who live a great deal better than we do. A man can worship God just as well in the woods and fields, or by merely contemplating the wide vault of heaven, like the ancients. My God is the God of Socrates, of Franklin, of Voltaire and of Béranger! I stand for the creed of the *Vicaire savoyard* and the immortal principles of '89. I have no use for any god who walks in his garden with his stick in his hand, entertains his friends in the bellies of whales, dies with a loud cry, and rises again after three days—all of them things which are not only absurd in themselves, but altogether contrary to the laws of the physical universe—which proves, by the way, that priests have always wallowed in slothful ignorance, and are for ever trying to drag down their flocks with them.

RODOLPHE

Upon his first sighting of Emma, Rodolphe schemes to seduce her while pondering the difficulties of disposing of her when he has had his fill.

That doctor's wife is charming, really charming: good teeth, black eyes, neat ankles, and carries herself like a Parisienne! Where the devil does she come from? and how on earth did that oaf manage to pick her up?

I should say he's as stupid as they make 'em, and it's pretty obvious that she's sick of him. His nails are dirty and he goes about with a three days' growth of beard on his chin. While he's off jogging on his rounds, she stays at home darning his socks. I bet she's bored!—wants to live in a town and go dancing the polka every night. Poor little woman—gasping for love like a carp on the kitchen table for water! If I paid her a few compliments, she'd be at my feet—I'm dam' sure of that! And a very charming, sweet little morsel she'd be. . . . But how to get rid of her afterwards 'd be a bit of a problem.

Madame Bovary is a great deal prettier, and quite unspoiled. Virginie is beginning to put on fat, and she's so fussy about her pleasures. Besides, she's got a perfect mania for shrimps!

I'll have her yet!

Where can I manage to meet her—and how? She's always got that kid hanging to her apron-strings, to say nothing of the servant, the husband and the neighbours—all sorts of tiresome obstacles. Bah! it's too much like work!

She's got eyes that go through you like a drill: and that wonderful pallor of hers—I adore pale women!

It's only a question of finding an opportunity. I'll call on them once or twice, send them some game and a few chickens. If need be, I'll have myself bled. We'll strike up a friendship: I'll invite them to my place. By Jove—the agricultural show'll be coming off shortly, she'll be there and I shall see her. That's where I'll make a beginning, and I'll go straight to the point—it's always the best way!

EMMA

In this climactic scene, Emma has come to Rodolphe to ask him for money to save Charles from ruin. When Rodolphe refuses, Emma angrily accuses him of having used her affection.

You haven't got it?

You haven't got it! . . . I might have spared myself this final humiliation. You never really loved me! You are just like all the others!

For that I am sorry, sincerely sorry. . . .

But a poor man like you doesn't lavish silver on the butt of a gun, or buy a clock inlaid with tortoiseshell or silver-gilt whistles for riding crops or trinkets for watch chains. I notice that you want for nothing, not even for a liqueur-stand in your bedroom. The only person you love is yourself. You live well, you have a château, farms, woods. You hunt, you take trips to Paris . . . and that's not all. Why, the smallest of these knick-knacks could be turned into money . . . Not that *I* want them . . . you can keep the lot for all I care!

I would have given you everything, would have sold all I had. I would have worked with my hands, would have begged along the roads, just for a smile, a look, just to hear you say "thank you." How can you sit there calmly in your chair, as though you hadn't made me suffer enough already? But for you, as you know full well, I might have lived happily. What was it induced you to come into my life? Was it a bet? . . . But you *did* love me, you told me so in the old days . . . and again, just now. Better far for me if you had turned me out of the house! My hands are still warm with your kisses. Here is the very spot on the carpet where you swore on your knees to love me for ever! You made me believe you meant it! For two years you led me on through the most glittering dream, the sweetest dream that ever was. . . . Do you remember what journeys we planned? Oh, that letter you wrote!— it tore my heart to shreds . . . and now that I come back to my rich, free, happy lover, to implore of him such help as any stranger would have given, kneeling to him with an offer of love and devotion, he pushes me away for no better reason than that it would cost him three thousand francs!

LES FLEURS DU MAL

by Charles Baudelaire

Translated by Richard Howard

1857

4 MONOLOGUES
The Poet 1
The Poet 2
The Poet 3
The Poet 4

SETTING: France, nineteenth century

Les Fleurs du Mal is the superlative work of France's greatest poet. A contemporary of such literary giants as Gustave Flaubert and Victor Hugo, Charles Baudelaire lived through the turbulent years leading to the uprising of 1848, when revolution stalked the streets of Paris. Revolution of a more personal nature boiled in the poet's blood, driving him to live a life of hedonistic debauchery, which led to his agonizing death of syphilis at age 46.

Baudelaire wrote as he lived: feverish, haunting passages about lust, death, drunkenness, and boredom combine in *Les Fleurs du Mal* to create a masterpiece of poetry that is as shocking as it is brilliant.

THE POET 1

In "As If a Serpent Danced," the poet describes with chilling sensuality the movement of a dancing woman.

AS IF A SERPENT DANCED

Dear indolent! I love to see
    with every move you make
the iridescence of your skin
    gleam like watered silk.

On your resilient head of hair,
    unfathomable sea
of acrid curls that veer from brown
    to blue inconstancies,

my dreamy soul weighs anchor, sails
    for undiscovered skies
like a galleon in the morning watch
    under a freshening wind.

Cruel? Kind? Your eyes reveal
    nothing but themselves:
cold as a pair of brooches made
    of gold inlaid with steel.

And when you walk to cadences
    of sinuous nonchalance,
it looks as if a serpent danced
    in rhythm to a wand.

Under the burden of your sloth,
    your head—just like a child's—
lolls with all the wobbly grace
    of a baby elephant;

your body lists and rights itself
    like a clipper in high seas,
rolling from side to side until
    the spray has soaked its spars.

And like a current swollen by
the melt of clashing ice,
when the saliva in your mouth
surges through your teeth,

I seem to drink a devil's brew,
salt and sovereign,
as if the sky had liquefied
and strewn my heart with stars!

THE POET 2

*"Conversation (One Side)" finds the poet made bitter by woman and the
power their beauty commands.*

CONVERSATION (ONE SIDE)

Fresh as an autumn morning you may be
yet sadness rises in me like the sea
that ebbing leaves a bitter after-taste
of iodine on my still-smarting lips.

No use your groping for my feeble heart—
what you are after is no longer there;
mauled by women's weapons, fangs and claws,
my heart is gone, the beasts have eaten it.

My heart! that palace ransacked by a mob
of drunken maenads at each other's throats . . .
What perfume hovers round *your* naked throat?

O Beauty, scourge of souls, thy will be done!
With eyes as bright as candles at a feast,
consume these scraps of flesh the beasts have spared!

THE POET 3

Obsessed with beauty, Baudelaire gives it its own personality in "Allegory."

ALLEGORY

It is a lovely woman, richly dressed,
who shares her wineglass with her own long hair;
the brothel's rotgut and the brawls of love
have left the marble of her skin unmarred.
She flouts Debauchery and flirts with Death,
monsters who maim what they do not mow down,
and yet their talons have not dared molest
the simple majesty of this proud flesh.
Artemis walking, a sultana prone,
she worships pleasure with a Moslem's faith
and summons to her breasts with open arms
the race of men enslaved by her warm eyes.
Sterile this virgin, yet imperative
to the world and its workings what she knows:
the body's beauty is a noble gift
which wrests a pardon for all infamy.
What is Purgatory, what is Hell
to her? When she must go into the Night,
her eyes will gaze upon the face of Death
without hate, without remorse—as one newborn.

THE POET 4

*"A Pagan's Prayer" is the poet's cry to the muse of pleasure to grant him
the pain that scourges the soul.*

A PAGAN'S PRAYER

No, no less than the worst of your fires will do
to warm my sluggish heart to life again . . .

Pleasure! sensual Pleasure, scourge of souls:
Diva, supplicem exaudi! Grant me pain!

Goddess brightening the air we breathe,
flame in the darkness following our feet,
hear the petition of a fallen soul
who consecrates to you a brazen song.

Pleasure, sensual Pleasure! Be my queen
forever! Wear the siren mask of flesh
and velvet that beguiles the skull beneath,

or fill my goblet with your heavy sleep
that shimmers in the mysteries of wine,
Pleasure, shifting phantom, shameless Muse!

A TALE OF TWO CITIES

by Charles Dickens

1859

1 MONOLOGUE
Sydney Carton

SETTING: Europe, late eighteenth century

The cities in the title of this novel are London and Paris during the turbulent years of the French Revolution. Dr. Manette, a French physician, is called to attend a young peasant and his sister who have been brutalized by the Marquis de St. Evrémonde. To ensure the doctor's silence, the Marquis has him imprisoned for eighteen years. When he is finally released, he is deranged. He is taken to London, where he eventually recovers. Charles Darnay, nephew of the evil Marquis, renounces the decadent practices of the aristocracy and moves to England, where he conceals his relationship to the Marquis. Charles falls in love with Dr. Manette's beautiful daughter, Lucie, and they marry. Charles then discovers that his faithful servant has been arrested in Paris for helping him to escape. He bravely returns to France during the Reign of Terror to rescue his friend, but is arrested and condemned to death. Charles is rescued at the last moment by Sydney Carton, an English barrister devoted to Lucie who also happens to bear a striking resemblance to Darnay. Sydney has led a profligate life and sees salvation for himself in saving the man that Lucie loves. He manages to have Charles smuggled out of the Bastille and takes his place. As he mounts the steps of the guillotine, he knows that he has, at last, done a noble thing.

SYDNEY CARTON

In one of the most famous monologues in literature, Sydney faces the blade of "Madame Guillotine" and allows himself to taste salvation. He becomes peaceful for the first and last time in his life and is thus empowered to look into the future to see the results of his great sacrifice.

I see Barsad, and Cly, Defarge, The Vengeance, the Juryman, the Judge, long ranks of the new oppressors who have risen on the destruction of the old, perishing by this retributive instrument, before it shall cease out of its present use. I see a beautiful city and a brilliant people rising from this abyss, and, in their struggles to be truly free, in their triumphs and defeats, through long long years to come, I see the evil of this time and of the previous time of which this is the natural birth, gradually making expiation for itself and wearing out.

I see the lives for which I lay down my life, peaceful, useful, prosperous and happy, in that England which I shall see no more. I see her with a child upon her bosom, who bears my name. I see her father, aged and bent, but otherwise restored, and faithful to all men in his healing office, and at peace. . . .

I see that I hold a sanctuary in their hearts, and in the hearts of their descendants, generations hence. I see her, an old woman, weeping for me on the anniversary of this day. I see her and her husband, their course done, lying side by side in their last earthly bed, and I know that each was not more honoured and held sacred in the other's soul, than I was in the souls of both.

I see that child who lay upon her bosom and who bore my name, a man winning his way up in that path of life which once was mine. I see him winning it so well, that my name is made illustrious there by the light of his. I see the blots I threw upon it, faded away. I see him, foremost of just judges and honoured men, bringing a boy of my name, with a forehead that I know and golden hair, to this place—then to look upon, with not a trace of this day's disfigurement—and I hear him tell the child my story, with a tender and faltering voice.

It is a far, far better thing that I do, than I have ever done; it is a far, far better rest that I go to than I have ever known.

SILAS MARNER

by George Eliot

1861

3 MONOLOGUES
Dolly Winthrop
Pricilla Lammeter
Silas Marner

SETTING: England, eighteenth century

Mary Ann Evans, who wrote under the pseudonym George Eliot, created such unforgettable works as *Middlemarch* and *Adam Bede*. One of her most popular works, *Silas Marner* is a powerful tale that may be seen as an allegorical accounting of love's ability to redeem.

Silas Marner is a man made bitter by the past who has withdrawn into his own world, where only his loom and his gold exist. When Marner's gold is stolen, he grieves as for a loved one. A few nights later, a little girl appears mysteriously in his cottage. The child's mother is found dead in the snow on the road and Marner feels compelled to adopt the girl, whom he names Eppie. She becomes the recluse's link to the world, drawing him out into the village of Raveloe and giving him the unconditional love that only a child can give.

As the years go by, the pain from Marner's past is eased by his relationship with Eppie. Eppie, in turn, adores her "father" and dotes on him. When Eppie's true father—the eldest son of the local squire—steps forward to claim her, she tells him that she will never acknowledge any other father except Silas Marner. Eppie soon marries Aaron, the son of her godmother, and they make the cottage their home. Silas's redemption is at last complete.

DOLLY WINTHROP

This kindhearted woman befriends Silas Marner and here offers him advice on how best to tend to a small child.

I've seen men as are wonderful handy wi' children. The men are awk'ard and contrairy mostly, God help 'em—but when the drink's out of 'em, they aren't unsensible, though they're bad for leeching and bandaging—so fiery and unpatient. . . . See there, she's fondest o' you. She wants to go o' your lap, I'll be bound. Go, then: take her, Master Marner; you can put the things on, and then you can say as you've done for her from the first of her coming to you. Why, you take to it quite easy, Master Marner, but what shall you do when you're forced to sit in your loom? For she'll get busier and mischievouser every day—she will, bless her. . . . I'll bring you my little chair, and some bits o' red rag and things for her to play wi'; an' she'll sit and chatter to 'em as if they was alive.

To be sure; you'll have a right to her if you're a father to her, and bring her up according. But you must bring her up like christened folks's children, and take her to church, and let her learn her catechise, as my little Aaron can say off—the "I believe," and everything, and "hurt nobody by word or deed,"—as well as if he was the clerk. That's what you must do, Master Marner, if you'd do the right thing by the orphin child.

PRICILLA LAMMETER

A housewife of Raveloe speaks out against the desires of men.

It drives me past patience. The way o' the men—always wanting and wanting, and never easy with what they've got: they can't sit comfortable in their chairs when they've neither ache nor pain, but either they must stick a pipe in their mouths, to make 'em better than well, or else they must be swallowing something strong, though they're forced to make haste before the next meal comes in. But joyful be it spoken, our father was never that sort o' man. And if it had pleased God to make you ugly, like me, so as the men wouldn't ha' run after you, we might have kept to our own family, and had nothing to do with folks as have got uneasy blood in their veins.

SILAS MARNER

The weaver tells Eppie of his love for her and that he feels blessed by God by her appearance in his life.

At first, I'd a sort o' feeling come across me now and then as if you might be changed into the gold again; for sometimes, turn my head which way I would, I seemed to see the gold; and I thought I should be glad if I could feel it, and find it come back. But that didn't last long. After a bit, I should have thought it was a curse to come again, if it had drove you from me, for I'd got to feel the need o' your looks and your voice and the touch o' your little fingers. You didn't know then, Eppie, when you were such a little un—you didn't know what your old father Silas felt for you.

Eh, my precious child, the blessing was mine. If you hadn't been sent to save me, I should ha' gone to the grave in my misery. The money was taken from me in time; and you see it's been kept—kept till it was wanted for you. It's wonderful—our life is wonderful.

It takes no hold of me now, the money doesn't. I wonder if it ever could again—I doubt it might, if I lost you, Eppie. I might come to think I was forsaken again, and lose the feeling that God was good to me.

NOTES FROM UNDERGROUND

by Fyodor Dostoevsky

1864

1 MONOLOGUE
The Underground Man

SETTING: Russia, late nineteenth century

In *Notes from Underground* we meet a man who is humanity's antithesis. He represents the part of man that hungers for anarchy and chaos, that questions faith and revels in suffering. In the first half of this novel, the "underground man" talks about himself to several unspecified gentlemen. He reveals to them the dark side of man's nature— a side that man must come to accept if he is ever to know truth.

In the second half of the novel, the underground man meets with Liza, a humble prostitute. He tries to reform her, convincing her of the error of her ways. He sees himself as her aristocratic savior, when he is actually her emotional inferior: poor, mean-spirited, and utterly wretched.

THE UNDERGROUND MAN

When Liza unexpectedly arrives at the underground man's hideous abode, catching him in his dirty old robe, his humiliation is so complete that he turns on her and lashes out in an attempt to degrade her as he has been degraded.

Why have you come to me, tell me that, please? Why have you come? Answer, answer. I'll tell you, my good girl, why you have come. You've

come because I talked sentimental stuff to you then. So now you are
soft as butter and longing for fine sentiments again. So you may as
well know that I was laughing at you then. And I am laughing at you
now. . . . Yes, I was laughing at you! . . . I had been humiliated, so
I wanted to humiliate; I had been treated like a rag, so I wanted to
show my power. . . .

. . . Power, power was what I wanted then, sport was what I
wanted, I wanted to wring out your tears, your humiliation, your hys-
teria—that was what I wanted then! . . . I know that I am a black-
guard, a scoundrel, an egoist, a sluggard. . . . And for what I am
confessing to you now, I shall never forgive *you* either! Yes—you must
answer for it all because you turned up like this, because I am a black-
guard, because I am the nastiest, stupidest, absurdest and most envious
of all the worms on earth, who are not a bit better than I am,
but, the devil knows why, are never put to confusion; while
I shall always be insulted by every louse, that is my doom! . . .
How I shall hate you now after saying this, for having been here
and listening. . . . What more do you want? Why do you still
stand confronting me, after all this? . . . Why don't you go?

O CAPTAIN! MY CAPTAIN!

by *Walt Whitman*

1865

1 MONOLOGUE
Young Sailor

SETTING: America, 1865

One of America's greatest poets, Walt Whitman sang through his work of the strength of the individual. His poetry has its roots in romanticism and an essentially pantheistic view of life.

Whitman became deeply involved in the Civil War, helping to nurse wounded soldiers while writing many poems of their bravery and sacrifice. His humanity is enhanced by a profound sense of beauty in all things, however small. This allegorical poem points to a nation's grief over losing its most beloved leader, Abraham Lincoln, to an assassin's bullet.

YOUNG SAILOR

In the poem "O Captain! My Captain!," a young sailor begs his captain to listen to the cheers that welcome them home from a victorious battle. The cheers go unheard, however, for the captain was slain in battle.

"O CAPTAIN! MY CAPTAIN!"

O Captain! my Captain! our fearful trip is done,
The ship has weathered every rack, the price we sought is won,
The port is near, the bells I hear, the people all exulting,

While follow eyes the steady keel, the vessel grim and daring;
But O heart! heart! heart!
O the bleeding drops of red,
Where on the deck my Captain lies,
Fallen cold and dead.

O Captain! my Captain! rise up and hear the bells;
Rise up—for you the flag is flung—for you the bugle trills,
For you bouquets and ribboned wreaths—for you the shores acrowding,
For you they call, the swaying mass, their eager faces turning;
Here Captain! dear father!
This arm beneath your head!
It is some dream that on the deck
You've fallen cold and dead.

My Captain does not answer, his lips are pale and still,
My father does not feel my arm, he has no pulse nor will,
The ship is anchored safe and sound, its voyage closed and done,
From fearful trip the victor ship comes in with object won;
Exult O shores, and ring O bells!
But I, with mournful tread,
Walk the deck my Captain lies,
Fallen cold and dead.

CRIME AND PUNISHMENT

by Fyodor Dostoevsky

1866

1 MONOLOGUE
Raskolnikov

SETTING: Russia, late nineteenth century

This great masterpiece of Russian literature tells the story of Raskolnikov, a young man driven by poverty and starvation to commit murder. Dostoevsky paints a stark and grim portrait of a Russia teeming with stricken masses crying for food and freedom. Raskolnikov isn't evil, but the horrendous conditions under which he lives force this rational young man to commit the most irrational of all acts when he takes the life of an old pawnbroker for a few rubles.

Raskolnikov is eventually apprehended and tried for his crime. His punishment is to be sent to Siberia to live out his days. There, in that cold and barren hell on earth, Raskolnikov finds both salvation and love.

RASKOLNIKOV

After the crime, Raskolnikov takes to his bed, suffering from malnutrition and pneumonia. As he recuperates, Sonia, his lover and lifelong friend, comes to see him. He then attempts to explain his reasons for killing the old lady to her and to himself.

I wanted to murder without casuistry, to murder for my own sake, for myself alone! I didn't want to lie about it even to myself. It wasn't to help my mother I did the murder—that's nonsense—I didn't do the murder to gain wealth and power and to become a benefactor of mankind. Nonsense! I simply did it; I did the murder for myself, for myself alone, and whether I became a benefactor to others, or spent my life like a spider catching men in my web and sucking the life out of men, I couldn't have cared at that moment. . . . And it was not the money I wanted [Sonia] when I did it. It was not so much the money I wanted, but something else. . . . I wanted to find out something else; it was something else led me on. I wanted to find out then and quickly whether I was a louse like everybody else or a man. Whether I can step over barriers or not, whether I dare stoop to pick up or not, whether I am a trembling creature or whether I have the right . . .

I want to prove one thing only, that the devil led me on then and he has shown me since that I had not the right to take that path, because I am just such a louse as all the rest. . . . Listen: when I went then to the old woman's I only went to try. . . . You may be sure of that!

But how did I murder her? Is that how men do murders? Do men go to commit a murder as I went then? I will tell you some day how I went! Did I murder the old woman? I murdered myself, not her!

BEHIND A MASK

by Louisa May Alcott

1866

4 MONOLOGUES
Jean Muir
Pauline 1
Pauline 2
Gilbert

SETTING: America, late nineteenth century

Louisa May Alcott is known primarily as the author of the ever-popular novel *Little Women*. Unknown to most people, when Louisa found herself low on funds, she wrote delicious "blood and thunder" thrillers which improved her finances considerably. They are beautifully written and show a new and intriguing aspect of the demure Miss Alcott. The characters in these stories are quite colorful and dramatic.

In "Behind a Mask," the protagonist, Jean Muir, an actress some thirty-five years of age, has succeeded in deceiving a wealthy family into believing that she is a young gentlewoman of charm and vulnerability who has fallen on hard times. Her goal is to marry the old uncle for his wealth and title. On the surface, Jean is a bubbly ingenue, but she is really a conniving woman who desperately means to secure a place for herself in the household.

A second story, "Pauline's Passion and Punishment," tells of a woman who seeks revenge on her lover, Gilbert, a married man who has rejected her. Hurt and furious, Pauline turns to Manuel, who adores her and agrees to marry him. Her only intent is to make Gilbert regret his choice to stay with his wife. Much to her surprise, she falls in love with her husband. Unfortunately, her plan to make Gilbert jealous has worked, and her former lover challenges her husband to a duel and kills him. In her desire to inflict pain on Gilbert, she has designed her own destruction.

JEAN MUIR

This monologue is actually two portions of a letter Jean has written to her confidante, whom she keeps informed of her progress.

One little event I must tell you, because I committed an actionable offense and was nearly discovered. I did not go down to supper, knowing that the moth would return to flutter around the candle, and preferring that the fluttering should be done in private, as Vashti's jealousy is getting uncontrollable. Passing through the gentlemen's dressing room, my quick eye caught sight of a letter lying among the costumes. It was no stage affair, and an odd sensation of fear ran through me as I recognized the hand of S. I had feared this, but I believe in chance; and having found the letter, I examined it. You know I can imitate almost any hand. When I read in this paper the whole story of my affair with S., truly told, and also that he had made inquiries into my past life and discovered the truth, I was in a fury. To be so near success and fail was terrible, and I resolved to risk everything. I opened the letter by means of a heated knife blade under the seal, therefore the envelope was perfect; imitating S.'s hand, I penned a few lines in his hasty style, saying he was at Baden, so that if Monsieur answered, the reply would not reach him, for he is in London, it seems. This letter I put into the pocket whence the other must have fallen, and was just congratulating myself on this narrow escape, when Dean, the maid of Vashti, appeared as if watching me. She had evidently seen the letter in my hand, and suspected something. I took no notice of her, but must be careful, for she is on the watch. After this the evening closed with strictly private theatricals, in which Monsieur and myself were the only actors. To make sure that he received my version of the story first, I told him a romantic story of S.'s persecution, and he believed it. This I followed up by a moonlight episode behind a rose hedge, and sent the young gentleman home in a half-dazed condition. What fools men are!

PAULINE 1

Pauline tells the devoted Manuel of Gilbert's rejection and asks whether he still loves her after knowing of her affair with a married man.

You know my past, happy as a dream till eighteen. Then all was swept away, home, fortune, friends, and I was left, like an unfledged bird, without even the shelter of a cage. For five years I have made my life what I could, humble, honest, but never happy, till I came here, for here I saw Gilbert. In the poor companion of your guardian's daughter he seemed to see the heiress I had been, and treated me as such. This flattered my pride and touched my heart. He was kind, I grateful; then he loved me, and God knows how utterly I loved him! A few months of happiness the purest, then he went to make home ready for me, and I believed him; for where I wholly love I wholly trust. While my own peace was undisturbed, I learned to read the language of your eyes, Manuel, to find the boy grown into the man, the friend warmed into a lover. Your youth had kept me blind too long. Your society had grown dear to me, and I loved you like a sister for your unvarying kindness to the solitary woman who earned her bread and found it bitter. I told you my secret to prevent the utterance of your own. . . . Now the storm is over, and I am ready for my work again, but it must be a new task in a new scene. I hate this house, this room, the faces I must meet, the duties I must perform, for the memory of that traitor haunts them all. I see a future full of interest, a stage whereon I could play a stirring part. I long for it intensely, yet cannot make it mine alone. Manuel, do you love me still?

PAULINE 2

Pauline resolves to revenge herself on Gilbert and invites Manuel to help her—by marrying her.

Listen, Manuel. A strange spirit rules me tonight, but I will have no reserves from you, all shall be told; then, if you will come, be it so; if not, I shall go my way as solitary as I came. If you think that this loss has broken my heart, undeceive yourself, for such as I live years in an hour and show no sign. I have shed no tears, uttered no cry, asked no comfort; yet, since I read that letter, I have suffered more than many suffer in a lifetime. I am not one to lament long over any hopeless sorrow. A single paroxysm, sharp and short, and it is over. Contempt has killed my love, I have buried it, and no power can make it live again, except as a pale ghost that will not rest till Gilbert shall pass through an hour as bitter as the last.

Yes, it is weak, wicked, and unwomanly; yet I persist as relentlessly as any Indian on a war trail. See me as I am, not the gay girl you have known, but a revengeful woman with but one tender spot now left in her heart, the place you fill. I have been wronged, and I long to right myself at once. Time is too slow; I cannot wait, for that man must be taught that two can play at the game of hearts, taught soon and sharply. I can do this, can wound as I have been wounded, can sting him with contempt, and prove that I too can forget.

Manuel, I want fortune, rank, splendor, and power; you can give me all these, and a faithful friend beside. I desire to show Gilbert the creature he deserted no longer poor, unknown, unloved, but lifted higher than himself, cherished, honored, applauded, her life one of royal pleasure, herself a happy queen. Beauty, grace, and talent you tell me I possess; wealth gives them luster, rank exalts them, power makes them irresistible. Place these worldly gifts in my hand and that hand is yours.

GILBERT

Gilbert confesses to Pauline that he never loved his wife and that he still loves her.

I can offer you a heart always faithful in truth though not in seeming, for I never loved that child. I would give years of happy life to undo that act and be again the man you trusted. I can offer you a name which shall yet be an honorable one, despite the stain an hour's madness cast upon it. You once taunted me with cowardice because I dared not face the world and conquer it. I dare do that now; I long to escape from this disgraceful servitude, to throw myself into the press, to struggle and achieve for your dear sake. I can offer you strength, energy, devotion—three gifts worthy any woman's acceptance who possesses power to direct, reward, and enjoy them as you do, Pauline. Because with your presence for my inspiration, I feel that I can retrieve my faultful past, and with time become God's noblest work—an honest man. . . . my earthly hope is in your hands, my soul's salvation in your love.

THROUGH THE LOOKING-GLASS

by Lewis Carroll

1871

2 MONOLOGUES
Alice 1
Alice 2

SETTING: Victorian England and the looking-glass world

Seven years after the publication of Lewis Carroll's endearing children's novel *Alice's Adventures in Wonderland*, his fans were treated to the further adventures of the precocious young girl in *Through the Looking-Glass*.

On a snowy winter's day, Alice is playing indoors with her kittens. As before, Alice's imagination leads her into a fantastic adventure, this time in the looking-glass that hangs above the fireplace. She finds that she is able to pass through the looking-glass into a fascinating world of talking chess pieces, Tweedledum, Tweedledee, and shoes and ships and sealing wax.

ALICE 1

When Alice first steps through the looking-glass, she discovers a book, but she must hold it to the looking-glass in order to read it. When the letters are reversed, she reads the immortal poem "Jabberwocky."

JABBERWOCKY

'Twas brillig, and the slithy toves
Did gyre and gimble in the wabe:

All mimsy were the borogoves,
    And the mome raths outgrabe.

"Beware the Jabberwock, my son!
    The jaws that bite, the claws that catch!
Beware the Jubjub bird, and shun
    The frumious Bandersnatch!"

He took his vorpal sword in hand:
    Long time the manxome foe he sought—
So rested he by the Tumtum tree,
    And stood awhile in thought.

And, as in uffish thought he stood,
    The Jabberwock, with eyes of flame,
Came whiffling through the tulgey wood,
    And burbled as it came!

One, two! One, two! And through and through
    The vorpal blade went snicker-snack!
He left it dead, and with its head
    He went galumphing back.

"And hast thou slain the Jabberwock?
    Come to my arms, my beamish boy!
O frabjous day! Callooh! Callay!"
    He chortled in his joy.

'Twas brillig, and the slithy toves
    Did gyre and gimble in the wabe:
All mimsy were the borogoves,
    And the mome raths outgrabe.

ALICE 2

On a snowy day, Alice plays with her kittens in the drawing room. In this monologue, she fondly admonishes Kitty for her faults and winds up musing about what it would be like if all her punishments were saved up for a year.

Do you know what tomorrow is, Kitty? You'd have guessed if you'd been up in the window with me—only Dinah was making you tidy, so you couldn't. I was watching the boys getting in sticks for the bonfire—and it wants plenty of sticks, Kitty! Only it got so cold, and it snowed so, they had to leave off. Never mind, we'll go and see the bonfire tomorrow.

Do you know, I was so angry, Kitty, when I saw all the mischief you had been doing. I was very nearly opening the window, and putting you out in the snow! And you'd have deserved it, you little mischievous darling! What have you got to say for yourself? Now don't interrupt me! I'm going to tell you all your faults. Number one: you squeaked twice while Dinah was washing your face this morning. Now you can't deny it, Kitty: I heard you! What's that you say? Her paw went into your eye? Well, that's *your* fault, for keeping your eyes open—if you'd shut them tight up, it wouldn't have happened. Now don't make any more excuses, but listen! Number two: you pulled Snowdrop away by the tail just as I had put down the saucer of milk before her. What, you were thirsty, were you? How do you know she wasn't thirsty too? Now for number three: you unwound every bit of worsted while I wasn't looking.

That's three faults, Kitty, and you've not been punished for any of them yet. You know I'm saving up all your punishments for Wednesday week—Suppose they had saved up all *my* punishments? What *would* they do at the end of the year? I should be sent to prison, I suppose, when the day came. Or—let me see—suppose each punishment was to be going without a dinner: then, when the miserable day came, I should have to go without fifty dinners at once! Well, I shouldn't mind *that* much! I'd far rather go without them than eat them!

A SEASON IN HELL

by Arthur Rimbaud

1873

3 MONOLOGUES
The Poet 1
The Poet 2
The Poet 3

SETTING: France, nineteenth century

Arthur Rimbaud was one of France's greatest poets, completing all of his work before he was twenty. At the age of sixteen, Rimbaud traveled to Paris where he was taken in by Paul Verlaine, a well-known poet ten years his senior. The two eventually became lovers, their stormy relationship ending two years later when a drunken Verlaine shot Rimbaud in the wrist for threatening to leave him.

Rimbaud composed his major works during and shortly after those two years. Condemning all but a few poets that preceded him, Rimbaud waged a personal war against beauty and order, his works taking on a feverish and haunting quality of hallucination. *A Season in Hell* is Rimbaud's cathartic exorcism of his life with Verlaine. Rimbaud was all of seventeen when he wrote it, and two years later he would write no more.

THE POET 1

Life has become a farce for Rimbaud, as this prose piece illustrates.

Boredom is no longer my love. Rages, debaucheries, madness, all of

whose transports and disasters I know,—my whole burden is set down.
Let's appreciate without giddiness the extent of my innocence.

I would no longer be capable of requesting the comfort of a bas-
tinado. I do not believe I have embarked on a wedding with Jesus
Christ as my father-in-law.

I am not a prisoner of my reason. I have said: God I wish for
freedom in salvation: how to pursue it? Frivolous tastes have left me.
No more need for devotion nor for divine love. I do not miss the age
of sensitive hearts. Everyone has his reason, scorn and charity: I retain
my place at the top of this angelic ladder of common sense.

As for established happiness, domestic or not . . . no, I cannot.
I am too dissipated, too weak. Life flowers through toil, an old truth:
as for me, my life is not sufficiently weighty, it takes wing and floats
far above the action, that cherished focus of the world.

What an old maid I'm becoming, to lack the courage to love death!

If only God would accord me heavenly, ethereal calmness,
prayer,—like the ancient saints—the saints! powerful men! the an-
chorites, artists such as are no longer needed!

An endless farce! My innocence would make me weep. Life is the
farce all have to perform.

THE POET 2

*In "The Flash of Lightning" Rimbaud reflects on his unyielding desire to
rebel, claiming that his "betrayal to the world would be too brief a torture."*

Human toil! this is the explosion that illuminates my abyss from time
to time. . . .

—What can I do? I know work; and science is too slow. Let prayer
gallop and let light roar . . . I see it plainly. It is too simple, and the
weather is too warm; they will do without me. I have my duty, I shall
be proud of it after the fashion of some people, by setting it aside.

My life is worn out. Come! let us dissemble, let us loaf, O mercy!
And we shall exist by amusing ourselves, by dreaming of monstrous
loves and fantastic universes, by complaining and quarreling with pre-

tenses of the world: buffoon, beggar, artist, bandit,—priest! On my hospital bed, the odor of incense, so overpowering, came back to me; guardian of the holy aromatics, confessor, martyr . . .

I recognize there my foul upbringing. What of it! . . . To reach my twenty years, if others are reaching twenty years . . .

No! no! right now I rebel against death! Work seems too trivial to my pride: my betrayal to the world would be too brief a torture. At the last moment, I'd attack on the right, on the left . . .

Then,—oh! poor dear soul, would eternity not be lost to us!

THE POET 3

Near the end of A Season in Hell, *this piece, called "Morning," looks to the future where the Poet sees the struggle to achieve a "new wisdom" as being won.*

Did I not *once* have a lovely youth, heroic, fabulous, to be inscribed on leaves of gold,—too much luck! Through what crime, through what error, have I deserved my present weakness? You who maintain that animals heave sobs of grief, that the sick despair, that the dead have bad dreams, try to recount my fall and my sleep. As for me, I can no more explain myself than the beggar with his perpetual *Paters* and *Ave Marias. I no longer know how to speak!*

Today, however, I think I have finished the account of my hell. It surely was hell; the old one, the one whose gates the son of man opened.

From the same wilderness, in the same night, always my tired eyes waken to the silver star, always, although the Kings of life, the three magi, the heart, the soul, the mind, are not moved. When shall we go, beyond the shores and the mountains, to acclaim the birth of the new work, the new wisdom, the flight of tyrants and of demons, the end of superstition, to adore—the first worshipers!—Christmas on earth!

The song of the heavens, the procession of peoples! Slaves, let us not blaspheme life.

ROSE IN BLOOM

by Louisa May Alcott

1876

2 MONOLOGUES
Rose
Mac

SETTING: America, late nineteenth century

Rose in Bloom tells the story of the orphan Rose, who has recently returned home after two years abroad. She is accompanied by Phebe, her companion and best friend. Rose's uncle, Dr. Alec Campbell, has been her legal guardian since the death of her parents, and meets Rose upon her return along with his wife and seven sons. *Rose in Bloom* relates the daily lives of the eight cousins, their romances, and Rose's decision to marry her cousin Mac.

ROSE

In this monologue, Rose announces to her uncle and cousins her extremely unconventional ideas about the role of women in society—a role that sounds decidedly twentieth century in this nineteenth-century novel.

Phebe and I believe that it is as much a right and a duty for women to do something with their lives as for men; and we are not going to be satisfied with such frivolous parts as you give us. I mean what I say, and you cannot laugh me down. Would *you* be contented to be told to enjoy yourself for a little while, then marry and do nothing more till you die?

. . . Neither should it be for a woman: for we've got minds and souls as well as hearts; ambition and talents, as well as beauty and accomplishments; and we want to live and learn as well as love and be loved. I'm sick of being told that is all a woman is fit for! I won't have anything to do with love till I prove that I am something beside a housekeeper and baby-tender!

Ah, you needn't pretend to be shocked; you will be in earnest presently; for this is only the beginning of my strong-mindedness. I have made up my mind not to be cheated out of the real things that make one good and happy; and just because I'm a rich girl, fold my hands and drift as so many do, I haven't lived with Phebe all these years in vain: I know what courage and self-reliance can do for one; and I sometimes wish I hadn't a penny in the world so that I could go and earn my bread with her, and be as brave and independent as she will be pretty soon.

MAC

At a male get-together before a ball, Mac becomes angry with several of his friends for tempting Charlie Prince, an alcoholic, to take a drink. He believes that offering liquor to one who is struggling to stay sober is both "cowardly and sinful."

I beg pardon, Van, for making a mess; but I can't stand by and see my own brother tempt another man beyond his strength, or make a brute of himself. That's plain English: but I can't help speaking out, for I know not one of you would willingly hurt Charlie, and you will if you do not let him alone.

. . . It is not civil to urge or joke a guest into doing what you know and he knows is bad for him. That's only a glass of wine to you, but it is perdition to Charlie; and, if Steve knew what he was about, he'd cut his right hand off before he'd offer it.

. . . Look here, boys: I know I ought not to explode in this violent sort of way, but upon my life I couldn't help it, when I heard what you were saying and saw what Steve was doing. Since I *have* begun I may as well finish, and tell you straight out that Prince can't stand this sort of thing. He is trying to flee temptation, and whoever leads him into it does a cowardly and sinful act: for the loss of one's own self-respect is bad enough without losing the more precious things that make life worth having. Don't tell him I've said this, but lend a hand if you can, and never have to reproach yourselves with the knowledge that you helped to ruin a fellow-creature, soul and body.

ANNA KARENINA

by Leo Tolstoy

1877

2 MONOLOGUES
Prince
Anna

SETTING: Russia, late nineteenth century

Anna Karenina is regarded as one of Tolstoy's greatest novels. It tells the story of Anna, a noblewoman who commits adultery and is subsequently condemned by society. Anna is a woman of great passion who is married to a dull man for whom she holds little affection. She meets the dashing Count Vronsky, a handsome young army officer, and falls in love. She renounces the duties placed upon her by society and becomes Vronsky's mistress, foolishly believing that her husband and society will forgive her.

Anna becomes dependent upon Vronsky for all her needs when she is openly condemned for her errant behavior. Vronsky, in turn, soon chafes under her possessive jealousy. When Anna comes to believe that he no longer loves her, she throws herself under a train. Stricken, Vronsky returns to army life, hoping to assuage his grief by volunteering for duty in a war between the Turks and the Serbians.

PRINCE

Kitty, a young princess in love with Vronsky, has a scheming mother who throws a party for her in hopes of attracting the eligible young count. Kitty's father, the prince, thinks that the party was a cheap and obvious lure to trap a man who does not love Kitty. Here, he chastises his wife for raising their daughter's hopes in vain.

What have you done? I'll tell you what. To begin with, you entice an eligible young man into your drawing room, which of course will become the talk of all Moscow and rightly so. If you give a party, invite everybody and not a selected number of eligible fools. Invite all the brainless puppies, engage a pianist and let them dance. But don't let us have the sort of thing we had tonight—don't throw them at her head. It makes me sick to look at it. I tell you it makes me sick! And you've got what you wanted, you've turned the poor girl's head. Levin is a thousand times the better man. As for that Petersburg coxcomb, they turn them out by machine. They're all the same, they're all trash. Even if he were a prince of the blood, my daughter has no need to run after him! . . .

. . . And what if she really falls in love with him and he has no more intention of marrying than I have? Oh, I wish I hadn't seen it! Oh, spiritualism! Oh, Nice! Oh, the ball!

I don't think, I know. We have eyes for these things and women haven't. I can see a man who has serious intentions—that's Levin. And I can see a popinjay like that conceited coxcomb who only wants to have a good time.

You'll remember my words, but it'll be too late.

ANNA

Convinced that Vronsky no longer loves her, Anna despairs over their hopeless situation. She commits suicide shortly after this scene.

My love grows more and more passionate and demanding and his dwindles and dwindles, and that is why we are drifting apart. And there's nothing one can do about it. He is everything in the world to me, and I demand that he should give himself up to me more and more completely. And he wants more and more to get away from me. Before we became lovers we were drawn together, but now we are irresistibly drifting apart. And nothing can be done to alter it. He tells me that I am insanely jealous, and I too have kept telling myself that I was insanely jealous. But that is not true. I am not jealous; I am discontented. If only I could be anything but his mistress, while caring passionately for nothing except his caresses! But I can't and I don't want to be anything else. And by this desire I arouse his disgust, which in turn arouses resentment and anger in me, and it cannot be otherwise. If, no longer loving me, he is kind and affectionate to me out of a sense of *duty* and what I desire is not there—why, that is a thousand times worse than hatred. It is hell! And that's just what it is. He has long stopped loving me. And where love ends, hate begins. . . . It is impossible! Life is pulling us apart, and I am the cause of his unhappiness and he of mine, and it is impossible to change either him or me.

TREASURE ISLAND

by Robert Louis Stevenson

1883

3 MONOLOGUES
Long John Silver 1
Jim Hawkins
Long John Silver 2

SETTING: England and the South Seas, nineteenth century

This adventure is narrated by Jim Hawkins, a boy who lives in the Admiral Benbow Inn on the west coast of England. An old buccaneer dies at the inn and Jim discovers a treasure map among the man's belongings. He and his mother flee the inn and find sanctuary with Squire Trelawney, before pirates in search of the map arrive.

Jim, the squire, and Dr. Livesey hire a ship and crew and set sail in search of the treasure. The ship's cook is the infamous Long John Silver, who plans to take the ship and the treasure for himself. Jim discovers Silver's plot and tells the squire and the doctor, who are able to thwart the pirate's efforts.

LONG JOHN SILVER 1

On Treasure Island, Jim accidentally stumbles upon Long John's campfire. Silver is happy to see Jim and asks the boy to join up with him.

So, here's Jim Hawkins, shiver my timbers! dropped in, like, eh? Well, come, I take that friendly.

Now, you see, Jim, so be as you *are* here, I'll give you a piece of my mind. I've always liked you, I have, for a lad of spirit, and the picter of my own self when I was young and handsome. I always wanted you to jine and take your share, and die a gentleman, and now, my cock, you've got to. Cap'n Smollett's a fine seaman, as I'll own up to any day, but stiff on discipline. "Dooty is dooty," says he, and right he is. Just you keep clear of the cap'n. The doctor himself is gone dead again you—"ungrateful scamp" was what he said; and the short and the long of the whole story is about here: you can't go back to your own lot, for they won't have you; and, without you start a third ship's company all by yourself, which might be lonely, you'll have to jine with Cap'n Silver.

I don't say nothing as to your being in our hands, though there you are, and you may lay to it. I'm all for argyment; I never seen good come o' threatening. If you like the service, well, you'll jine; and if you don't, Jim, why, you're free to answer no—free and welcome, shipmate; and if fairer can be said by mortal seaman, shiver my sides!

JIM HAWKINS

Jim is determined not to show any fear when he is captured by the pirates. He defiantly tells Long John that it was he who stole the ship away from the pirates and caused Long John no end of trouble.

I am not such a fool but I know pretty well what I have to look for. Let the worst come to the worst, it's little I care. I've seen too many die since I fell in with you. But there's a thing or two I have to tell you, and the first is this: here you are, in a bad way: ship lost, treasure lost, men lost; your whole business gone to wreck; and if you want to know who did it—it was I! I was in the apple barrel the night we sighted land, and I heard you, John, and you, Dick Johnson, and Hands, who is now at the bottom of the sea, and told every word you said before the hour was out. And as for the schooner, it was I who cut her cable, and it was I that killed the men you had aboard of her, and it was I who brought her where you'll never see her more, not one of you. The laugh's on my side; I've had the top of this business from the first; I no more fear you than I fear a fly. Kill me, if you please, or spare me. But one thing I'll say, and no more; if you spare me, bygones are bygones, and when you fellows are in court for piracy, I'll save you all I can. It is for you to choose. Kill another and do yourselves no good, or spare me and keep a witness to save you from the gallows.

LONG JOHN SILVER 2

The other pirates want to kill Jim, but Long John defends him, claiming that anyone who tries to harm the boy has to deal with him.

Did any of you gentlemen want to have it out with *me*? Put a name on what you're at; you ain't dumb, I reckon. Him that wants shall get it. Have I lived this many years, and a son of a rum puncheon cock his hat athwart my hawse at the latter end of it? You know the way; you're all gentlemen o' fortune, by your account. Well, I'm ready. Take a cutlass, him that dares, and I'll see the colour of his inside, crutch and all, before that pipe's empty.

That's your sort, is it? Well, you're a gay lot to look at, anyway. Not much worth to fight, you ain't. P'r'aps you can understand King George's English. I'm cap'n here by 'lection. I'm cap'n here because I'm the best man by a long sea-mile. You won't fight as gentlemen o' fortune should; then, by thunder, you'll obey, and you may lay to it! I like that boy, now; I never seen a better boy than that. He's more a man than any pair of rats of you in this here house, and what I say is this: let me see him that'll lay a hand on him—that's what I say, and you may lay to it.

THE ADVENTURES OF HUCKLEBERRY FINN

by Mark Twain

1884

3 MONOLOGUES
Huck 1
Huck 2
Pap

SETTING: pre–Civil War America

Considered by many literary critics to be the greatest American novel, *The Adventures of Huckleberry Finn* is a profound treatise on the evils of slavery and a vivid portrait of pre–Civil War America. Using the innocence of Huck's character, Twain comments on the faults of his day. Although Huck describes himself as being "lowdown and ornery," he has a sense of honor and nobility despite his lowly origins and personal privations. Relying on instinct, he always seems to do the right and moral thing.

Huck manages to escape from his brutal father by faking his own death and sets off down the Mississippi River with Jim, a runaway slave. This odd couple encounter many adventures on their journey, including an involvement with two confidence men who sell Jim back into slavery. Huck's best friend, Tom Sawyer, arrives in time to help rescue Jim who, unknown to them, has already been freed by Miss Watson in her will. Written in a native dialect, we see in one boy the wonderful heroism of the American spirit.

HUCK 1

Our young hero introduces himself, revealing a boy struggling to reconcile his buoyant soul with the constraints of society. Here we see him living under the protection of the Widow Douglas, a kindhearted woman devout in her Christian beliefs and forever hounding Huck about his errant ways.

You don't know about me without you have read a book by the name of *The Adventures of Tom Sawyer,* but that ain't no matter. That book was made by Mr. Mark Twain, and he told the truth, mainly. There was things which he stretched, but mainly he told the truth. . . .

. . . The Widow Douglas she took me for her son, and allowed she would sivilize me; it was rough living in the house all the time, considering how dismal regular and decent the widow was in all her ways; and so when I couldn't stand it no longer I lit out. . . . But Tom Sawyer he hunted me up and said he was going to start a band of robbers, and I might join if I would go back to the widow and be respectable. So I went back.

The widow she cried over me, and called me a poor lost lamb, and she called me a lot of other names, too, but she never meant no harm by it. . . .

After supper she got out her book and learned me about Moses and the Bulrushers, and I was in a sweat to find out all about him; but by and by she let it out that Moses had been dead a considerable long time; so then I didn't care no more about him, because I don't take no stock in dead people.

HUCK 2

Huckleberry deals with the prickly question of religion, resolving it for himself with characteristically practical results.

[Miss Watson] told me to pray every day, and whatever I asked for I would get it. But it warn't so. I tried it. Once I got a fishline, but no hooks. It warn't any good to me without hooks. I tried for the hooks three or four times, but somehow I couldn't make it work. One day I asked Miss Watson to try for me, but she said I was a fool. She never told me why, and I couldn't make it out no way.

I set down one time back in the woods and had a long think about it. I says to myself, if a body can get anything they pray for, why don't Deacon Winn get back the money he lost on pork? Why can't the widow get back her silver snuffbox that was stole? . . . No, says I to myself, there ain't nothing in it. I went and told the widow about it, and she said the thing a body could get by praying for it was "spiritual gifts." This was too many for me, but she told me what she meant— I must help other people, and do everything I could for other people, and look out for them all the time, and never think about myself. This was including Miss Watson, as I took it. I went out in the woods and turned it over in my mind a long time, but I couldn't see no advantage about it—except for the other people; so at last I reckoned I wouldn't worry about it any more, but just let it go.

PAP

Here we meet Huck's drunken, abusive, and bigoted father. Pap rails against all those whom he believes have done him an injustice. In this character we see a frightening portrait of ignorance and racism.

Call this a govment! why, just look at it and see what it's like. Here's the law a-standing ready to take a man's son away from him—a man's own son, which he has had all the trouble and all the anxiety and all the expense of raising. Yes, just as that man has got that son raised at last, and ready to go to work and begin to do suthin' for *him* and give him a rest, the law up and goes for him. And they call *that* govment! . . . Sometimes I've a mighty notion to just leave the country for good and all. Says I, for two cents I'd leave the blamed country and never come a-near it ag'in. . . .

Oh, yes, this is a wonderful govment, wonderful. Why, looky here. There was a free nigger there from Ohio—a mulatter, most as white as a white man. He had the whitest shirt on you ever see, too, and the shiniest hat; and there ain't a man in town that's got as fine clothes as what he had; and he had a gold watch and chain, and a silver-headed cane—the awfulest old grayheaded nabob in the state. They said he was a p'fessor in a college, and could talk all kinds of languages, and knowed everything. And that ain't the wust. They said he could *vote* when he was at home. Thinks I, what is the country a-coming to? It was 'lection day, and I was just about to go and vote myself if I warn't too drunk to get there; but when they told me there was a state in this country where they'd let that nigger vote, I drawed out. I says I'll never vote ag'in. Them's the very words I said; they all heard me; and the country may rot for all me—I'll never vote ag'in as long as I live.

SELECTED TALES OF
GUY DE MAUPASSANT

1887, 1890

3 MONOLOGUES
Roger de Salnis
The Countess
The Protagonist

SETTING: France, late nineteenth century

The two stories given here show Guy de Maupassant at his best.

"Vain Beauty" is the tale of a beautiful woman who has told her husband that one of their children is not his, but not which one. Because of this, the husband has broken off physical relations with her and torments himself in trying to discover which child he should love less.

In "The Horla," de Maupassant explores mental illness, paranoia, and despair, all of which the writer suffered. The protagonist comes to believe that an invisible being is trying to destroy him. The entity, which he calls "the Horla," becomes so real to him that he actually burns down his house in a desperate effort to kill it. Realizing that the creature did not perish in the flames, he is finally driven to suicide.

ROGER DE SALNIS

While observing the beautiful Countess at the opera, Roger expresses his disgust with the vulgarity of sex as a means of reproduction. He claims that

*it is God's great joke on mankind to give him a sense of beauty and romance
while providing such a base method of fulfilling it.*

Poor women! Ah! my dear fellow, just consider! Eleven years of maternity, for such a woman! What a hell! All her youth, all her beauty,
every hope of success, every poetical ideal of a bright life, sacrificed
to that abominable law of reproduction which turns the normal woman
into a mere machine for maternity. I say that Nature is our enemy,
that we must always fight against Nature, for she is continually bringing us back to an animal state. . . .

God only created coarse beings full of the germs of disease, and
who, after a few years of bestial enjoyment, grow old and infirm, with
all the ugliness and all the want of power of human decrepitude. He
only seems to have made them in order that they may reproduce their
species in a repulsive manner, and then die like ephemeral insects.

One might say that the Creator wished to prohibit men from ever
ennobling and idealizing their commerce with women. . . . Those
among us who are powerless to deceive themselves have invented vice
and refined debauchery, which is another way of laughing at God,
and of paying homage, immodest homage, to beauty.

THE COUNTESS

*The beautiful Countess de Mascaret reveals to her husband that she has
not been unfaithful to him. She lied in order to get him to leave her alone,
for she simply cannot bear to have another child.*

I have been more guilty than you think, perhaps, but I could no longer
endure that life of continual pregnancy, and I had only one means of
driving you from my bed. I lied before God, and I lied, with my hand
raised to my children's heads, for I have never wronged you. . . . I
do not at all feel that I am the mother of children who have never
been born. It is enough for me to be the mother of those that I have,
and to love them with all my heart. I am—we are—women who

belong to the civilized world, Monsieur, and we are no longer, and we refuse to be, mere females who restock the earth.

THE PROTAGONIST

The obsessed man watches as his house is devoured by flames. Though he hears his servants scream as they are killed in the fire he has set, his thoughts are only of the Horla. Realizing that it has not perished in the pyre he made for it, he contemplates suicide.

I already began to think that the fire had gone out of its own accord, or that He had extinguished it, when one of the lower windows gave way under the violence of the flames, and a long, soft, caressing sheet of red flame mounted up the white wall, and kissed it as high as the roof. . . . I saw that the whole of the lower part of my house was nothing but a terrible furnace. But a cry, a horrible, shrill, heartrending cry, a woman's cry, sounded through the night, and two garret windows were opened! I had forgotten the servants! I saw the terror-struck faces, and the frantic waving of their arms! By this time the house was nothing but a horrible and magnificent funeral pile, a monstrous pyre which lit up the whole country, a pyre where men were burning, and where He was burning also, He, He, my prisoner, that new Being, the new Master, the Horla! . . . I saw the flames darting, and I reflected that He was there, in that kiln, dead.

Dead? Perhaps? Was not his body, which was transparent, indestructible by such means as would kill ours? . . . Perhaps time alone has power over that Invisible and Redoubtable Being. . . . No—no—there is no doubt about it—He is not dead. Then—then—I suppose I must kill *myself*!

REBECCA OF SUNNYBROOK FARM

by Kate Douglas Wiggin

1903

4 MONOLOGUES
Rebecca 1
Mr. Cobb
Rebecca 2
Huldah

SETTING: rural Maine, early twentieth century

Rebecca Randall is one of seven children who live on Sunnybrook Farm with their mother and father. When Rebecca's father dies, her mother sends her to live with her two maiden aunts, Miranda and Jane. The two aunts are unprepared for the vivacious ten-year-old who so exuberantly enters their lives.

Rebecca soon settles down to her new life. Lively, talkative, and intelligent, Rebecca charms almost everyone—except Aunt Miranda. The prim spinster had never approved of Rebecca's artistic father, and she sees the same traits in her young niece. Rebecca gradually wins Aunt Miranda's love before she is sent to a seminary to study. There she writes a story for which she receives a cash prize. She gives the prize to her aunts who have lost money in a bad investment. When Aunt Miranda suffers a stroke, Rebecca helps Aunt Jane to nurse her until she is called back to Sunnybrook Farm to help her mother. During her absence, Aunt Miranda dies and leaves her beautiful home to Rebecca.

Long considered a classic, *Rebecca of Sunnybrook Farm* has charmed readers of all ages for over eighty years. Rebecca is a wonderful character for a young actress to portray.

REBECCA 1

Mr. Cobb, a taciturn Yankee, has picked up the loquacious Rebecca at the train station. He asks Rebecca the name of her folks and gets a real earful.

Randall. My mother's name is Aurelia Randall; our names are Hannah Lucy Randall, Rebecca Rowena Randall, John Halifax Randall, Jenny Lind Randall, Marquis Randall, Fanny Ellsler Randall, and Miranda Randall. Mother named half of us and father the other half, but we didn't come out even, so they both thought it would be nice to name Mira after aunt Miranda in Riverboro; they hoped it might do some good, but it didn't, and now we call her Mira. We are all named after somebody in particular. Hannah is Hannah at the Window Binding Shoes, and I am taken out of Ivanhoe; John Halifax was a gentleman in a book; Mark is after his uncle Marquis de Lafayette that died a twin. (Twins very often don't live to grow up, and triplets almost never—did you know that, Mr. Cobb?) We don't call him Marquis, only Mark. Jenny is named for a singer and Fanny for a beautiful dancer, but mother says they're both misfits, for Jenny can't carry a tune and Fanny's kind of stiff-legged. Mother would like to call them Jane and Frances and give up their middle names, but she says it wouldn't be fair to father. She says we must always stand up for father, because everything was against him, and he would n't have died if he had n't had such bad luck. I think that's all there is to tell about us.

MR. COBB

Mr. Cobb is so taken with Rebecca that he tells Mrs. Cobb all about her, expressing his concern as to how she will get along with Aunt Miranda.

Stranger or no stranger, 't would n't make no difference to her. She'd talk to a pump or a grinestun; she'd talk to herself ruther 'n keep still.

Blamed if I can repeat any of it. She kep' me so surprised I did n't have my wits about me. She had a little pink sunshade—it kind of looked like a doll's amberill, 'n' she clung to it like a burr to a woolen stockin'. I advised her to open it up—the sun was so hot; but she said no, 't would fade and she tucked it under her dress. "It's the dearest thing in life to me," says she, "but it's a dreadful care." Them's the very words, an' it's all the words I remember. "It's the dearest thing in life to me, but it's an awful care."

There was another thing, but I can't get it right exactly. She was talkin' 'bout the circus parade an' the snake charmer in a gold chariot, an' says she, "She was so beautiful beyond compare, Mr. Cobb, that it made you have lumps in your throat to look at her." She'll be comin' over to see you, mother, an' you can size her up for yourself. I don' know how she'll git on with Mirandy Sawyer—poor little soul!

REBECCA 2

The minister is so grateful to Rebecca because of her generosity in offering to house visiting missionaries in her aunt's home that he invites Rebecca to deliver a sermon, given here.

Our Father who art in Heaven, . . . Thou art God in Syria just the same as in Maine; . . . over there today are blue skies and yellow stars and burning suns . . . the great trees are waving in the warm air, while here the snow lies thick under our feet, . . . but no distance is too far for God to travel and so He is with us here as He is with them there, . . . and our thoughts rise to Him "as doves that to their windows fly". . .

We cannot all be missionaries, teaching people to be good, . . . some of us have not learned yet how to be good ourselves, but if thy kingdom is to come and thy will is to be done on earth as it is in heaven, everybody must try and everybody must help, . . . those who are old and tired and those who are young and strong. . . . The little children of whom we have heard, those born under Syrian skies, have strange and interesting work to do for Thee, and some of us would like to travel in far lands and do wonderful brave things for the heathen and gently take away their idols of wood and stone. But perhaps we have to stay at home and do what is given us to do . . . sometimes

even things we dislike, . . . but that must be what it means in the
hymn we sang, when it talked about the sweet perfume that rises with
every morning sacrifice. . . . This is the way that God teaches us to
be meek and patient and the thought that He has willed it so should
rob us of our fears and help us bear the years. Amen.

HULDAH

*At fifteen, Rebecca enters a boarding school, where she meets Huldah Mes-
erve, a girl who is a little older than Rebecca, silly and vain. Huldah reveals
her bubbly personality and an inordinate preoccupation with clothes.*

How d' ye do, girls? Can you stop studying a minute and show me
your room? Say, I've just been down to the store and bought me these
gloves, for I was bound I would n't wear mittens this winter; they're
simply too countrified. It's your first year here, and you're younger
than I am, so I s'pose you don't mind, but I simply suffer if I don't
keep up some kind of style. Say, your room is simply too cute for
words! I don't believe any of the others can begin to compare with
it! I don't know what gives it that simply gorgeous look, whether it's
the full curtains, or that elegant screen, or Rebecca's lamp; but you
certainly do have a faculty for fixing up. I like a pretty room too, but
I never have a minute to attend to mine; I'm always so busy on my
clothes that half the time I don't get my bed made up till noon; and
after all, having no callers but the girls, it don't make much difference.
When I graduate, I'm going to fix up our parlor at home so it'll be
simply regal. I've learned decalcomania, and after I take up lustre
painting I shall have it simply stiff with drapes and tidies and plaques
and sofa pillows, and make mother let me have a fire, and receive my
friends there evenings. May I dry my feet at your register? I can't bear
to wear rubbers unless the mud or the slush is simply knee-deep, they
make your feet look so awfully big. I had such a fuss getting this pair
of French-heeled boots that I don't intend to spoil the looks of them
with rubbers any oftener than I can help. I believe boys notice feet
quicker than anything. Elmer Webster stepped on one of mine yes-

terday when I accidentally had it out in the aisle, and when he apol-
ogized after class, he said he was n't so much to blame, for the foot
was so little he really couldn't see it! Is n't he perfectly great? Of course
that's only his way of talking, for after all I only wear a number two,
but these French heels and pointed toes do certainly make your foot
look smaller, and it's always said a high instep helps, too. I used to
think mine was almost a deformity, but they say it's a great beauty.
Just put your feet beside mine, girls, and look at the difference; not
that I care much, but just for fun.

PATTERNS

by Amy Lowell

1915

1 MONOLOGUE
Young Englishwoman

SETTING: England, eighteenth century

Amy Lowell was a wealthy Bostonian who was greatly influenced by
such poets as Ezra Pound. "Patterns" is Lowell's best-known poem and
is generally considered a masterpiece. First published in 1915, "Patterns" takes the perspective of an eighteenth-century Englishwoman.
The poem deals with the universal patterns of society and war, giving
it timeless significance. Both the woman and the garden in which she
walks represent her civilization's paradigm of beauty, ordered and re-
strained.

YOUNG ENGLISHWOMAN

*A woman walks the paths of a beautiful garden as she reflects on the many
patterns of life that bind us. She has just received news that her fiancé has
been killed in action, and she mourns his loss as well as the loss of opportunity
to free herself of her stiff brocade and to break the patterns of society.*

"PATTERNS"

I walk down the garden-paths,
And all the daffodils
Are blowing, and the bright blue squills.

I walk down the patterned garden-paths
In my stiff, brocaded gown.
With my powdered hair and jewelled fan,
I too am a rare
Pattern. As I wander down
The garden-paths
My dress is richly figured,
And the train
Makes a pink and silver stain
On the gravel, and the thrift
Of the borders.
Just a plate of current fashion,
Tripping by in high-heeled, ribboned shoes.
Not a softness anywhere about me,
Only whale-bone and brocade.
And I sink on a seat in the shade
Of a lime-tree. For my passion
Wars against the stiff brocade.
The daffodils and squills
Flutter in the breeze
As they please.
And I weep;
For the lime-tree is in blossom
And one small flower has dropped upon my bosom.

And the plashing of waterdrops
In the marble fountain
Comes down the garden-paths.
The dripping never stops.
Underneath my stiffened gown
Is the softness of a woman bathing in a marble basin,
A basin in the midst of hedges grown
So thick, she cannot see her lover hiding.
But she guesses he is near,
And the sliding of the water
Seems the stroking of a dear

Hand upon her.
What is Summer in a fine brocaded gown?
I should like to see it lying in a heap upon the ground,
All the pink and silver upon the ground.

I would be the pink and silver as I ran along the paths,
And he would stumble after,
Bewildered by my laughter.
I should see the sun flashing from his sword-hilt and the buckles on
    his shoes.
I would choose
To lead him in a maze along the patterned paths,
A bright and laughing maze for my heavy-booted lover,
Till he caught me in the shade,
And the buttons of his waistcoat bruised my body as he clasped me
Aching, melting, unafraid.
With the shadows of the leaves and the sundrops,
And the plopping of the waterdrops,
All about us in the open afternoon—
I am very like to swoon
With the weight of this brocade,
For the sun sifts through the shade.

Underneath the fallen blossom
In my bosom,
Is a letter I have hid.
It was brought to me this morning by a rider from the Duke,
"Madam, we regret to inform you that Lord Hartwell
Died in action Thursday se'ennight."
As I read it in the white, morning sunlight,
The letters squirmed like snakes.
"Any answer, Madam?" said my footman.
"No," I told him.
"See that the messenger takes some refreshment.
No, no answer."
And I walked down the patterned paths,

In my stiff, correct brocade.
The blue and yellow flowers stood up proudly in the sun,
Each one.
I stood upright too,
Held rigid to the pattern
By the stiffness of my gown.
Up and down I walked,

Up and down.
In a month he would have been my husband.
In a month, here, underneath this lime,
We would have broke the pattern;
He for me, and I for him,
He as Colonel, I as Lady,
On this shady seat.
He had a whim
That sunlight carried blessing.
And I answered, "It shall be as you have said."

In Summer and in Winter I shall walk
Up and down
The patterned garden-paths
In my stiff brocaded gown.
The squills and daffodils
Will give place to pillared roses, and to asters, and to snow.
I shall go
Up and down,
In my gown.
Gorgeously arrayed,
Boned and stayed.
And the softness of my body will be guarded from embrace
By each button, hook and lace.
For the man who should loose me is dead,
Fighting with the Duke in Flanders,
In a pattern called a war.
Christ! What are patterns for?

THE RAINBOW

by D. H. Lawrence

1915

4 MONOLOGUES
Ursula 1
Ursula 2
Ursula 3
Ursula 4

SETTING: rural England, turn of the century

D. H. Lawrence was a man with the rare gift of using the passion in his life to give emotional meaning to his writing. He was a man out of synch with his time. His books were suppressed, banned, or thought to be so risqué that no publisher would touch them. His two greatest works, *The Rainbow* and its sequel, *Women in Love*, were denounced for their "obscene" qualities, as was his final and most famous novel, *Lady Chatterley's Lover*.

The Rainbow begins the epic of the Brangwen family of Marsh Farm in Nottinghamshire. The Brangwens are honest, hard-working, solid people. They feel a special affinity with the land and espouse a quiet passion for living that is handed down from generation to generation. Into this proud family is born Ursula, the eldest of the children that will eventually have their stories told in *Women in Love*. This is Ursula's story. It chronicles her childhood on the farm and her eventual entrance into womanhood. Ursula is a young woman of torrential passion, torn between the need to belong to her lover, Anton Skrebensky, and the more powerful need to belong to herself.

Ursula defies tradition and contemporary morality by attending college. She wishes to be responsible for her own destiny and finds that she may do so by teaching school. Anton is shallow and incapable of understanding her need for independence. To him a woman is something beautiful to be possessed, and nothing more.

The book reaches its tragic climax when Ursula loses Anton's child in a feverish illness, and then receives word that he has married his colonel's daughter. Finally free of the past, Ursula is able to begin life anew. She will become the school mistress of Beldover, responsible for her own destiny. The book closes with Ursula studying a rainbow that points away from the corruption of the earth to the Truth of the heavens.

URSULA 1

Young Ursula shows her pride and passion in this monologue, in which she reveals a child's bitterness at her simple life, and her desire for wealth and station.

I hate the Wherrys, and I wish they were dead. Why does my father leave us in the lurch like this, making us poor and insignificant? Why is he not more? If we had a father as he ought to be, he would be Earl William Brangwen, and I should be the Lady Ursula! What right have *I* to be poor, crawling along the lane like vermin? If I had my rights I should be seated on horseback in a green riding-habit, and my groom would be behind me. And I should stop at the gates of the cottages, and inquire of the cottage woman who came out with a child in her arms, how did her husband, who had hurt his foot. And I would pat the flaxen head of the child, stooping from my horse, and I would give her a shilling from my purse, and order nourishing food to be sent from the hall to the cottage.

URSULA 2

During her last year at college, Ursula becomes obsessed with the pretense of people and their "mechanization." Here, she muses on the false quality of one of her professors while sitting in class.

What are you, you pale citizens? You subdued beast in sheep's clothing, you primeval darkness falsified to a social mechanism.

They assume selves as they assume suits of clothing. They think it better to be clerks or professors than to be the dark, fertile beings that exist in the potential darkness. What do you think you are? What do you think you are, as you sit there in your gown and your spectacles? You are a lurking, blood-sniffing creature with eyes peering out of the jungle darkness, snuffing for your desires. That is what you *are*, though nobody would believe it, and you would be the very last to allow it.

URSULA 3

Torn between Anton and her degree, Ursula describes her rather modern concept of love to her friend Dorothy.

It isn't a question of loving him. I love him well enough—certainly more than I love anybody else in the world. And I shall never love anybody else the same again. We have had the flower of each other. But I don't *care* about love. I don't value it. I don't care whether I love or whether I don't, whether I have love or whether I haven't. What is it to me? I don't know. Love—love—love—what does it mean—what does it amount to? So much personal gratification. It doesn't lead anywhere. Then what does it matter to me? As an end in itself, I could love a hundred men, one after the other. Why should I not go on, and love all the types I fancy, one after another, if love is an end in itself? There are plenty of men who aren't Anton, whom I could love—whom I would like to love.

. . . there are plenty of things that aren't in Anton that I would love in the other men. A sort of strong understanding, in some men, and then a dignity, a directness, something unquestioned that there is in working men, and then a jolly, reckless passionateness that you see—a man who could really let go—

URSULA 4

When she discovers that she is pregnant, Ursula writes this pathetic letter to Anton, who has been stationed in India and has married his colonel's

*daughter. Not knowing that he is now married, Ursula begs his forgiveness
and promises to marry him.*

Since you left me I have suffered a great deal, and so have come to
myself. I cannot tell you the remorse I feel for my wicked, perverse
behaviour. It was given to me to love you, and to know your love for
me. But instead of thankfully, on my knees, taking what God had
given, I must have the moon in my keeping, I must insist on having
the moon for my own. Because I could not have it, everything else
must go.

I do not know if you can ever forgive me. I could die with shame
to think of my behaviour with you during our last times, and I don't
know if I could ever bear to look you in the face again. Truly the best
thing would be for me to die, and cover my fantasies for ever. But I
find I am with child, so that cannot be.

It is your child, and for that reason I must revere it and submit
my body entirely to its welfare, entertaining no thought of death,
which once more is largely conceit. Therefore, because you once loved
me, and because this child is your child, I ask you to have me back.
If you will cable me one word, I will come to you as soon as I can. I
swear to you to be a dutiful wife, and to serve you in all things. For
now I only hate myself and my own conceited foolishness. I love you—
I love the thought of you—you were natural and decent all through,
whilst I was so false. Once I am with you again, I shall ask no more
than to rest in your shelter all my life—

GREEN MANSIONS

by W. H. Hudson

1916

3 MONOLOGUES
Abel
Rima
Nuflo

SETTING: the tropical rain forest of South America
in the early twentieth century

Green Mansions, written by W. H. Hudson, a distinguished naturalist, bears the subtitle: "A Romance of the Tropical Forest." Lushly exquisite, passionate, and spiritual, this tale symbolizes man's eternal quest for perfect love.

At the beginning of the story, Mr. Abel, a Venezuelan, confides to a friend his secret adventures among the savages of the South American jungle. As a young man, he was forced to flee Caracas for political reasons. He journeyed ever deeper into the jungle, living with the Indians and learning their culture. Abel is puzzled by the fact that the tribesmen refuse to hunt in the nearby forest, but hunt in areas farther away. It seems they believe the forest to be possessed by the "Daughter of Didi," an evil spirit. Filled with curiosity, Abel enters the forbidding forest, where he catches glimpses of a beautiful girl. On a subsequent visit to the forest, he is bitten by a poisonous snake. It is then that Rima, the lovely bird-girl, reveals herself. She rescues Abel and brings him to the hut where she lives with an old man she calls "Grandfather." Abel falls in love with Rima, who believes in the sanctity of all living things.

Abel vows to protect her from the superstitious Indians, but Rima's destruction is inevitable. Following her death, Abel goes mad with grief. He eventually makes his way back to civilization, where he lives out his life, a quiet, gentle man who has learned much from his beloved Rima.

ABEL

In this monologue, Abel seeks to console Rima, who has discovered that she is the last of her people. He holds her in his arms and tells her that he will be her family and that they share the language of love.

Sweetest Rima, it is so sad that I can never hope to talk with you in your way; but a greater love than this that is ours we could never feel, and love will make us happy, unutterably happy, in spite of that one sadness. And perhaps, after a while, you will be able to say all you wish in my language, which is also yours, as you said some time ago. When we are back again in the beloved wood, and talk once more under that tree where we first talked, and under the old mora, where you hid yourself and threw down leaves on me, and where you caught the little spider to show me how you made yourself a dress, you shall speak to me in your own sweet tongue, and then try to say the same things in mine. . . . And in the end, perhaps, you will find that it is not so impossible as you think.

RIMA

Rima realizes that she and Abel will always be separated by their differences. She tells him of the pain that her mother felt, knowing that she and Rima were the last of their people.

Look, grandfather lying asleep by the fire. So far away from us—oh, so far! But if we were to go out from the cave, and on and on to the great mountains where the city of the sun is, and stood there at last in the midst of great crowds of people, all looking at us, talking to us, it would be just the same. They would be like the trees and rocks and animals—so far! Not with us nor we with them. But we are everywhere alone together, apart—we two. It is love; I know it now, but I did not know it before because I had forgotten what she told me. Do you think I can tell you what she said when I asked her why she cried? Oh no! Only this, she and another were like one, always, apart from the others. Then something came—something came! O Abel, was that the something you told me about on the mountain? And the other was lost for ever, and she was alone in the forests and mountains of the world. Oh, why do we cry for what is lost? Why do we not quickly forget it and feel glad again? Now only do I know what you felt, O sweet mother, when you sat still and cried, while I ran about and played and laughed! O poor mother! Oh, what pain!

NUFLO

The old man who lives with Rima expounds on his favorite grievance: that God simply doesn't have the time to watch over every little incident. And just like any bureaucracy, He doesn't always send the best of angels for the job.

Señor, we are never sure of anything in this world. Not absolutely sure. Thus, it may come to pass that you will one day marry, and that your wife will in due time present you with a son—one that will inherit your fortune and transmit your name to posterity. And yet, sir, in this world, you will never know to a certainty that he is your son.

Here we are, compelled to inhabit this land and do not meet with proper protection from the infidel. Now, sir, this is a crying evil, and it is only becoming in one who has the true faith, and is a loyal subject of the All-Powerful, to point out with due humility that He is growing very remiss in His affairs, and is losing a good deal of His prestige. And what, señor, is at the bottom of it? Favoritism. We know that the Supreme cannot Himself be everywhere, attending to each little trike-traka that arises in the world—matters altogether beneath His notice; and that He must, like the President of Venezuela or the

Emperor of Brazil, appoint men—angels if you like—to conduct His
affairs and watch over each district. And it is manifest that . . . the
proper person has not been appointed. Every evil is done and there
is no remedy, and the Christian has no more consideration shown
him than the infidel. . . . I once saw on a church the archangel Michael, made of stone, and twice as tall as a man, with one foot on a
monster shaped like a cayman, but with bat's wings, and a head and
neck like a serpent. Into this monster he was thrusting his spear. That
is the kind of person that should be sent to rule these latitudes—a
person of firmness and resolution, with strength in his wrist. And yet
it is probable that this very man—this St. Michael—is hanging about
the palace, twirling his thumbs, waiting for an appointment, while
other weaker men, and Heaven forgive me for saying it, not above a
bribe, perhaps—are sent out to rule over this province.

NEW ORLEANS SKETCHES

by William Faulkner

Edited by Carvel Collier

1925

3 MONOLOGUES
Johnny
The Cop
Magdalen

SETTING: New Orleans, 1920s

The following monologues are taken from the first fiction written by William Faulkner. The great American author lived in New Orleans for six months in 1925. These sketches of his impressions of life in the French Quarter were first submitted to the New Orleans *Times-Picayune* and were his first departure from poetry and reviews. They are examples of the early bloom of a complex writer and are rich character studies of the people of New Orleans.

JOHNNY

In this monologue, taken from a short story called "Frankie and Johnny," a young street tough expresses his love for Frankie in astonishingly poetic language.

Listen, baby, before I seen you it was like I was one of them ferry boats yonder, crossing and crossing a dark river or something by myself; acrossing and acrossing and never getting nowheres and not knowing it and thinking I was all the time. You know—being full of a lot of names of people and things busy with their own business, and thinking I was the berries all the time. And say, listen:

When I seen you coming down the street back yonder it was like them two ferry boats hadn't seen each other until then, and they would stop when they met instead of crossing each other, and they would turn and go off side by side together where they wasn't nobody except them. Listen, baby: before I seen you I was just a young tough like what old Ryan, the cop, says I was, not doing nothing and not worth nothing and not caring for nothing except old Johnny. But when that drunk bum stopped you and said what he said to you and I walked up and slammed him, I done it for you and not for me; and it was like a wind had blew a lot of trash and stuff out of the street.

And when I put my arm around you and you was holding to me and crying, I knowed you was meant for me even if I hadn't never seen you before, and that I wasn't no longer the young tough like what old Ryan, the cop, says I was; and when you kissed me it was like . . . when you are in a dark room or something, and all of a sudden somebody turns up the light, and that's all. When I seen your yellow hair and your gray eyes it was like that: It was like a wind had blew clean through me and there was birds singing somewheres. And then I knowed it was all up with me.

THE COP

In this character study entitled "The Cop," we meet the local policeman, who likes to reflect on his life and how it hasn't exactly turned out as he had planned as a boy so many years ago.

When I was young, running about like a puppy or a colt, doing all the things which seemed to me grander than kings or even policemen could do . . . and being heartily wished dead by half the neighborhood in consequence, there was but one person in the world with whom I would have exchanged. . . . I would be a patrolman; in a blue coat and swinging a casual stick and with a silver shield on my breast, I would space the streets away with the measured beat of my footsteps.

What to compare to this grandeur? To be the idol and fear of the lads, to be looked upon with respect by even grown people; to be the personification of bravery and the despair of criminals; to have a real pistol in my pocket! . . . Or, foiling the murderer, shooting him dead in the spitting darkness, and sorely wounded, to be nursed to health again by a beautiful girl, whom I would marry.

But now that lad is grown up. Sometimes I think he still lurkes somewhere within me, reproaching me because the man has been unable to give to the lad that high desire which life has promised him. . . . Certainly man does not ever get exactly what he wants in this world, and who can say that a wife and a home and a position in the world are not, after all, the end of every man's desire. Anyway, I prefer to believe that this creature fronting the world bravely in a blue coat and a silver shield is quite a fellow, after all.

MAGDALEN

A middle-aged courtesan ruminates with bitter irony about her life. She has forgotten love and grief, living from night to night instead of day to day.

God, the light in my eyes, the sunlight flashing through the window, crashing in my poor head like last night's piano. Why didn't I close them damn shutters?

I can remember when I found days gold, but now the gold of days hurts my head. 'Tis night only is gold now, and that not often. Men aint what they used to be, or money aint, or something. Or maybe its I that aint like I was once. God knows, I try to treat 'em like they'd want I should. I treat 'em white as any, and whiter than some—not calling no names. I'm an American girl with an American smile I am, and they know it.

There was wild blood in my veins; when I was young the blood sang like shrill horns through me. I saw women who had the bright things I wanted—dresses and shoes and golden rings, lifting no finger to get them. And lights and sultry music, and all the bright chimaerae of the brain! And ah! my body like music, my body like the flame crying for silken sheens a million worms had died to make, and that my body has died a hundred times to wear them. Yes, a thousand worms made this silk, and died; I have died a thousand deaths to wear it; and sometime a thousand worms, feeding upon this body which has betrayed me, feeding, will live.

Was there love once? I have forgotten her. Was there grief once? Yes, long ago. Ah, long ago.

THE PORTABLE DOROTHY PARKER

1926, 1939

4 MONOLOGUES
Woman in Love
Bitter Person
Waiting Woman
New York City Lady

SETTING: America, 1920s and 1930s

Dorothy Parker was a much-touted member of an elite New York literary set whose ranks included Robert Benchley, George S. Kaufman, and Edna Ferber. The group's favorite haunt was the bar at the Algonquin Hotel, where they came to be known as the "Round Table."

A poet, drama critic, and short story writer renowned for her acerbic wit, Parker wrote with caustic candor and moral outrage of the excesses of New York in the 1920s, as well as with poignancy of lost love and loneliness. Her complex and multilayered writing is too often neglected in favor of her glib and memorable turn of phrase.

WOMAN IN LOVE

In the poem "Love Song," Parker juxtaposes the romantic language of young love with dashes of jaded reality. This is a true acting challenge—the actress must contradict herself in the last phrase of every stanza.

LOVE SONG

My own dear love, he is strong and bold
And he cares not what comes after.

His words ring sweet as a chime of gold,
  And his eyes are lit with laughter.
He is jubilant as a flag unfurled—
  Oh, a girl, she'd not forget him.
My own dear love, he is all my world—
  And I wish I'd never met him.

My love, he's mad, and my love, he's fleet,
  And a wild young wood thing bore him!
The ways are fair to his roaming feet,
  And the skies are sunlit for him.
As sharply sweet to my heart he seems
  As the fragrance of acacia.
My own dear love, he is all my dreams—
  And I wish he were in Asia.

My love runs by like a day in June,
  And he makes no friends of sorrows.
He'll tread his galloping rigadoon
  In the pathway of the morrows.
He'll live his days where the sunbeams start,
  Nor could storm or wind uproot him.
My own dear love, he is all my heart—
  And I wish somebody'd shoot him.

BITTER PERSON

In "Symptom Recital," we are presented with an apparent misanthrope, only to discover a person falling in love.

SYMPTOM RECITAL

I do not like my state of mind;
I'm bitter, querulous, unkind.
I hate my legs, I hate my hands,

I do not yearn for lovelier lands.
I dread the dawn's recurrent light;
I hate to go to bed at night.
I snoot at simple, earnest folk.
I cannot take the gentlest joke.
I find no peace in paint or type.
My world is but a lot of tripe.
I'm disillusioned, empty-breasted.
For what I think, I'd be arrested.
I am not sick, I am not well.
My quondam dreams are shot to hell.
My soul is crushed, my spirit sore;
I do not like me any more.
I cavil, quarrel, grumble, grouse.
I ponder on the narrow house.
I shudder at the thought of men. . . .
I'm due to fall in love again.

WAITING WOMAN

*In "A Telephone Call," the protagonist is a young woman anxiously await-
ing a phone call from a man she hopes will ask her out on a date.*

Please, God, let him telephone me now. Dear God, let him call me
now. I won't ask anything else of You, truly I won't. It isn't very much
to ask. It would be so little to You, God, such a little, little thing.
Only let him telephone now. Please, God. Please, please, please.

This is the last time I'll look at the clock. I will not look at it
again. It's ten minutes past seven. He said he would telephone at five
o'clock: "I'll call you at five, darling." I think that's where he said
"darling." I'm almost sure he said it there. I know he called me "darling" twice, and the other time was when he said good-by. "Good-
by, darling."

I must stop this. I mustn't be this way. Look. Suppose a young
man says he'll call a girl up, and then something happens, and he

doesn't. That isn't so terrible, is it? Why, it's going on all over the world, right this minute. Oh, what do I care what's going on all over the world? Why can't that telephone ring? Why can't it, why can't it? Couldn't you ring? Ah, please, couldn't you? You damned, ugly, shiny thing. It would hurt you to ring, wouldn't it? Oh, that would hurt you. Damn you, I'll pull your filthy roots out of the wall, I'll smash your smug black face in little bits. Damn you to hell.

NEW YORK CITY LADY

"From the Diary of a New York City Lady" reveals the exploits of a lady of leisure—a member of the smart set.

Monday. Breakfast tray about eleven; didn't want it. The champagne at the Amorys' last night was *too* revolting, but what *can* you do? You can't stay until five o'clock on just *nothing*. They had those *divine* Hungarian musicians in the green coats, and Stewie Hunter took off one of his shoes and led them with it, and it *couldn't* have been funnier. He is *the* wittiest number in the *entire* world; he *couldn't* be more perfect. . . . Every time I look at my finger nails, I could *spit*. *Damn* Miss Rose.

Tuesday. Joe came barging in my room this morning at *practically* nine o'clock. Couldn't have been more furious. Started to fight, but *too* dead. . . . Tried to read a book, but couldn't sit still. *Can't* decide to wear the red lace or the pink with the feathers. Feel *too* exhausted, but what *can* you do?

Wednesday. The most terrible thing happened *just this minute*. Broke one of my finger nails *right off short*. Absolutely *the* most horrible thing I ever had happen to me in my life. Called up Miss Rose to come over and shape it for me, but she was out for the day. I do have *the* worst luck in the *entire* world. Now I'll have to go around like this all day and all night, but what *can* you do? *Damn* Miss Rose. . . .

Thursday. Simply *collapsing* on my *feet*. Last night *too* marvelous. . . . Took Ollie to the Watsons' party; *couldn't* have been more thrilling. Everybody simply *blind*. They had those Hungarians in the green coats and Stewie Hunter was leading them with a lamp, and, after the lamp got broken, he and Tommy Thomas did adagio dances—*too* wonderful. . . . Miss Rose came at noon to shape my nail, *couldn't* have been more fascinating. . . . Made her take that *vile* tangerine polish off my nails and put on dark red. Didn't notice until after she had gone that it's practically *black* in electric light; *couldn't* be in a worse state. *Damn* Miss Rose. . . .

Friday. Absolutely *sunk; couldn't* be worse. Last night *too* divine, movie simply deadly. Took Ollie to the Kingslands' party, *too* unbelievable, everybody simply *rolling.* They had those Hungarians in the green coats, but Stewie Hunter wasn't there. He's got a *complete* nervous breakdown. . . . Absolutely *walking the floor* like a *panther* all day. . . . Can't *face* deciding whether to wear the blue with the white jacket or the purple with the beige roses. Every time I look at those *revolting* black nails, I want to absolutely *yip.* I really have *the* most horrible things happen to me of anybody in the *entire* world. *Damn* Miss Rose.

LOST HORIZON

by James Hilton

1933

1 MONOLOGUE
High Lama

·SETTING: Shangri-La, a hidden city in the Himalayas,
twentieth century

Lost Horizon is the fascinating tale of a secret valley in the majestic
mountains at the top of the world. The story is told by Conway, a
British pilot whose plane mysteriously vanishes in the mountains of
Tibet. Conway and his passengers are rescued and brought to Shangri-
La, a wondrous place where men and women live for hundreds of
years. They are each given the opportunity to stay in Shangri-La, and
several decide happily to do so. Others of the party wish to return to
the outside world, and Conway decides to accompany them although
he has lost his heart to a beautiful woman of Shangri-La. Months after
their departure, Conway stumbles, near death, into a Tibetan mon-
astery. The gentle monks nurse him back to health as he tells his
remarkable tale. Then, one day, Conway mysteriously leaves the mon-
astery, heading back through the forbidding towers of snow to reclaim
the valley of Shangri-La and his love.

HIGH LAMA

This monologue is delivered to Conway by the High Lama of Shangri-La,
a man of indeterminate age and great wisdom. The High Lama reveals to

Conway the joys of living far beyond his imagining and the hope of preserving a life which he believes is in imminent danger of being destroyed.

There *is* a reason, and a very definite one indeed. It is the whole reason for this colony of chance-sought strangers living beyond their years. We do not follow an idle experiment, a mere whimsy. We have a dream and a vision. It is a vision that first appeared to old Perrault when he lay dying in this room in the year 1789. He looked back then on his long life, as I have already told you, and it seemed to him that all the loveliest things were transient and perishable, and that war, lust, and brutality might some day crush them until there were no more left in the world. He remembered sights he had seen with his own eyes, and with his mind he pictured others; he saw the nations strengthening, not in wisdom, but in vulgar passions and the will to destroy; he saw their machine power multiplying until a single-weaponed man might have matched a whole army of the Grand Monarque. And he perceived that when they had filled the land and sea with ruin, they would take to the air. . . .

We may expect no mercy, but we may faintly hope for neglect. Here we shall stay with our books and our music and our meditations, conserving the frail elegancies of a dying age, and seeking such wisdom as men will need when their passions are all spent. We have a heritage to cherish and bequeath. Let us take what pleasure we may until that time comes.

Then, my son, when the strong have devoured each other, the Christian ethic may at last be fulfilled, and the meek shall inherit the earth.

FOR WHOM THE BELL TOLLS

by Ernest Hemingway

1940

2 MONOLOGUES
Pilar
Robert Jordan

SETTING: Spain, 1936

The bloody Spanish Civil War rages across Spain, drawing together the many political factions that vie for power following the deposing of the king and his government.

Robert Jordan is an American partisan who has been hired by the Popular Front to blow up a bridge that is critical to winning the war. Anselmo is a sixty-eight-year-old Segovian who acts as Robert's guide to the bridge. The two run into a group of guerrillas led by a man and his wife. Jordan asks for their help in accomplishing his goal and is surprised at the infighting this causes in the group. He falls in love with and marries Maria, a woman traveling with the guerrillas who has been tortured by the Fascists. Love, passion, and patriotism blend vividly with the tempestuousness of war, creating an unforgettable classic.

PILAR

In this monologue, the guerrilla's woman tells a story of an idyllic time in her life when she and a young lover stayed in Valencia, where they ate melons, drank cold beer, and made love.

We made love in the room with the strip wood blinds hanging over the balcony and a breeze through the opening of the top of the door which turned on hinges. We made love there, the room dark in the day time from the hanging blinds, and from the streets there was the scent of the flower market and the smell of burned powder from the firecrackers of the *traca* that ran through the streets exploding each noon during the Feria. It was a line of fireworks that ran through all the city, the firecrackers linked together and the explosions running along on poles and wires of the tramways, exploding with a great noise and jumping from pole to pole with a sharpness and a cracking of explosion you could not believe.

We made love and then sent for another pitcher of beer with the drops of its coldness on the glass and when the girl brought it, I took it from the door and I placed the coldness of the pitcher against the back of Finito as he lay, now, asleep, not having wakened when the beer was brought and he said, "No, Pilar. No, woman, let me sleep." And I said, "No, wake up and drink this to see how cold," and he drank without opening his eyes and went to sleep again and I lay with my back against a pillow at the foot of the bed and watched him sleep, brown and dark-haired and young and quiet in his sleep, and drank the whole pitcher, listening now to the music of a band that was passing.

ROBERT JORDAN

As Robert marches along with Anselmo, Maria, and the guerrillas, he ponders the future. Although he loves Maria, he is forced to wonder what life back in Montana would be like for her.

Spanish girls make wonderful wives. I've never had one so I know. And when I get my job back at the university she can be an instructor's wife and when undergraduates who take Spanish IV come in to smoke pipes in the evening and have those so valuable informal discussions about Quevedo, Lope de Vega, Galdós and the other always admirable dead, Maria can tell them about how some of the blue-shirted crusaders for the true faith sat on her head while others twisted her arms and pulled her skirts up and stuffed them in her mouth.

I wonder how they will like Maria in Missoula, Montana? That is if I can get a job back in Missoula. I suppose that I am ticketed as a Red there now for good and will be on the general blacklist. Though you never know. You can never tell. They've no proof of what you do, and as a matter of fact they would never believe it if you told them, and my passport was valid for Spain before they issued the restrictions.

The time for getting back will not be until the fall of thirty-seven. I left in the summer of thirty-six and though the leave is for a year you do not need to be back until the fall term opens in the following year. There is a lot of time between now and day after tomorrow if you want to put it that way. No. I think there is no need to worry about the university. Just you turn up there in the fall and it will be all right. Just try and turn up there.

THE WHITE CLIFFS

by Alice Duer Miller

1940

3 MONOLOGUES
Susan's Father
Susan 1
Susan 2

SETTING: England at the outbreak of World War II

"The White Cliffs" is a narrative poem describing an American woman's experiences living in England at the advent of World War II. Married to an Englishman, Susan learns to adjust to a new family and a different way of life. Just as she settles into her new life, England is drawn into war and her husband must go to fight. The tension-fraught process of waiting is shared by her mother-in-law, a woman she admires and grows to love as the two are drawn together by their mutual anxiety. John and Susan's son is born and grows up in his father's absence, seeing him only once before he is killed in combat. In her grief, Susan knows that if there were to be another war, her son would also fight and possibly die for his country.

SUSAN'S FATHER

This monologue is a letter to Susan from her staunchly Yankee father. With a wry sense of humor, he reminds her not to forget her roots.

> So, Susan, my dear,
> You've fallen in love with an Englishman.
> Well, they're a manly, attractive lot,

If you happen to like them, which I do not.
I am a Yankee through and through,
And I don't like them, or the things they do.

....

Your man may be all that a man should be,
Only don't you bring him back to me,
Saying he can't get decent tea—
He could have got his tea all right
In Boston Harbor a certain night,

....

All very long ago, you'll say,
But whenever I go up Boston-way,
I drive through Concord—that neck of the wood,
Where once the embattled farmers stood,
And I think of Revere, and the Old South Steeple,
And I say, by heck, we're the only people
Who licked them not only once, but twice.
Never forget it—that's my advice.
They have their points—they're honest and
     brave,
Loyal and sure—as sure as the grave;
They make other nations seem pale and flighty,
But they do think England is God almighty,
And you must remind them now and then
That other countries breed other men.
From all of which you will think me rather
Unjust. I am.
Your devoted
Father.

SUSAN 1

Susan describes the unexpected and exquisite joy of motherhood.

Maternity is common, but not so
It seemed to me. Motherless, I did not know—

I was all unprepared to feel this glow,
Holy as a Madonna's, and as crude
As any animal's beatitude—
Crude as my own black cat's, who used to bring
Her newest litter to me every spring,
And say, with green eyes shining in the sun:
"Behold this miracle that I have done."

. . . .

"I want him called John after you, or if not that I'd rather. . . ."
"But the eldest son is always called Percy, dear."
"I don't ask to call him Hiram, after my father—"
"But the eldest son is always called Percy, dear."
"But I hate the name Percy. I like Richard or Ronald,
Or Peter like your brother, or Ian or Noel or Donald—"
"But the eldest is always called Percy, dear."

. . . .

So the Vicar christened him Percy; and Lady Jean
Gave to the child and me the empty place
In her heart. Poor Lady, it was as if she had seen
The world destroyed—the extinction of her race,
Her country, her class, her name—and now she saw
Them live again. And I would hear her say:
"No. I admire Americans; my daughter-in-law
Was an American." Thus she would well repay
The debt, and I was grateful—the English made
Life hard for those who did not come to her aid.

SUSAN 2

Susan expresses both her own feelings and those of her father about the Americans' entering the war.

What could I do, but ache and long
That my country, peaceful, rich, and strong,
Should come and do battle for England's sake.
What could I do, but long and ache.

And my father's letters I hid away
Lest someone should know the things he'd say.
"You ask me whether we're coming in—
We are. The English are clever as sin,
Silently, subtly they inspire
Most of our youth with a holy fire
To shed their blood for the British Empire.
We'll come in—we'll fight and die
Humbly to help them, and by and by,
England will do us in the eye.
They'll get colonies, gold, and fame,
And we'll get nothing at all but blame.
Blame for not having come before,
Blame for not having sent them more
Money and men and war supplies,
Blame if we venture to criticize.
We're so damn simple—our skins so thin,
We'll get nothing whatever, but we'll come in."
And at last—at last—like the dawn of a calm fair day
After a night of terror and storm, they came—
My young light-hearted countrymen, tall and gay,
Looking the world over in search of fun and fame,
Marching through London to the beat of a boastful air,
Seeing for the first time Piccadilly and Leicester Square,
All the bands playing: "Over There, Over There,
Send the word, send the word to beware—"
And as the American flag went fluttering by,
Englishmen uncovered, and I began to cry.

WHY I LIVE AT THE P.O.

by Eudora Welty

1941

4 MONOLOGUES
Sister 1
Sister 2
Sister 3
Sister 4

SETTING: China Grove, Mississippi, 1940s

"Why I Live at the P.O.," one of Eudora Welty's best-loved short stories, is the acerbically funny first-person account of the craziest family in China Grove, Mississippi. Spend a Fourth of July with Mama, Papa-Daddy, Uncle Rondo, Stella-Rondo, Shirley T., and Sister. Sister narrates the tale of Stella-Rondo's homecoming—an event that leads to Sister's decision to move into the P.O., where she is postmistress. From cranky Papa-Daddy to drunken Uncle Rondo, Sister's family is impossibly funny and thoroughly unforgettable.

SISTER 1

Stella-Rondo has returned to China Grove with a child that she claims is adopted. Sister speculates that the little girl bears a striking family resemblance.

I was getting along fine with Mama, Papa-Daddy and Uncle Rondo until my sister Stella-Rondo just separated from her husband and came back home again. Mr. Whitaker! Of course I went with Mr. Whitaker first, when he first appeared here in China Grove, taking "Pose Your-self" photos, and Stella-Rondo broke us up. Told him I was one-sided. Bigger on one side than the other, which is a deliberate, calculated falsehood: I'm the same. Stella-Rondo is exactly twelve months to the day younger than I am and for that reason she's spoiled.

She's always had anything in the world she wanted and then she'd throw it away. Papa-Daddy gave her this gorgeous Add-a-Pearl neck-lace when she was eight years old and she threw it away playing base-ball when she was nine, with only two pearls.

So as soon as she got married and moved away from home the first thing she did was separate! From Mr. Whitaker! This photog-rapher with the popeyes she said she trusted. Came home from one of those towns up in Illinois and to our complete surprise brought this child of two. . . .

"Here you had this marvelous blonde child and never so much as wrote your mother a word about it," says Mama. "I'm thoroughly ashamed of you." But of course she wasn't.

Stella-Rondo just calmly takes off this *hat*, I wish you could see it. She says, "Why, Mama, Shirley-T.'s adopted, I can prove it."

"How?" says Mama, but all I says was, "H'm!" . . .

"What do you mean—'H'm!'?" says Stella-Rondo, and Mama says, "I heard that, Sister."

I said that oh, I didn't mean a thing, only that whoever Shirley-T. was, she was the spit-image of Papa-Daddy if he'd cut off his beard, which of course he'd never do in the world. Papa-Daddy's Mama's papa and sulks.

Stella-Rondo got furious! She said, "Sister, I don't need to tell you you got a lot of nerve and always did have and I'll thank you to make no future reference to my adopted child whatsoever." . . .

"She looks exactly like Shirley Temple to me," says Mama, but Shirley-T. just ran away from her.

SISTER 2

Uncle Rondo is drunk again, and Sister complains that Papa-Daddy uses Rondo's drunkenness to turn him against her.

It wasn't five minutes before Uncle Rondo suddenly appeared in the hall in one of Stella-Rondo's flesh-colored kimonos, all cut on the bias. . . .

"Uncle Rondo!" I says. "I didn't know who that was! Where are you going?"

"Sister," he says, "get out of my way, I'm poisoned."

"If you're poisoned stay away from Papa-Daddy," I says. "Keep out of the hammock. Papa-Daddy will certainly beat you on the head if you come within forty miles of him. He thinks I deliberately said he ought to cut off his beard after he got me the P.O., and I've told him and told him and told him, and he acts like he just don't hear me. Papa-Daddy must of gone stone deaf."

"He picked a fine day to do it then," says Uncle Rondo, and before you could say "Jack Robinson" flew out in the yard.

What he'd really done, he'd drunk another bottle of that prescription. He does it every single Fourth of July as sure as shooting, and it's horribly expensive. . . . So he insisted on zigzagging right on out to the hammock, looking like a half-wit.

Papa-Daddy woke up with this horrible yell and right there without moving an inch he tried to turn Uncle Rondo against me. . . . Oh, he told Uncle Rondo I didn't learn to read till I was eight years old and he didn't see how in the world I ever got the mail put up at the P.O., much less read it all. . . . All the time he was just lying there swinging as pretty as you please and looping out his beard, and poor Uncle Rondo was *pleading* with him to slow down the hammock, it was making him as dizzy as a witch to watch it. But that's what Papa-Daddy likes about a hammock. So Uncle Rondo was too dizzy to get turned against me for the time being. He's Mama's only brother and is a good case of a one-track mind. Ask anybody.

SISTER 3

Uncle Rondo throws a package of firecrackers into Sister's bedroom at 6:30
A.M. and she decides to move into the P.O.

At 6:30 A.M. the next morning, he threw a whole five-cent package
of some unsold one-inch firecrackers from the store as hard as he could
into my bedroom and they every one went off. . . .

Well, I'm just terribly susceptible to noise of any kind, and the
doctor has always told me I was the most sensitive person he had ever
seen in his whole life, and I was simply prostrated. I couldn't eat!
People tell me they heard it as far as the cemetery, and old Aunt Jep
Patterson, that had been holding her own so good, thought it was
Judgment Day and she was going to meet her whole family. . . .

And I'll tell you it didn't take me any longer than a minute to
make up my mind what to do. There I was with the whole entire
house on Stella-Rondo's side and turned against me. If I have anything
at all I have pride.

So I just decided I'd go straight down to the P.O. There's plenty
of room there in back, I says to myself.

Well! I made no bones about letting the family catch on to what
I was up to. . . .

The first thing they knew, I marched in where they were all playing
Old Maid and pulled the electric oscillating fan out by the plug, and
everything got real hot. . . .

"So that's the way the land lies," says Uncle Rondo. . . . "Well,
Sister, I'll be glad to donate my army cot if you got any place to set
it up, providing you'll leave right this minute and let me get some
peace."

"Thank you kindly for the cot and 'peace' is hardly the word I
would select if I had to resort to firecrackers at 6:30 A.M. in a young
girl's bedroom," I says back to him. "And as to where I intend to go,
you seem to forget my position as postmistress of China Grove, Mississippi," I says. "I've always got the P.O."

Well, that made them all sit up and take notice.

SISTER 4

The postmistress now calls the P.O. home and is happy enough, though she can still spare a nasty thought or two for Stella-Rondo.

That's the last I've laid eyes on any of my family or my family laid eyes on me for five solid days and nights. . . .

But, oh, I like it here. It's ideal, as I've been saying. You see, I've got everything cater-cornered, the way I like it. Hear the radio? All the war news. Radio, sewing machine, book ends, ironing board and that great big piano lamp—peace, that's what I like. Butter-bean vines planted all along the front where the strings are.

Of course, there's not much mail. My family are naturally the main people in China Grove, and if they prefer to vanish from the face of the earth, for all the mail they get or the mail they write, why, I'm not going to open my mouth. Some of the folks here in town are taking up for me and some turned against me. I know which is which. . . .

But here I am, and here I'll stay. I want the world to know I'm happy.

And if Stella-Rondo should come to me this minute, on bended knees, and *attempt* to explain the incidents of her life with Mr. Whitaker, I'd simply put my fingers in both my ears and refuse to listen.

A TREE GROWS IN BROOKLYN

by Betty Smith

1943

3 MONOLOGUES
Johnny
Katie
Francie

SETTING: Brooklyn, New York, early twentieth century

This is the story of the Nolan family of Brooklyn, New York. Johnny Nolan is a loving dreamer, a singer of Irish ballads, and a drunk. His wife, Katie, is a down-to-earth woman who eventually becomes hardened by the burden of poverty. Their adored son, Neeley, is much like his father. Daughter Francie has the poetic soul of her father and the steely resolve of her mother. She is the small "tree" that grows anywhere in Brooklyn—through cracks in the concrete, through garbage; in short, where nothing else will grow. Francie thrives in spite of, or perhaps because of, hardships and adversity. Like the tree, she is at first unnoticed and unappreciated, yet possessed of an indestructible nature. She is beauty blooming in the tenements of Brooklyn, reaching ever toward the sky.

JOHNNY

Johnny is a dreamer who drinks because of his many responsibilities. Here, he reminisces to Francie about his life and failures.

Take me. I'm nobody. My folks came over from Ireland the year the potatoes gave out. Fellow ran a steamship company said he'd take my father to America—had a job waiting for him. Said he'd take the boat fare from his wages. So my father and mother came over.

My father was like me—never held the job long.

My folks never knew how to read or write. I only got to the sixth grade myself—had to leave school when the old man died. . . .

I was a boy of twelve then. I sang in saloons for the drunks and they threw pennies at me. Then I started working around saloons and restaurants . . . waiting on people. . . .

I always wanted to be a real singer, the kind that comes out on the stage all dressed up. But I didn't have no education and I didn't know the first way about how to start in being a stage singer. Mind your job, my mother told me. You don't know how lucky you are to have work, she said. So I drifted into the singing waiter business. It's not steady work. I'd be better off if I was just a plain waiter. That's why I drink.

I drink because I don't stand a chance and I know it. I couldn't drive a truck like other men and I couldn't get on the cops with my build. I got to sling beer and sing when I just want to sing. I drink because I got responsibilities that I can't handle. I am not a happy man. I got a wife and children and I don't happen to be a hard-working man. I never wanted a family.

KATIE

Thinking aloud, Katie realizes that Francie needs an education to help her to become somebody. She knows that her daughter will grow away from her but that her son will stay. She also realizes that drink has ruined her husband's life.

Francie is smart. She must go to high school and maybe beyond that. She's a learner and she'll be somebody someday. But when she gets educated, she will grow away from me. Why, she's growing away from me now. She does not love me the way the boy loves me. I feel her turn away from me. She does not understand me. All she understands is that I don't understand her. Maybe when she gets education, she will be ashamed of me—the way I talk. But she will have too much character to show it. Instead she will try to make me different. She will come to see me and try to make me live in a better way and I will be mean to her because I'll know she's above me. She will figure out too much about things as she grows older; she'll get to know too much for her own happiness. She'll find out that I don't love her as much as I love the boy. I cannot help it that this is so. But she won't understand that. Sometimes I think she knows that now. Already she is growing away from me; she will fight to get away soon. Changing over to that far-away school was the first step in her getting away from me. But Neeley will never leave me, that is why I love him best. He will cling to me and understand me. I want him to be a doctor. He *must* be a doctor. Maybe he will play the fiddle, too. There is music in him. He got that from his father. Yes, his father has the music in him but it does him no good. It is ruining him. If he couldn't sing, those men who treat him to drinks wouldn't want him around. What good is the fine way he can sing when it doesn't make him or us any better? With the boy, it will be different. He'll be educated. I must think out ways. We'll not have Johnny with us long. Dear God, I loved him so much once—and sometimes I still do. But he's worthless . . . worthless. And God forgive me for ever finding it out.

FRANCIE

Now fifteen years old and wise beyond her years, Francie hopes for a love that may someday be hers.

Oh, I want to hold it all! I want to hold the way the night is—cold without wind. And the way the stars are so near and shiny. I want to hold all of it tight until it hollers out, "Let me go! Let me go!"

I need someone. I need someone. I need to hold somebody close. And I need more than this holding. I need someone to understand how I feel at a time like now. And the understanding must be part of the holding.

I love mama and Neeley and Laurie. But I need someone to love in a different way from the way I love them.

If I talked to mama about it, she'd say, "Yes? Well, when you get that feeling don't linger in dark hallways with the boys." She'd worry, too, thinking I was going to be the way Sissy used to be. But it isn't an Aunt Sissy thing because there's this understanding that I want almost more than I want the holding. If I told Sissy or Evy, they'd talk the same as mama, although Sissy was married at fourteen and Evy at sixteen. Mama was only a girl when she married. But they've forgotten . . . and they'd tell me I was too young to be having such ideas. I'm young, maybe, in just being fifteen. But I'm older than those years in some things. But there is no one for me to hold and no one to understand. Maybe someday . . . someday. . . .

FAHRENHEIT 451

by Ray Bradbury

1953

4 MONOLOGUES
Clarisse
Beatty 1
Beatty 2
Beatty 3

SETTING: The future

Bradbury's chilling masterpiece describes a technocratic future in which every aspect of life is controlled by the government and reading is the ultimate sin. The book's central character is Guy Montag, a member of the firemen, an elite corps whose responsibility is to hunt out illegal libraries and burn them.

Montag is reasonably content with his life until he meets Clarisse, a young girl who challenges him to question life. As if waking from a dream, Montag realizes that his life is a sham. He becomes obsessed with saving books and starts his own secret library. Beatty, the chief of the firemen, suspects Montag and raids his house. Montag escapes with his life and travels to the wilds beyond the city, where he meets Granger, a member of a group of deposed college professors, authors, and the like who carry the world's precious literature in their heads, becoming the books that they memorize while awaiting the war that will destroy the society that has banned them.

CLARISSE

This lively young girl paints a grim picture of her society as she describes violence and alienation among her peers.

I'm antisocial, they say. I don't mix. It's so strange. I'm very social indeed. It all depends on what you mean by social, doesn't it? . . . Being with people is nice. But I don't think it's social to get a bunch of people together and then not let them talk, do you? That's not social to me at all. . . . They run us so ragged by the end of the day we can't do anything but go to bed or head for a Fun Park to bully people around, break windowpanes in the Window Smasher place or wreck cars in the Car Wrecker place with the big steel ball. . . . I guess I'm everything they say I am, all right. I haven't any friends. That's supposed to prove I'm abnormal. But everyone I know is either shouting or dancing around like wild or beating up one another. . . .

I'm afraid of children my own age. They kill each other. Did it always used to be that way? . . . Six of my friends have been shot in the last year alone. . . . I'm afraid of them and they don't like me because I'm afraid. . . .

I like to watch people. Sometimes I ride the subway all day and look at them and listen to them. I just want to figure out who they are and what they want and where they're going. . . . Sometimes I sneak around and listen in subways. Or I listen at soda fountains, and do you know what? People don't talk about anything.

. . . And at the museums, have you *ever* been? *All* abstract. That's all there is now. My uncle says it was different once. A long time back sometimes pictures said things or even showed *people*.

Well, I got to be going. Good-bye.

BEATTY 1

The fire chief tells Montag the story of how books first came to be burned. This is a chilling account of a society closely resembling our own.

Every fireman, sooner or later, hits this. They only need understanding, to know how the wheels run. Need to know the history of our profession. They don't feed it to rookies like they used to. Damn shame. Only fire chiefs remember it now. I'll let you in on it.

. . . The fact is we didn't get along well until photography came into its own. Then—motion pictures in the early twentieth century. Radio. Television. Things began to have *mass*.

And because they had mass, they became simpler. Once, books appealed to a few people here, there, everywhere. But then the world got full of eyes and elbows and mouths. Double, triple, quadruple population. Films and radios, magazines, books leveled down to a sort of pastepudding norm, do you follow me?

Classics cut to fit fifteen-minute radio shows, then cut again to fill a two-minute book column, winding up at last as a ten or twelve-line dictionary resume. I exaggerate, of course. . . . But many were those whose sole knowledge of *Hamlet* . . . was a one-page digest in a book that claimed: *now at last you can read all the classics; keep up with your neighbors.* . . .

Speed up the film, Montag, quick. *Click, Pic, Look, Eye, Now, Flick, Here, There, Swift, Pace, Up, Down, In, Out, Why, How, Who, What, Where, Eh? Uh! Bang! Smack! Wallop, Bing, Bong, Boom!* Digest-digests, digest-digest-digests. . . . Whirl man's mind around about so fast under the pumping hands of publishers, exploiters, broadcasters that the centrifuge flings off all unnecessary, time-wasting thought!

. . . Authors, full of evil thoughts, lock up your typewriters. They *did*. Magazines became a nice blend of vanilla tapioca. . . . No *wonder* books stopped selling, the critics said. But the public, knowing what it wanted, spinning happily, let the comic books survive. . . .

We must all be alike. . . . Each man the image of the other; then all are happy, for there are no mountains to make them cower, to judge themselves against. So! A book is a loaded gun in the house next door. Burn it. . . . Who knows who might be the target of the well-read man? . . . And so when the houses were finally fireproofed completely, all over the world . . . there was no longer need of firemen for the old purposes. They were given the new job, as custodians of our peace of mind, the focus of our understandable and rightful dread of being inferior: official censors, judges, and executors. That's you, Montag, and that's me.

BEATTY 2

Montag's superior explains that burning offensive materials is the most expedient way to control all of the minority groups in the country.

You must understand that our civilization is so vast that we can't have our minorities upset and stirred. Ask yourself, What do we want in this country, above all? People want to be happy, isn't that right? Haven't you heard it all your life? I want to be happy, people say. Well, aren't they? Don't we keep them moving, don't we give them fun? That's all we live for, isn't it? For pleasure? For titillation? And you must admit our culture provides plenty of these.

Colored people don't like *Little Black Sambo*. Burn it. White people don't feel good about *Uncle Tom's Cabin*. Burn it. Someone's written a book on tobacco and cancer of the lungs? The cigarette people are weeping? Burn the book. Serenity, Montag. Peace, Montag. Take your fight outside. Better yet, into the incinerator. Funerals are unhappy and pagan? Eliminate them, too. Five minutes after a person is dead he's on his way to the Big Flue, the Incinerators serviced by helicopters all over the country. Ten minutes after death a man's a speck of black dust. Let's not quibble over individuals with memoriums. Forget them. Burn all, burn everything. Fire is bright and fire is clean.

BEATTY 3

While trying to get Montag to reveal his obsession with books, Beatty demonstrates the power of words and how they may be twisted to fit any argument.

I had a dream an hour ago. I lay down for a catnap and in this dream you and I, Montag, got into a furious debate on books. You towered with rage, yelled quotes at me. I calmly parried every thrust. *Power*, I said. And you, quoting Dr. Johnson, said "Knowledge is more than equivalent to force!" And I said, "Well, Dr. Johnson also said, dear boy, that 'He is no wise man that will quit a certainty for an uncertainty.'" Stick with the firemen, Montag. All else is dreary chaos!

And you said quoting, "Truth will come to light, murder will not be hid long!" And I cried in good humor, "Oh God, he speaks only of his horse!" And "The Devil can cite scripture for his purpose." And you yelled, "This age thinks better of a gilded fool than of a threadbare saint in wisdom's school!" and I whispered gently, "The dignity of truth is lost with much protesting." And you screamed, "Carcasses bleed at the sight of the murderer!" And I said, patting your hand, "What, do I give you trench mouth?" And you shrieked, "Knowledge is power!" and "A dwarf on a giant's shoulders sees the farthest of the two!" and I summed my side up with rare serenity in, "The folly of mistaking a metaphor for a proof, a torrent of verbiage for a spring of capital truths, and oneself as an oracle, is inborn in us, Mr. Valery once said."

God, what a pulse! I've got you going, have I, Montag? Jesus God, your pulse sounds like the day after the war. Everything but sirens and bells! Shall I talk some more? I like your look of panic. Swahili, Indian, English Lit., I speak them all. A kind of excellent dumb discourse.

. . . What traitors books can be! You think they're backing you up, and they turn on you. Others can use them, too, and there you are, lost in the middle of the moor, in a great welter of nouns and verbs and adjectives. And at the very end of my dream, along I came with the Salamander and said, "Going my way?" And you got in and we drove back to the firehouse in beatific silence all dwindled away to peace.

ON THE ROAD

by Jack Kerouac

1955

1 MONOLOGUE
Sal

SETTING: post–World War II America

On the Road is a picture of America as seen by a small group of young men and women who travel by foot, car, and rail across the land in search of themselves and the heart of a nation. Considered a landmark in American literature, the story follows Sal Paradise, a young World War II veteran, as he makes several pilgrimages from coast to coast in the wake of Dean, his mentor. Dean is a self-proclaimed noble savage whose simplistic philosophies stand in vivid contrast to the social confusion following the war.

Sal has many adventures and meets an amazing cast of characters in his pursuit of Dean. The two meet and separate several times before their final good-bye in New York City. Dean must return to his wife and Sal must get on with his life. He has finally learned that the wilderness that he sought on the open road can only be found within his own heart.

SAL

Cold and hungry, Sal must spend the night on a bench at the Harrisburg, Pennsylvania, railroad station. Here he denounces both Harrisburg and starvation.

That night in Harrisburg I had to sleep in the railroad station on a bench; at dawn the station masters threw me out. Isn't it true that you start your life a sweet child believing in everything under your father's roof? Then comes the day of the Laodiceans, when you know you are wretched and miserable and poor and blind and naked, and with the visage of a gruesome grieving ghost you go shuddering through nightmare life. I stumbled haggardly out of the station; I had no more control. All I could see of the morning was a whiteness like the whiteness of the tomb. I was starving to death. All I had left in the form of calories were the last of the cough drops I'd bought in Shelton, Nebraska, months ago; these I sucked for their sugar. I didn't know how to panhandle. I stumbled out of town with barely enough strength to reach the city limits. I knew I'd be arrested if I spent another night in Harrisburg. Cursed city! The ride I proceeded to get was with a skinny, haggard man who believed in controlled starvation for the sake of health. When I told him I was starving to death as we rolled east he said, "Fine, fine, there's nothing better for you. I myself haven't eaten for three days. I'm going to live to be a hundred and fifty years old." He was a bag of bones, a floppy doll, a broken stick, a maniac. I might have gotten a ride with an affluent fat man who'd say, "Let's stop at this restaurant and have some pork chops and beans." No, I had to get a ride that morning with a maniac who believed in controlled starvation for the sake of health. After a hundred miles he grew lenient and took out bread-and-butter sandwiches from the back of the car. They were hidden among his salesman samples. He was selling plumbing fixtures around Pennsylvania. I devoured the bread and butter. Suddenly I began to laugh. I was all alone in the car, waiting for him as he made business calls in Allentown, and I laughed and laughed. Gad, I was sick and tired of life. But the madman drove me home to New York.

ATLAS SHRUGGED

by Ayn Rand

1957

2 MONOLOGUES
Lillian Rearden
Dagny Taggart

SETTING: America, the future

Ayn Rand was the founder of the philosophical school of objectivism and the author of novels, screenplays, and works of nonfiction. *Atlas Shrugged* is her signature piece. It is a brilliantly conceived manifesto that chronicles one man's attempt to stop the world and make it work *his* way.

"Who is John Galt?" is a question on everyone's lips in this tale of a futuristic world—not at all unlike the one we now inhabit. The identity of the mysterious John Galt is particularly perplexing to beautiful and powerful Dagny Taggart, head of Taggart Transcontinental. Over the course of this sweeping epic, Dagny is drawn closer and closer to the answers she seeks.

The world dangles precariously upon a precipice; it can either plunge into the endless night of moral mediocrity or it may be elevated to a new stage of human spiritual development. John Galt and his followers seek to achieve the latter by drawing the world's most powerful industrialists into their ranks and then destroying all their power bases. Galt seeks to liberate humankind from centuries of altruistic philosophies with his own brand of selfishness. In his own words: "I swear—by my life and my love of it—that I will never live for the sake of another man, nor ask the man to live for mine."

When Dagny and Galt finally meet, they experience a love that is as passionate as it is profound.

LILLIAN REARDEN

The selfish wife of steel magnate Henry Rearden panics when she realizes that she has lost her husband and lashes out in a desperate attempt to hurt him as he heads for the door.

You think you're so good, don't you? You're so good! . . . You're so proud of yourself! Well, *I* have something to tell you! . . . I have something to tell you! You're so proud of yourself, aren't you? You're so proud of your name! Rearden Steel, Rearden Metal, Rearden Wife! That's what I was, wasn't I? Mrs. Rearden! Mrs. Henry Rearden! Well, I think you'd like to know that your wife's been laid by another man! I've been unfaithful to you, do you hear me? I've been unfaithful, not with some great, noble lover, but with the scummiest louse, with Jim Taggart! Three months ago! Before your divorce! While I was your wife! While I was still your wife! . . . I've been unfaithful to you! Don't you hear me, you stainless Puritan? I've slept with Jim Taggart, you incorruptible hero! Don't you hear me? . . . Don't you hear me? . . . Don't you . . . ?

DAGNY TAGGART

In John Galt's secret mountain valley, Dagny meets men and women who are living a life that she has always longed for. In this monologue she tells Galt of her intention to return to the outside world to fight for the valley and what it represents to humankind.

I want you to know this. I started my life with a single absolute: that the world was mine to shape in the image of my highest values and never to be given up to a lesser standard, no matter how long or how hard the struggle. Now I know that I was fighting for this valley—it is my love for you that had kept me moving—it was this valley that I saw as possible and would exchange for nothing less and would not give up to a mindless evil. I am going back to fight for this valley— to release it from its underground, to regain for it its full and rightful realm, to let the earth belong to you in fact, as it does in spirit—and to meet you again on the day when I'm able to deliver to you the whole of the world—or, if I fail, to remain in exile from this valley to the end of my life—but what is left of my life will still be yours, and I will go on in your name, even though it is a name I'm never to pronounce, I will go on serving you, even though I'm never to win, I will go on, to be worthy of you on the day when I would have met you. Even though I won't—I will fight for it, even if I have to fight against you, even if you damn me as a traitor . . . even if I am never to see you again.

THINGS FALL APART

by Chinua Achebe

1959

3 MONOLOGUES
Uchendu
Obierika
Okika

SETTING: Colonial Nigeria

Chinua Achebe's powerful first novel, *Things Fall Apart* tells the tragic story of one African's struggle to cling to old values as his world is destroyed by the invasion of white men.

Okonkwo is a strong man of a tribal village who dreams of being a leader of his people. Unfortunately, his strength is not enough to sustain either himself or his people as white men arrive and things begin to change. Forced into exile by the accidental killing of a young boy, Okonkwo wanders the land until he is taken in by his mother's kinsmen. He lives with their tribe, all the time despairing that he will never be a leader.

Over the years Okonkwo hears stories of the white man's arrival and of the subsequent destruction that is wrought upon his clan. Okonkwo's own son is converted by Christian missionaries, and he grieves as if the boy has died. After seven years in exile, Okonkwo returns to his village to find that nothing is the same. He is arrested and imprisoned when he speaks out against the whites. Upon his release he kills a white messenger. In the end, Okonkwo hangs himself, for he knows that there is no longer a place for him in the new world of white domination.

UCHENDU

The oldest member of Okonkwo's mother's clan addresses the family in an effort to bring Okonkwo out of his despair.

It is Okonkwo that I primarily wish to speak to. But I want all of you to note what I am going to say. I am an old man and you are all children. I know more about the world than any of you. If there is any one among you who thinks he knows more let him speak up.

Why is Okonkwo with us today? This is not his clan. We are only his mother's kinsmen. He does not belong here. He is an exile, condemned for seven years to live in a strange land. And so he is bowed with grief. But there is just one question I would like to ask him. Can you tell me, Okonkwo, why it is that one of the commonest names we give our children is Nneka, or "Mother is Supreme"? We all know that a man is the head of the family and his wives do his bidding. A child belongs to its father and his family and not to its mother and her family. A man belongs to his fatherland and not to his motherland. And yet we say Nneka—"Mother is Supreme." Why is that?

I want Okonkwo to answer me.

You do not know the answer? So you see that you are a child. You have many wives and many children—more children than I have. You are a great man in your clan. But you are still a child, my child. Listen to me and I shall tell you. But there is one more question I shall ask you. Why is it that when a woman dies she is taken home to be buried with her own kinsmen? She is not buried with her husband's kinsmen. Why is that? Your mother was brought home to me and buried with my people. Why was that?

He does not know that either, and yet he is full of sorrow because he has come to live in his motherland for a few years. What about you? Can you answer my question?

Then listen to me. It's true that a child belongs to its father. But when a father beats his child, it seeks sympathy in its mother's hut. A man belongs to his fatherland when things are good and life is sweet. But when there is sorrow and bitterness he finds refuge in his motherland. Your mother is there to protect you. She is buried there.

And that is why we say that mother is supreme. Is it right that you, Okonkwo, should bring to your mother a heavy face and refuse to be comforted? Be careful or you may displease the dead. Your duty is to comfort your wives and children and take them back to your fatherland after seven years. But if you allow sorrow to weigh you down and kill you, they will all die in exile. These are now your kinsmen. You think you are the greatest sufferer in the world? Do you know that men are sometimes banished for life? Do you know that men sometimes lose all their yams and even their children? I had six wives once. I have none now except that young girl who knows not her right from her left. Do you know how many children I have buried—children I begot in my youth and strength? Twenty-two. I did not hang myself, and I am still alive. If you think you are the greatest sufferer in the world ask my daughter, Akueni, how many twins she has borne and thrown away. Have you not heard the song they sing when a woman dies?

"For whom is it well, for whom is it well? There is no one for whom it is well."

I have no more to say to you.

OBIERIKA

Okonkwo's friend visits him in exile and tells him the story of the arrival of the first white man.

Three moons ago, on an Eke market day a little band of fugitives came into our town. Most of them were sons of our land whose mothers had been buried with us. But there were some too who came because they had friends in our town, and others who could think of nowhere else open to escape. And so they fled into Umuofia with a woeful story.

During the last planting season a white man had appeared in their clan.

He was not an albino. He was quite different. And he was riding an iron horse. The first people who saw him ran away, but he stood beckoning to them. In the end the fearless ones went near and even touched him. The elders consulted their Oracle and it told them that the strange man would break their clan and spread destruction among them. And so they killed the white man and tied his iron horse to their sacred tree because it looked as if it would run away to call the man's friends. I forgot to tell you another thing which the Oracle said. It said that other white men were on their way. They were locusts, it said, and that first man was their harbinger sent to explore the terrain. And so they killed him.

He said something, only they did not understand him. He seemed to speak through his nose.

Anyway, they killed him and tied up his iron horse. This was before the planting season began. For a long time nothing happened. The rains had come and yams had been sown. The iron horse was still tied to the sacred silk-cotton tree. And then one morning three white men led by a band of ordinary men like us came to the clan. They saw the iron horse and went away again. Most of the men and women of Abame had gone to their farms. Only a few of them saw these white men and their followers. For many market weeks nothing else happened. They have a big market in Abame on every Afo day and, as you know, the whole clan gathers there. That was the day it happened. The three white men and a very large number of other men surrounded the market. They must have used a powerful medicine to make themselves invisible until the market was full. And they began to shoot. Everybody was killed, except the old and the sick who were at home and a handful of men and women whose *chi* were wide awake and brought them out of that market.

Their clan is now completely empty. Even the sacred fish in their mysterious lake have fled and the lake has turned the color of blood. A great evil has come upon their land as the Oracle had warned.

OKIKA

A man imprisoned with Okonkwo speaks to the clan, urging them to take up arms against the white man.

Umuofia kwenu!
  Umuofia kwenu!
  You all know why we are here, when we ought to be building our
barns or mending our huts, when we should be putting our compounds
in order. My father used to say to me: "Whenever you see a toad
jumping in broad daylight, then know that something is after its life."
When I saw you all pouring into this meeting from all the quarters of
our clan so early in the morning, I knew that something was after our
life.
  All our gods are weeping. Idemili is weeping, Ogwugwu is weeping,
Agbala is weeping, and all the others. Our dead fathers are weeping
because of the shameful sacrilege they are suffering and the abomination we have all seen with our eyes.
  This is a great gathering. No clan can boast of greater numbers
or greater valor. But are we all here? I ask you: Are all the sons of
Umuofia with us here?
  They are not. They have broken the clan and gone their several
ways. We who are here this morning have remained true to our fathers,
but our brothers have deserted us and joined a stranger to soil their
fatherland. If we fight the stranger we shall hit our brothers and perhaps shed the blood of a clansman. But we must do it. Our fathers
never dreamed of such a thing, they never killed their brothers. But
a white man never came to them. So we must do what our fathers
would never have done. . . . We must root out this evil. And if our
brothers take the side of evil we must root them out too. And we
must do it *now*. We must bale this water now that it is only ankle-
deep. . . .

THE APPLICANT

by Sylvia Plath

1963

1 MONOLOGUE
Interviewer

SETTING: contemporary America

Sylvia Plath's poetry, often noted for its confessional style and emotional ferocity, displays a craftsmanship and brilliance that have secured her place among the greatest twentieth-century poets. In the last year of her life, Plath was separated from her poet husband, Ted Hughes, living in a small flat in London, taking care of her two children on her own, and suffering from ill health and depression. It was during this time that she started writing at the incredible rate of almost one poem a day before committing suicide on February 11, 1963. "The Applicant" is a poem from the collection entitled *Ariel*.

INTERVIEWER

This sardonic interview masks the despair and rage a woman feels over her helplessness in her role as wife and mother, according to society's expectations of the perfectly dutiful, submissive "living doll."

THE APPLICANT

First, are you our sort of a person?
Do you wear
A glass eye, false teeth or a crutch,

A brace or a hook,
Rubber breasts or a rubber crotch,

Stitches to show something's missing? No, no? Then
How can we give you a thing?
Stop crying.
Open your hand.
Empty? Empty. Here is a hand

To fill it and willing
To bring teacups and roll away headaches
And do whatever you tell it.
Will you marry it?
It is guaranteed

To thumb shut your eyes at the end
And dissolve of sorrow.
We make new stock from the salt.
I notice you are stark naked.
How about this suit—

Black and stiff, but not a bad fit.
Will you marry it?
It is waterproof, shatterproof, proof
Against fire and bombs through the roof.
Believe me, they'll bury you in it.

Now your head, excuse me, is empty.
I have the ticket for that.
Come here, sweetie, out of the closet.
Well, what do you think of that?
Naked as paper to start

But in twenty-five years she'll be silver,
In fifty, gold.
A living doll, everywhere you look.

It can sew, it can cook.
It can talk, talk, talk.

It works, there is nothing wrong with it.
You have a hole, it's a poultice.
You have an eye, it's an image.
My boy, it's your last resort.
Will you marry it, marry it, marry it.

SLAUGHTERHOUSE FIVE

by Kurt Vonnegut, Jr.

1969

2 MONOLOGUES
Narrator 1
Narrator 2

SETTING: Post–World War II America

Billy Pilgrim is a man trying to find his way through life in Kurt Vonnegut, Jr.'s classic tale of one man's alienation and eventual withdrawal from the banalities of the American middle class. Unable to please his domineering father and demanding mother, Billy learns to become passive in order to survive. As a young man, he fights in World War II and experiences the horrors of the firebombing of Dresden.

After the war, he becomes an optometrist and marries the boss's daughter. His two children develop personality problems with which Billy is unable to cope. The absurd nature of reality drives him into a fantasy world in which he is brought to the planet Tralfamadore, where he is able to observe the world through the eyes of the impassionate aliens who in turn observe him.

NARRATOR 1

As the narrator, the author speaks of his procrastination in writing of his war experiences on the grounds that they are impossible to convey.

When I got home from the Second World War twenty-three years ago, I thought it would be easy for me to write about the destruction of Dresden, since all I would have to do would be to report what I had seen. And I thought, too, that it would be a masterpiece or at least make me a lot of money, since the subject was so big.

But not many words about Dresden came from my mind then— not enough of them to make a book, anyway. And not many words come now, either, when I have become an old fart with his memories and his Pall Malls, with his sons full grown.

I think of how useless the Dresden part of my memory has been, and yet how tempting Dresden has been to write about, and I am reminded of the famous limerick:

There was a young man from Stamboul,
Who soliloquized thus to his tool:
"You took all my wealth
And you ruined my health,
And now you won't *pee*, you old fool."

And I'm reminded, too, of the song that goes:
My name is Yon Yonson,
I work in Wisconsin,
I work in a lumbermill there.
The people I meet when I walk down the street,
They say, "What's your name?"
And I say,
"My name is Yon Yonson,
I work in Wisconsin . . ."

And so on to infinity.

Over the years, people I've met have often asked me what I'm working on, and I've usually replied that the main thing was a book about Dresden.

I said that to Harrison Starr, the movie-maker, one time, and he raised his eyebrows and inquired, "Is it an anti-war book?"

"Yes," I said. "I guess."

"You know what I say to people when I hear they're writing anti-war books?"

"No. What *do* you say, Harrison Starr?"

"I say, 'Why don't you write an anti-*glacier* book instead?'"

What he meant, of course, was that there would always be wars, that they were as easy to stop as glaciers. I believe that, too.

And, even if wars didn't keep coming like glaciers, there would still be plain old death.

NARRATOR 2

The narrator expresses a wistful desire to call up old girlfriends late at night.

Sometimes I try to call up old girl friends on the telephone late at night, after my wife has gone to bed. "Operator, I wonder if you could give me the number of a Mrs. So-and-So. I think she lives at such-and-such."

"I'm sorry, sir. There is no such listing."

"Thanks, Operator. Thanks just the same."

And I let the dog out, or I let him in, and we talk some. I let him know I like him, and he lets me know he likes me. He doesn't mind the smell of mustard gas and roses.

"You're all right, Sandy," I'll say to the dog. "You know that, Sandy? You're O.K."

Sometimes I'll turn on the radio and listen to a talk program from Boston or New York. I can't stand recorded music if I've been drinking a good deal.

Sooner or later I go to bed, and my wife asks me what time it is. She always has to know the time. Sometimes I don't know, and I say, "Search *me*."

THE FRENCH
LIEUTENANT'S WOMAN

by John Fowles

1969

3 MONOLOGUES
Sarah 1
Sarah 2
Charles

SETTING: Victorian England

This is a complex, intriguing story about Charles Smithson, a Victorian gentleman of independent means, who becomes hopelessly obsessed with an enigmatic woman. The woman, Sarah Woodruff, is an outcast in the village of Lyme Regis because of a liaison with a French lieutenant, who has abandoned her. Smithson is irresistibly drawn to the proud and mysterious Sarah. Forsaking his conventional love, Tina, he consummates his desire for Sarah in one night of raging passion. She subsequently disappears, leaving him bereft and determined to find her.

Although the story is set in England of the 1860s, Fowles weaves a modern perspective into the tale by interpolating commentary in the text, allowing the reader to glimpse the Victorian mind as it relates to our own.

SARAH 1

In this monologue, Sarah reveals to Charles how she became the French lieutenant's "whore." She had made an unconscious decision to abandon

her respectability because of the frustration of living in a world where she
was an outsider, a world in which her position was nebulous. She was neither
a gentlewoman nor a peasant, neither a wife nor a prostitute.

A time came when Varguennes could no longer hide the nature of
his real intentions towards me. Nor could I pretend to surprise. My
innocence was false from the moment I chose to stay. . . . I know
very well that I could still, even after the door closed on the maid
who cleared away our supper, I could still have left. I could pretend
to you that he overpowered me, that he drugged me . . . what you
will. But it is not so. He was a man without scruples, a man of caprice,
of a passionate selfishness. But he would never violate a woman against
her will.

I gave myself to him.

So I am a doubly dishonored woman. By circumstances. And by
choice.

What I beg you to understand is not that I did this shameful thing,
but why I did it. Why I sacrificed a woman's most precious possession
for the transient gratification of a man I did not love. I did it so that
I should never be the same again. I did it so that people *should* point
at me, *should* say, there walks the French Lieutenant's Whore—oh
yes, let the word be said. So that they should know I have suffered,
and suffer, as others suffer in every town and village in this land. I
could not marry that man. So I married shame. . . . It seemed to me
then as if I threw myself off a precipice or plunged a knife into my
heart. It was a kind of suicide. An act of despair. I know it was wicked
. . . blasphemous, but I knew no other way to break out of what I
was. What has kept me alive is my shame, my knowing that I am
truly not like other women. I shall never have children, a husband,
and those innocent happinesses they have. And they will never understand the reason for my crime. Sometimes I almost pity them. I
think I have a freedom they cannot understand. No insult, no blame,
can touch me. Because I have set myself beyond the pale. I am nothing, I am hardly human any more. I am the French Lieutenant's
Whore.

SARAH 2

After two years of searching, Charles has at last found Sarah living with an artist—not as his mistress, but as companion and muse. Here she attempts to explain to Charles why she is happy and why she will not leave with him. She treasures the independence her situation has brought, an independence completely unknown to Victorian women. Sarah needs not only independence but power, the kind of power she has had over Charles.

There is another. . . . He is . . . an artist I have met here. He wishes to marry me. I admire him, I respect him both as man and as artist. But I shall never marry him. If I were forced this moment to choose between Mr. . . . between him and yourself, you would not leave this house the unhappier. I beg you to believe that. The rival you both share is myself. I do not wish to marry. I do not wish to marry because . . . first, because of my past, which habituated me to loneliness. I had always thought that I hated it. I now live in a world where loneliness is most easy to avoid. And I have found that I treasure it. I do not want to share my life. I wish to be what I am, not what a husband, however kind, however indulgent, must expect me to become in marriage.

My second reason is my present. I never expected to be happy in life. Yet I find myself happy where I am situated now. I have varied and congenial work—work so pleasant that I no longer think of it as such. . . . I am happy, I am at last arrived, or so it seems to me, where I belong. . . . You may think what you will of me, but I cannot wish my life other than it is at the moment. And not even when I am besought by a man I esteem, who touches me more than I show, from whom I do not deserve such a faithful generosity of affection. And whom I beg to comprehend me.

CHARLES

Charles has at last come to understand Sarah's nature. He realizes that behind her mysterious exterior is a calculating woman with a need to dominate and triumph.

You have not only planted the dagger in my breast, you have delighted in twisting it. A day will come when you shall be called to account for what you have done to me. And if there is justice in heaven—your punishment shall outlast eternity.

Your logic assumes that I knew your real nature. I did not.

I thought your mistress in Lyme a selfish and bigoted woman. I now perceive she was a saint compared to her companion.

There was a time when you spoke of me as your last resource. As your one remaining hope in life. Our situations are now reversed. You have no time for me. Very well. But don't try to defend yourself. It can only add malice to an already sufficient injury.

BULLET PARK

by John Cheever

1969

1 MONOLOGUE
Mrs. Hammer

SETTING: Suburban New York, 1960s

In *Bullet Park* we meet Eliot Nailles and Paul Hammer, suburban neighbors whose fates are intertwined. Nailles and his family have lived in relative happiness until the arrival of the Hammers. Hammer is not as he appears. A psychotic, he hides from the world behind the veneer of a mild-mannered man, a nice guy. An entrepreneur who has traveled extensively, Hammer has settled down in the bucolic suburb of Bullet Park for the express purpose, it seems, of destroying Nailles and all that he stands for: middle-class morality, children, and a wife who actually loves him.

MRS. HAMMER

At a party, Mrs. Hammer launches into a drunken diatribe against her husband, whom she despises.

Oh what's wrong with you? What are you so cross about? You've been cross all week. Are you sore because I bought this dress? Is that your trouble? Do you think I ought to buy my clothes at Macy's or Alexander's or someplace like that? Do you think I ought to make my own clothes, for Christ's sake. So it cost four hundred dollars but it looks good on me and I need something to wear. And I don't have many clothes. Well I don't have very many clothes. All right I *do* have a lot of clothes and I've said something stupid and now you're going to gloat over it. Oh Jesus, I wish you could see your face. You make me laugh.

You're a doormat. You're a henpecked doormat and don't try and blame me for it. You're the kind of a man who thinks someday, someday, some slender, well-bred, beautiful, wealthy, passionate, and intelligent blonde will fall in love with you. Oh God, I can imagine the whole thing. It's so disgusting. She'll have long hair and long legs and be about twenty-eight, divorced, but without any children. I'll bet she's an actress or a night-club singer. . . . What do you do with her, chump, what do you do with her besides tying on a can. What is a henpecked doormat up to. Do you take her to the theater? Do you buy her jewelry? Do you travel? I'll bet you travel. That's your idea of a big thing. Ten days on the *Raffaello*, tying on a can morning, noon and night and drifting into the first-class bar at seven in your beautifully cut dinner jacket. What a distinguished couple! What crap. But I guess it would be the *France*, someplace where you can show off your lousy French. I suppose you'd drag her around Paris in her high heels, showing her all your old haunts. I feel sorry for her, I really do. But get this straight, chump, get this straight. If this blonde showed up you wouldn't have the guts to take her to bed. You'd just moon around, kissing her behind pantry doors, and finally decide not to be unfaithful to me. That's if a blonde showed up, but no blonde is going to show up. There isn't any such blonde. You're going to be lonely for the rest of your life. You're a lonely man and a lonely man is a lonesome thing, a stick, a stone, a bone, a doormat, an empty gin bottle . . .

MANDALA

by Pearl S. Buck

1970

2 MONOLOGUES
Grandmother
Brooke

SETTING: India, 1960s

Mandala is the romantic and mysterious story of Maharana Prince Jagat and his love for an American woman, Brooke Westly. It is also the story of Jagat's quest for the spirit of his dead son, Jai, who was killed in a border skirmish with the Chinese. When Jagat travels to Delhi to learn the details of his son's death, he sees a beautiful American woman playing the piano in the lobby of a hotel. For the first time in his life he meets someone with whom he can communicate, whose spirit touches his.

GRANDMOTHER

Before she dies, Brooke's grandmother tells Brooke of the many times she has been in love. She encourages Brooke to seek love and to embrace it in all of its forms.

I would like to tell you of men whom I have loved—and shall always love. . . . What you don't know, child, is that the heart never grows old. I've watched with amusement my aging body, knowing that the eternal flame in my heart does not so much as flicker. Yes, after your grandfather's death, twenty years ago, I have been in love several times—three times, to be exact, three times really in love, and other times, too many to remember, on the brink of love. You need not look shocked, my child—it was intentional, constantly intentional, and I was never unfaithful to your grandfather, my husband, who remains the love of my life. Indeed, it was he who told me to keep loving. We had a long last talk—at first I could only cry, and then he actually grew impatient with me. He scolded me—

Oh, the darling! He knew me so well! I was too young, of course, when we married and he was old enough—almost—to be my father.

"Stop crying," he ordered me. "I haven't much strength and I know that without me you will feel lost. And you're too young not to fall in love. Listen to me! I *want* you to fall in love—as often as possible. I want you to know that wherever I am, I'll *approve*. I don't want you to be what's called faithful to me. You'll be faithful to me by doing what your heart desires. I'm not afraid of your doing anything stupid and tasteless, because you are intelligent and a woman of taste. And I don't want you, above all, to feel what's called a sense of sin. Love can never be a sin. It can be only a blessing. Even if you're not loved in return—though I can't imagine that—to love is a proof of life—indeed, it's the only proof, for once you can't love another human being, you're not alive."

That is what he told me, Brooke—such wise, wise words! He gave me my freedom. Of course I told him I'd never love any man again, and he just smiled.

"When you do," he said, "remember, I'll be glad."

BROOKE

On their second meeting, Brooke tries to explain to Jagat her strong attraction toward him.

You are a stranger to me. I have no wish to know you and yet I long to be with you wherever you are. I don't even understand what sort of man you are, because I don't know your country or your language and yet I know I have been looking for you all my life. I don't know how you feel toward me, and I ought to care, but I don't. My half of the world is not yours nor yours mine, and yet until we know each other in some way I don't comprehend, we'll never be whole. You're old—yes, you are, because the age of your people is in you, and I'm young, because my people are young and youth is all we have, but until we teach each other whatever it is that each does not know, we can't know enough to live—perhaps even to survive. And I don't know what I am saying or why except that wherever you are, there I must be.

QB VII

by Leon Uris

1970

1 MONOLOGUE
Dr. Adam Kelno

SETTING: London, 1970s

"QB VII" stands for Queen's Bench Courtroom Number Seven in London, where an electrifying trial is about to take place. A highly respected and knighted physician has been accused—in a novel—of committing Nazi atrocities. The American author of the novel claims that the doctor conducted medical experiments too horrifying to describe. Is this a slanderous ploy for publicity by a fame-hungry author, or has he spoken the truth? Dr. Adam Kelno's life has been happy and satisfying; his work is held in great esteem by the medical community and he is revered by his son. Now his carefully ordered world threatens to come crashing down around him. The trial in Courtroom Seven is Dr. Kelno's libel suit against the novelist.

This sweeping and powerful saga takes the reader on a long journey from Europe to Borneo, from Virginia to Jerusalem, in search of the dark secrets of the human heart.

DR. ADAM KELNO

In this monologue, Dr. Kelno defends himself to his son, who has just read the infamous novel.

You are naïve, Terry. Before the war there were several million Jews in Poland. We had only gained our own liberation at the end of the First World War. The Jews were always strangers in our midst, always attempting to overthrow us again. They were the soul of the Communist Party and the ones guilty of giving Poland back to Russia. From the beginning it was always a life and death struggle.

In my village all of us owed money to the Jew. Do you know how poor I was when I got to Warsaw? For my first two years my room was a large closet, and my bed was of rags. I had to lock myself in the bathroom in order to have a place to study. I waited and waited to gain admittance to the university but there was no room because the Jews lied about themselves to find ways around the quota system. You think a quota system is wrong. If there hadn't been one they would have bought every seat in every classroom. They are cunning beyond imagination. The Jewish professors and teachers tried to control every facet of university life. Always pushing their way in. I joined the Nationalist Students Movement, proudly, because it was a way to combat them. And afterwards, it was always a Jewish doctor getting the prime positions. Well, my father drank himself to death and my mother worked her way into an early grave paying off the Jewish moneylender. All the way to the end, I stood for my Polish nationalism and because of it I have been driven to hell.

PORTNOY'S COMPLAINT

by Philip Roth

1969

4 MONOLOGUES
Portnoy 1
Portnoy 2
Portnoy 3
Portnoy 4

SETTING: New Jersey and New York

Alexander Portnoy is a brilliant Jewish man emotionally stuck in perpetual adolescence. His psyche is constantly warring between extreme sexual longings and extraordinary guilt. As a child, he was under the rigid control of an omniscient, omnipotent mother and an uptight, frustrated, eternally constipated father. From an early age, masturbation becomes his source of release and rebellion. Add to this a secret yearning to revenge himself on the Waspy Gentiles who have used his father and given Portnoy deep feelings of inferiority. This complex ailment is "Portnoy's Complaint." Although Alexander had been a brilliant student and is highly successful at his job as the Assistant Commissioner of Human Opportunity for the city of New York, he is plagued by feelings of guilt over his nonstop sexual exploits and his failure to provide his needy parents with grandchildren. He comes to see himself as the punchline of a Jewish joke. As a result, Alexander is as emotionally immature at age thirty-three as he was at age thirteen. Portnoy tells his story to an ever-present, invisible psychiatrist, Dr. Spielvogel.

PORTNOY 1

In this monologue, Portnoy describes his father's eternal, futile battle with constipation.

He drank—of course, not whiskey like a *goy*, but mineral oil and milk of magnesia; and chewed on Ex-Lax; and ate All-Bran morning and night; and downed mixed dried fruits by the pound bag. He suffered—did he suffer!—from constipation. . . . He used to brew dried senna leaves in a saucepan, and that, along with the suppository melting invisibly in his rectum, comprised *his* witchcraft; brewing those veiny green leaves, stirring with a spoon the evil-smelling liquid, then carefully pouring it in a strainer, and hence into his blockaded body, through that weary and afflicted expression on his face. And then hunched silently above the empty glass, as though listening for distant thunder, he awaits the miracle.

. . . As a little boy I sometimes sat in the kitchen and waited with him. But the miracle never came, not at least as we imagined and prayed it would, as a lifting of the sentence, total deliverance from the plague. I remember that when they announced over the radio the explosion of the first atom bomb, he said aloud, "Maybe that would do the job." But all catharses were in vain for that man; his *kishkas* were gripped by the iron hand of outrage and frustration.

PORTNOY 2

Here Portnoy describes his mother, a determined woman who takes motherhood to its devoted extreme.

It was my mother who could accomplish anything, who herself had to admit that it might even be that she was actually too good. And could a small child with my intelligence, with my powers of observation, doubt that this was so? She could make jello, for instance, with sliced peaches *hanging* in it, peaches just *suspended* there, in defiance of the law of gravity. She could bake a cake that tasted like a banana. Weeping suffering, she grated her own horseradish rather than buy the *pishachs* they sold in a bottle at the delicatessen. She watched the butcher, as she put it, "like a hawk," to be certain that he did not forget to put her chopped meat through the kosher grinder. She would telephone all the other women in the building drying clothes on the back lines—called even the divorced *goy* on the top floor one magnanimous day—to tell them rush, take in the laundry, a drop of rain had fallen on our windowpane. What radar on that woman! And this is *before* radar! The energy on her! The thoroughness! For mistakes she checked my sums; for holes, my socks; for dirt, my nails, my neck, every seam and crease of my body. She even dredges the furthest recesses of my ears by pouring cold peroxide into my head. It tingles and pops like an earful of ginger ale, and brings to the surface, in bits and pieces, the hidden stores of yellow wax, which can apparently endanger a person's hearing. A medical procedure like this . . . takes time, of course; it takes effort, to be sure—but where health and cleanliness are concerned, germs and bodily secretions, she will not spare herself and sacrifice others. She lights candles for the dead— others invariably forget, she religiously remembers, and without even the aid of a notation on the calendar. Devotion is just in her blood. She seems to be the only one, she says, who when she goes to the cemetery has "the common sense," "the ordinary common decency," to clear the weeds from the graves of our relatives. . . . She is never ashamed of her house: a stranger could walk in and open any closet, any drawer, and she would have nothing to be ashamed of. You could even eat off her bathroom floor, if that should ever become neces- sary. . . . She sews, she knits, she darns—she irons better even than the *schvartze*, to whom, of all of her friends who each possess a piece of this grinning childish black old lady's hide, she alone is good. "I'm the only one who's good to her. I'm the only one who gives her a whole can of tuna for lunch, and I'm not talking *dreck*, either. I'm talking Chicken of the Sea, Alex. I'm sorry, I can't be a stingy per- son." . . . Once Dorothy chanced to come back into the kitchen while my mother was still standing over the faucet marked H, sending tor- rents down upon the knife and fork that had passed between the *schvartze*'s thick pink lips. "Oh, you know how hard it is to get mayonnaise off silverware these days, Dorothy," says my nimble-tongued mother—and thus, she tells me later, by her quick thinking, has managed to spare the colored woman's feelings.

PORTNOY 3

In this monologue, a very young Portnoy tries his first profitless attempt at rebellion.

I would refuse to eat, and my mother would find herself unable to submit to such willfulness—and such idiocy. And unable to for my own good. She is only asking me to do something *for my own good*—and still I say *no?* Wouldn't she give me the food out of her own mouth, don't I know that by now?

But I don't want the food from her mouth. I don't even want the food from my plate—that's the whole point. . . .

Which do I want to be when I grow up, weak or strong, a success or a failure, a man or a mouse?

I just don't want to eat, I answer.

So my mother sits down in a chair beside me with a long bread knife in her hand. It is made of stainless steel, and has little sawlike teeth. . . .

Why, why oh why oh why oh why does a mother pull a knife on her own son? I am six, seven years old, how do I know she really wouldn't use it? What am I supposed to do, try bluffing her out, at seven? I have no complicated sense of strategy, for Christ's sake—I probably don't even weigh sixty pounds yet! Someone waves a knife in my direction, I believe there is an intention lurking somewhere to draw my blood! Only *why?* What can she possibly be thinking in *her brain?* How crazy can she possibly be? Suppose she had let me win—what would have been lost? Why a *knife*, why the threat of a *murder*, why is such total and annihilating victory necessary—when only the day before she set down her iron on the ironing board and *applauded* as I stormed around the kitchen rehearsing my role as Christopher

Columbus in the third-grade production of *Land Ho!* . . . Oh, *how*, how can she spend such glorious afternoons in that kitchen polishing silver, chopping liver, threading new elastic in the waistband of my little jockey shorts—and feeding me all the while my cues from the mimeographed script, playing Queen Isabella to my Columbus, Betsy Ross to my Washington, Mrs. Pasteur to my Louis—how can she rise with me on the crest of my genius during those dusky beautiful hours after school, and then at night, because I will not eat some string beans and a baked potato, point a bread knife at my heart?

And why doesn't my father stop her?

PORTNOY 4

When adolescence hits Portnoy, he discovers a whole new wonderful way to rebel and enjoy himself at the same time—"whacking off."

Then came adolescence—half my waking life spent locked behind the bathroom door, firing my wad down the toilet bowl, or into the soiled clothes in the laundry hamper, or *splat*, up against the medicine-chest mirror, before which I stood in my dropped drawers so I could see how it looked coming out. Or else I was doubled over my flying fist, eyes pressed closed but mouth wide open, to take that sticky sauce of buttermilk and Clorox on my own tongue and teeth—though not infrequently, in my blindness and ecstasy, I got it all in the pompadour, like a blast of Wildroot Cream Oil. Through a world of matted handkerchiefs and crumpled Kleenex and stained pajamas, I moved my raw and swollen penis, perpetually in dread that my loathsomeness would be discovered by someone stealing upon me just as I was in the frenzy of dropping my load. Nevertheless, I was wholly incapable of keeping my paws from my dong once it started the climb up my belly. In the middle of a class I would raise a hand to be excused, rush down the corridor to the lavatory, and with ten or fifteen savage strokes, beat off standing up into a urinal. At the Saturday afternoon movie I would leave my friends to go off to the candy machine—and wind up in a distant balcony seat, squirting my seed into an empty wrapper from a Mounds bar. On an outing of our family association, I once cored an apple, saw to my astonishment (and with the aid of my obsession) what it looked like, and ran off into the woods to fall upon the orifice of the fruit, pretending that the cool and mealy hole was actually between the legs of that mythical being who always called me Big Boy when she pleaded for what no girl in all recorded history had ever had. "Oh, shove it in me, Big Boy," cried the cored apple that I banged silly on that picnic. "Big Boy, Big Boy, oh give me all you've got," begged the empty milk bottle that I kept hidden in our storage bin in the basement, to drive wild after school with my vaselined upright. "Come, Big Boy, come," screamed the maddened piece of liver that, in my own insanity, I bought one afternoon at a butcher shop and, believe it or not, violated behind a billboard on the way to a bar mitzvah lesson.

THE GAZEBO

by Raymond Carver

1974

1 MONOLOGUE
Holly

SETTING: contemporary America

What We Talk About When We Talk About Love is a group of short stories about everyday events in the lives of Americans—the displaced, the homeless, the jobless, the ordinary, and the perplexed.

"Gazebo" tells the tale of a married couple—Holly and Duane—both in their early thirties. Together they manage a motel, for which they receive free room and board. Duane keeps the pool clean, mows the grass, and does small repairs. Holly keeps the books and rents out the units. They are happy, saving their money to buy a home of their own, until Duane develops a passion for the Mexican maid who cleans the rooms.

HOLLY

After learning of the affair, Holly sadly remembers a time when she and Duane met an old couple who showed them kindness and realizes that her dream of being like that old couple has been shattered.

You weren't my first, you know. My first was Wyatt. Imagine. Wyatt. And your name's Duane. Wyatt and Duane. Who knows what I was missing all those years? You were my everything, just like the song.

I couldn't go outside the marriage.

Listen, you remember the time we drove out to that old farm place outside of Yakima, out past Terrace Heights? We were just driving around? We were on this little dirt road and it was hot and dusty? We kept going and came to that old house, and you asked if we could have a drink of water? Can you imagine us doing that now? Going up to a house and asking for a drink of water?

Those old people must be dead now, side by side out there in some cemetery. You remember they asked us in for cake? And later on they showed us around? And there was this gazebo there out back? It was out back under some trees? It had a little peaked roof and the paint was gone and there were these weeds growing up over the steps. And the woman said that years before, I mean a real long time ago, men used to come around and play music out there on a Sunday, and the people would sit and listen. I thought we'd be like that too when we got old enough. Dignified. And in a place. And people would come to our door.

IF BEALE STREET COULD TALK

by James Baldwin

1974

4 MONOLOGUES
Tish 1
Tish 2
Tish 3
Ernestine

SETTING: contemporary America

If Beale Street Could Talk is the story of two young lovers, Tish and Fonny. Tish is pregnant but they can't be together, for Fonny has been falsely accused and imprisoned for raping a Puerto Rican girl. As told by Tish, this is a story of love, pain, hope, and despair. It is the story of the two families as they look for evidence to clear Fonny. Their search takes them from New York to San Juan and back again. It is a touching affirmation of love and its ultimate triumph over adversity.

TISH 1

The plight of the poor, as described by Tish with stunning clarity, eventually sets such people apart from society.

If you cross the Sahara, and you fall, by and by vultures circle around you, smelling, sensing, your death. They circle lower and lower: they wait. They know. They know exactly when the flesh is ready, when the spirit cannot fight back. The poor are always crossing the Sahara.

And the lawyers and bondsmen and all that crowd circle around the poor, exactly like vultures. Of course, they're not any richer than the poor, really, that's why they've turned into vultures, scavengers, indecent garbage men, and I'm talking about the black cats, too, who, in so many ways, are worse. I think that, personally, I would be ashamed. But I've had to think about it and now I think that maybe not. I don't know what I wouldn't do to get Fonny out of jail. I've never come across any shame down here, except shame like mine, except the shame of the hardworking black ladies, who call me Daughter, and the shame of proud Puerto Ricans, who don't understand what's happened—no one who speaks to them speaks Spanish, for example—and who are ashamed that they have loved ones in jail. But they are wrong to be ashamed. The people responsible for these jails should be ashamed.

TISH 2

Here is Tish's indictment of New York, a city she finds cold, indifferent, and horrible.

If I ever get out of this, if we ever get out of this, I swear I'll never set foot in downtown New York again.

Maybe I used to like it, a long time ago, when Daddy used to bring me and Sis here and we'd watch the people and the buildings and Daddy would point out different sights to us and we might stop in Battery Park and have ice cream and hot dogs. Those were great days and we were always very happy—but that was because of our father, not because of the city. It was because we knew our father loved us. Now, I can say, because I certainly know it now, the city didn't. They looked at us as though we were zebras—and, you know, some people like zebras and some people don't. But nobody ever asks the zebra.

It's true that I haven't seen much of other cities, only Philadelphia and Albany, but I swear that New York must be the ugliest and the dirtiest city in the world. It must have the ugliest buildings and the nastiest people. It's got to have the worst cops. If any place is worse, it's got to be so close to hell that you can smell the people frying. And, come to think of it, that's exactly the smell of New York in the summertime.

TISH 3

In this monologue, Tish describes her feelings for Fonny and the control that men have over women.

I had never seen Fonny outside of the world in which I moved. I had seen him with his father and his mother and his sisters, and I had seen him with us. But I'm not sure, now that I think about it, that I had ever really seen him with *me*. . . . He was a stranger to me, but joined. I had never seen him with other men. I had never seen the love and respect that men can have for each other.

I've had time since to think about it. I think that the first time a woman sees this—though I was not yet a woman—she sees it, first of all, only because she loves the man: she could not possibly see it otherwise. It can be a very great revelation. And, in this fucked up time and place, many women, perhaps most women, feel, in this warmth and energy, a threat. They think that they feel locked out. The truth is that they sense themselves in the presence, so to speak, of a language which they cannot decipher and therefore cannot manipulate, and, however they make a thing about it, so far from being locked out, are appalled by the apprehension that they are, in fact, forever locked in. . . . But men have no secrets, except from women, and never grow up in the way that women do. It is very much harder, and it takes much longer, for a man to grow up, and he could never do it at all without women. This is a mystery which can terrify and immobilize a woman, and it is always the key to her deepest distress. She must watch and guide, but he must lead, and he will always appear to be giving far more of his real attention to his comrades than he is giving to her. But that noisy, outward openness of men with each other enables them to deal with the silence and secrecy of women,

that silence and secrecy which contains the truth of a man, and re-
leases it. . . . Anyway, in this fucked up time and place, the whole
thing becomes ridiculous when you realize that women are supposed
to be more imaginative than men. This is an idea dreamed up by men,
and it proves exactly the contrary. The truth is that dealing with the
reality of men leaves a woman very little time, or need, for imagination. And you can get very fucked up, here, once you take seriously
the notion that a man who is not afraid to trust his imagination . . .
is effeminate. It says a lot about this country, because, of course, if
all you want to do is make money, the very last thing you need is
imagination. Or women, for that matter: or men.

ERNESTINE

*Tish's sister verbally attacks Fonny's mother and sisters because they have
rejected Tish and the baby she is carrying.*

Ladies, don't worry. We'll never tell the baby about you. There's no
way to tell a baby how obscene human beings can be! Blessed be the
next fruit of thy womb. I hope it turns out to be uterine cancer. And
I mean that. If you come anywhere near this house again in life, *I
will kill you*. This child is not your child—you have just said so. If I
hear that you have so much as crossed a playground and *seen* the child,
you won't live to get any *kind* of cancer. Now. I am not my sister.
Remember that. My sister's nice. I'm not. My father and my mother
are nice. I'm not. I can tell you why Adrienne can't get fucked—you
want to hear it? I could tell you about Sheila, too, and all those cats
she jerks off in their handkerchiefs, in cars and movies—now, you
want to hear *that*? You just cursed the child in my sister's womb. Don't
you *never* let me see you again, you broken down half-white bride of
Christ! That's your flesh and blood you were cursing, you sick, filthy
dried-up cunt! And you carry that message to the Holy Ghost and if
He don't like it you tell Him I said He's a faggot and He better not
come nowhere near me.

THE BOARDING

by Denis Johnson

1974

1 MONOLOGUE
Bag Lady

SETTING: contemporary America

"The Boarding" is a dramatic monologue from Denis Johnson's collection of poems, *The Incognito Lounge*. The powerful voice of this elderly bag lady insists on being heard amidst the flux of an apathetic and dangerous city.

BAG LADY

While trying to board a bus, an old bag woman rails against the diseases from which she suffers and those who stare.

THE BOARDING

> One of these days under the white
> clouds onto the white
> lines of the goddamn PED
> X-ING I shall be flattened,
> and I shall spill my bag of discount
> medicines upon the avenue,
> and an abruptly materializing bouquet
> of bums, retirees, and Mexican
> street-gangers will see all what

kinds of diseases are enjoying me
and what kind of underwear and my little
old lady's legs spidery with veins.
So Mr. Young and Lovely Negro Bus
Driver I care exactly this: zero,
that you see these things
now as I fling my shopping
up by your seat, putting
this left-hand foot way up
on the step so this dress rides up,
grabbing this metal pole like
a beam of silver falling down
from Heaven to my aid, thank-you,
hollering, "Watch det my medicine
one second for me will you dolling,
I'm four feet and det's a tall bus
you got and it's hot and I got
every disease they are making
these days, my God, Jesus Christ,
I'm telling you out of my soul."

EVEN COWGIRLS GET THE BLUES

by Tom Robbins

1976

6 MONOLOGUES
Sissy
The Countess 1
Julian
The Countess 2
Bonanza Jellybean
The Chink

SETTING: contemporary America

This is the story of Sissy Hankshaw, a small-town girl who is lovely to look at and has one remarkable feature: gigantic thumbs. Sissy's thumbs take her everywhere. A professional hitchhiker, she considers herself to be the best.

Sissy finds her way to New York, where she begins modeling for the Countess, who makes Sissy the "Yoni Yum Dew" girl—a spokeswoman for scented douches. She meets and marries Julian Gitsche, an urban American Indian who is fascinated by Sissy's thumbs and her free spirit.

Sissy is sent by the Countess to investigate reports of a Cowgirl Rebellion at his Rubber Rose Ranch in the Dakotas. There, Sissy meets the perkiest cowgirl since Dale Evans—Bonanza Jellybean, an exuberant young woman who would like to run the Rubber Rose her own way. Sissy also meets the Chink, a strange old holy man who lives in the hills above the ranch. He bestows upon Sissy the meaning of life, telling her that "if civilization is ever going to be anything . . . more than a can of deodorizer in the shithouse of existence, the statesmen are going to have to concern themselves with magic and poetry."

The cowgirls take over the ranch and lead a rebellion against the government to save the whooping cranes. When the dust settles, Jellybean is a casualty—"roping clouds on the prairies of paradise." The Chink returns to his own people. The Countess takes a job in a maternity ward to overcome his aversion to feminine odor. Sissy is living in a cave about to give birth to a half-Chink with enormous thumbs, and the whooping cranes abandon their natural migratory patterns to hitchhike around the world.

SISSY

Here, Sissy describes her hitchhiking skills to a psychiatrist.

Please don't think me immodest, but I'm really the best. When my hands are in shape and my timing is right, I'm the best there is, ever was or ever will be.

When I was younger, . . . I hitchhiked one hundred and twenty-seven hours without stopping, without food or sleep, crossed the continent twice in six days, cooled my thumbs in both oceans and caught rides after midnight on unlighted highways, such was my skill, persuasion, rhythm. I set records and immediately cracked them; went farther, faster than any hitchhiker before or since. . . . Daylight, I would sleep in ditches and under bushes, crawling out in the afternoon like the first fish crawling from the sea, stopping car after car and often as not refusing their lift, or riding only a mile and starting over again. . . . Overpasses, cloverleafs, exit ramps took on the personality of Mayan ruins for me. . . . Then I began to juxtapose slow, extended runs with short, furiously fast ones—until I could compose melodies, concerti, entire symphonies of hitch. When poor Jack Kerouac heard about this, he got drunk for a week. I added dimensions to hitchhiking that others could not even understand. In the Age of the Automobile—and nothing has shaped our culture like the motor car—there have been many great drivers but only one great passenger. I have hitched and hiked over every state and half the nations, through blizzards and under rainbows, in deserts and in cities, backward and sideways, upstairs, downstairs and in my lady's chamber. There is no road that did not expect me. Fields of daisies bowed and gas pumps gurgled when I passed by. Every moo cow dipped toward me her full udder. . . . I am the spirit and the heart of hitchhiking, I am its cortex and its medulla, I am its foundation and its culmination, I am the jewel in its lotus. And when I am really moving, stopping car after car after car, moving so freely, so clearly, so delicately that even the sex maniacs and the cops can only blink and let me pass, then I embody the rhythms of the universe, I feel what it is like to *be* the universe, I am in a state of grace.

THE COUNTESS 1

This monologue is the Countess's indictment of marriage.

Heterosexual relationships seem to lead only to marriage, and for most poor dumb brainwashed women marriage is the climactic experience. For men, marriage is a matter of efficient logistics: the male gets his food, bed, laundry, TV, pussy, offspring and creature comforts all under one roof, where he doen't have to dissipate his psychic energy thinking about them too much—then he is free to go out and fight the battles of life, which is what existence is all about. But for a woman, marriage is surrender. Marriage is when a girl gives up the fight, walks off the battlefield and from then on leaves the truly interesting and significant action to her husband, who has bargained to "take care" of her. What a sad bum deal. Women live longer than men because they really haven't been living. Better blue-in-the-face dead of a heart attack at fifty than a healthy seventy-year-old widow who hasn't had a piece of life's action since girlhood. Shit O goodness, how I do go on.

JULIAN

This Indian artist with asthma tells Sissy that her ideas of Indians are romantic and out of touch.

You have a romantic concept of Indians. They are people, like any other; a people whose time has passed. I see no virtue in wallowing in the past, especially a past that was more often miserable than not. I am a Mohawk Indian in the same sense that Spiro Agnew is a Greek: a descendant, nothing more. And believe me, the Mohawk never approximated the glory that was Greece. My grandfather was one of the first Mohawks to work as a steel-rigger in New York City; you know Mohawks are used extensively on skyscraper construction because they have no fear of height. My dad helped build the Empire State Building. Later, he founded his own steeplejack service, and despite prejudices against him by the unions and so forth for being an uppity redskin, he made a great deal of money. Enough to send me to Yale. I have a masters degree in fine arts and fairly good connections in Manhattan art circles. Primitive cultures, Indian or otherwise, hold a minimum of attraction for me. I cherish the firm order of symmetry that marks Western civilization off from the more heterogeneous, random societies in an imperfect world.

THE COUNTESS 2

The douche queen here plans to counteract the government's decision to call for all douches to be labeled with warnings by throwing a major media blitz starring Sissy.

I'm going to film a commercial such as television has never seen.

. . . Shit O dear, I've got to go back to TV. I've no choice anymore. Didn't you read about it in the papers? Those bleeding-heart do-gooders in the government are out to ruin me! Listen to this.

WASHINGTON (UPI)—The Food and Drug Administration (FDA) said Wednesday female deodorant sprays are medically and hygienically worthless, and may cause such harmful reactions as blisters, burns and rashes.

It proposed a warning label on each can of spray to tell the consumer:

"Caution: For external use only. Spray at least eight inches from skin. Use sparingly and not more than once daily to avoid irritation. Do not use this product with a sanitary napkin. Do not apply to broken, irritated or itching skin. Persistent or unusual odor may indicate the presence of a condition for which a physician should be consulted. If a rash, irritation, unusual vaginal discharge or discomfort develops, discontinue use immediately and consult a physician."

Shit O dear, that's enough to make *me* asthmatic. The nerve of those twits. What do they know about female odor? None of those politicos sleeps with his wife. They all go to whores and whores know how to take care of themselves. They're my best customers. I'll bet Ralph Nader is behind this. Why he's probably got his kiddie corps of Ivy League law students out inspecting vaginas from coast to coast, looking for fresh blisters and unusual discharges. It's an affront to a Christian nation. I'm the one who's trying to clean things up, rid the human race of its most pagan stench. But do you think those dupes understand that? And after my sizable contribution to the President's campaign fund! I'm going to bend ears in the White House about this. I'll get action, too; you wait and see. They accepted my donation, so they're aware they'd better serve my interests or I'll buy some leadership that will. These swine are not the pearls I've dreamed of.

But it'll take time, precious time, to head off this FDA plot. The government moves slower than a candied turd. So, meanwhile, to offset their monkey business, I plan to hit TV with a commercial that'll spin eyeballs and win hearts by the millions.

BONANZA JELLYBEAN

The cowgirl tells Sissy how her childhood dreams were discouraged.

I'm talking about our fantasies. You know the difference between fantasy and reality, don't you? Fantasy is when you wake up at four o'clock on Christmas morning and you're so crazy excited you can't possibly go back to sleep. But when you go downstairs and look under the tree—podner, that's reality.

They teach us to believe in Santa Claus, right? And the Easter Bunny. Wondrous critters, both of 'em. Then one day they tell us, "Well, there really isn't any Santa Claus or Easter Bunny, it was Mama and Daddy all along." So we feel a bit cheated, but we accept it because, after all, we got the goodies, no matter where they came from, and the Tooth Fairy never had much credibility to begin with. Okay. So they let you dress up like a cowgirl, and when you say, "I'm gonna be a cowgirl when I grow up," they laugh and say, "Ain't she cute." Then one day they tell you, "Look, honey, cowgirls are only play. You can't *really* be one." And that's when I holler, "Wait a minute! Hold on! Santa and the Easter Bunny, I understand; they were nice lies and I don't blame you for them. But now you're screwing around with my personal identity, with my plans for the future. What do you mean I can't be a cowgirl?" When I got the answer, I began to realize there was a lot bigger difference between me and my brother than what I could see in the bathtub.

. . . Yep, it's true; any boy anywhere can grow up to be a cowpoke even today if he wants to bad enough. One of the top wranglers on the circuit right now was born and raised in the Bronx. Little boys may be discouraged from adventurous yearnings by parents and teachers, but their dreams are indulged, nevertheless, and the possibilities of fulfilling their childhood expectations do exist. But little girls? Podner, you know that story as well as me. Give 'em doll babies, tea sets and toy stoves. And if they show a hankering for more bodacious playthings, call 'em tomboy, humor 'em for a few years and then slip 'em the bad news. If you've got a girl who persists in fantasizing a more exciting future for herself than housewifery, desk-jobbing or motherhood, better hustle her off to a child psychologist. Force her to face up to reality. And the reality is, we got about as much chance of growing up to be cowgirls as Eskimos have got being vegetarians.

THE CHINK

The wise man gives Sissy a little of his philosophy of life.

Life isn't simple; it's overwhelmingly complex. The love of simplicity is an escapist drug, like alcohol. It's an antilife attitude. These "simple" people who sit around in drab clothes in bleak rooms sipping peppermint tea by candlelight are mocking life. They are unwittingly on the side of death. Death is simple but life is rich. I embrace that richness, the more complicated the better. I revel in disorder.

I'm not a slob. . . . Slobs don't *love* disorder. They're ineffectual people who are disorderly because they can't help themselves. It's not the same. I set my cave in order knowing that life's disorder will only mess it up again. That's beautiful, that's right, that's part of the paradox. The beauty of simplicity is the complexity it attracts. . . .

Of course I've contradicted myself. I always do. Only cretins and logicians don't contradict themselves. And in their consistency, they contradict life.

THE MAGUS

by John Fowles

1977

3 MONOLOGUES
Conchis
Alison 1
Alison 2

SETTING: Greece, 1970s

Nicolas Urfe, a young Englishman, travels to Greece, where he accepts a teaching post. Rebounding from his failed relationship with Alison, Nicolas is happy to live away from her in a country that he has always admired. He soon becomes involved in the life of a complicated, sinister man on an island retreat. The man, Conchis, draws Nicolas into a bizarre game of deception, hallucination, and riddles. Caught in this maze, Nicolas becomes fascinated with Lily, a young woman who works in some mysterious capacity for Conchis. The delicate, otherworldly Lily is quite a contrast to the sensual and earthy Alison.

Why does Conchis want Nicolas in his domain? What sort of game is he playing? Who is Lily? And finally, what is Nicolas himself searching for? These are some of the questions that must be answered in this complex novel.

CONCHIS

The enigmatic Conchis tells Nicolas about his experience in war and how it forever changed his attitudes toward life.

You cannot imagine what the first few minutes of that bombardment were like. It was the first massive artillery barrage of the war, the heaviest ever delivered.

A runner came from the front trenches, down the communicating trench. His face and uniform were streaked with red. Montague asked if he was hit. He said everyone in the front trenches was splashed with blood from the German trenches. They were so close. If only they could have stopped to think how close . . .

After half an hour the barrage was moving over the village. Montague, at the periscope, cried "They're up!" . . . The men about me began to shout as the line reached the first houses and a cheer came back. A red light soared up, and then we in our turn advanced. It was difficult to walk. And as we went forward, fear was driven out by horror. Not a shot was fired at us. But the ground became increasingly hideous. Nameless things, pink, white, red, mud-bespattered, still with rags of grey or khaki. We crossed our own front trench and traversed the no-man's-land. When we came to the German trenches there was nothing to see. Everything had either been buried or blown out of them. Then we halted for a moment, lying down in the craters, almost in peace. . . .

Figures appeared between the wrecked cottages ahead, their hands high. Some of them being held up by friends. They were the first prisoners. . . . One walked straight towards me, lurching, with his head tilted, as if in a dream, and fell straight into a deep crater. . . . Other prisoners came weeping. One vomited blood in front of us, and collapsed.

Then we were running towards the village. We came into what must have once been a street. Desolation. Rubble, fragments of plastered wall, broken rafters, the yellow splashes of lyddite everywhere. . . . In ten minutes I saw a summary of the whole butcher's shop of war. The blood, the gaping holes, the bone sticking out of flesh, the stench of burst intestines—I am telling you this only because the effect on me, a boy who had never seen even a peacefully dead body before that day, was one I should never have predicted. It was not nausea and terror. I saw several men being sick. But I was not. It was an intense new conviction. Nothing could justify this. It was a thousand times better that England should be a Prussian colony. One reads that such scenes give the green soldier nothing but a mad lust to kill in his turn. But I had exactly the contrary feeling. I had a mad lust not to be killed.

ALISON 1

Now an airline hostess, Alison tells Nicolas that she is very much like him. She is unhappy with her career and feels homeless.

O Jesus, excitement. That lasts about a couple of duties. New faces, new cities, new romances with handsome pilots. Most of the pilots think we're part of the aircrew amenities. Just queueing up to be blessed by their miserable old Battle-of-Britain cocks.

It's not funny. It destroys you. That bloody tin pipe. And all that freedom, that space outside. Sometimes I just want to pull the safety handle and be sucked out. Just falling, a minute of wonderful lovely passengerless falling . . .

. . . We call it charm depression. When you get so penny-in-the-slot charming that you stop being human any more. It's like . . . sometimes we're so busy after take-off we don't realize how far the plane's climbed and you look out and it's a shock . . . it's like that, you suddenly realize how far you are from what you really are. Or you were, or something. . . .

You begin to feel you don't belong anywhere any more. You know, as if I didn't have enough problems that way already, I mean England's impossible, it becomes more *honi soit qui* smelly pants every day, it's a graveyard. And Australia . . . Australia. God how I hate my country. The meanest stupidest blindest . . .

It's just I haven't roots anywhere any more, I don't belong anywhere. They're all places I fly to or from. Or over. I just have people I like. Or love. They're the only homeland I have left.

ALISON 2

After Nicolas has confessed his infatuation with Lily, Alison, in an anguished rage, tells him exactly what she thinks of him.

I think you're so blind you probably don't even know you love me. You don't even know you're a filthy selfish bastard who can't, can't like being impotent, can't *ever* think of anything except number one. Because nothing can hurt you, Nicko. Deep down, where it counts. You've built your life so that nothing can ever reach you. So whatever you do you can say, I couldn't help it. You can't lose. You can always have your next adventure. Your bloody next affaire. . . .

All that mystery balls. You think I fall for that? There's some girl on your island and you want to lay her. That's all. But of course that's nasty, that's crude. So you tart it up. As usual. Tart it up so it makes you seem the innocent one, the great intellectual who must have his experience. Always both ways. Always cake and eat it. . . .

That reminds me. That child. You thought I didn't notice. That little girl with the boil. It made you furious. Alison showing how good she is with kids. Doing the mother act. . . . Just for a moment, when she smiled, I did think that. I did think how I'd like to have your children and . . . have my arm round them and have you near me. Isn't that terrible? I have this filthy disgusting stinking-taste thing called love . . . God, syphilis is *nice* compared to love . . . and I'm so depraved, so colonial, so degenerate that I actually dare show you . . .

I realized as soon as we met on Friday. For you I'll always be Alison who slept around. That Australian girl who had an abortion. The human boomerang. Throw her away and she'll always come back for another week-end of cheap knock.

All that time, last autumn . . . I didn't realize then. I didn't realize you can get softer. I thought you went on getting harder. God only knows why, I felt closer to you than I've ever felt to any other man. God only knows why. In spite of all your smart-alec Pommie ways. Your bloody class mania. So I never really got over your going. I tried Pete, I tried another man, but it didn't work. Always this stupid, pathetic little dream. That one day you'd write . . . so I went mad trying to organize these three days. Betting everything on them. Even though I could see, God how I could see you were just bored.

JUST ABOVE MY HEAD

by James Baldwin

1978

4 MONOLOGUES
Hall 1
Arthur
Hall 2
Hall 3

SETTING: America and France, 1970s

Just Above My Head is the haunting saga of three people whose lives are irrevocably bound together. Julia is the "fire-baptised" child evangelist who loses her faith as a result of her abusive relationship with her father. She escapes by moving in with the Montana family, eventually having an affair with the oldest son, Hall. Confused, and seeking spiritual solace, Julia breaks with Hall and goes to Africa, where she lives for many years. Hall's younger brother, Arthur Montana, is a gifted soul singer, whose career takes him all over the world. Jimmy, Julia's brother, is his accompanist and his lover. And it is Jimmy who tries to save Arthur from his self-destructive behavior and promiscuousness.

Hall narrates this epic tale, spanning three decades, moving from Harlem to Paris. It is, as Hall says, "a love song to my brother," the story of three people who, while fighting tremendous odds, attempt to triumph over life's adversities.

HALL 1

Hall describes his brother's anonymous death in a restroom in London. He relives his own pain and feelings of inadequacy.

I: sat by the telephone. I looked at the marvel of human effort, the telephone. The telephone beside my bed was black—like me, I think I thought, God knows why I thought it, if I did. The telephone in the bathroom was gray. The telephone in the kitchen was blue, bright blue.

The sun was shining in the morning, like I've never known the sun to shine before.

He had been found lying in a pool of blood—why does one say a pool?—a storm, a violence, a miracle of blood: his blood, my brother's blood, my brother's blood, my brother's blood! My blood, Arthur's blood, soaking into the sawdust of some grimy men's room in the filthy basement of some filthy London pub. . . .

My brother. Do you know, friend, how a brother loves his brother, how mighty. how unanswerable it is to be confronted with the truth beneath that simple word? Simple. Word. Yes. No. Everything becomes unanswerable, unreadable, in the face of an event yet more unimaginable than one's own death. It is one's death, occurring far beyond the confines of one's imagination. . . . And do you know, do you know, how much my brother loved me? how much he loved me! And do you know I did not know it? did not dare to know it: do you know? No. No. No.

I looked and looked and looked at the telephone: I looked at the telephone and I looked at the telephone. The telephone was silent. . . . Oh. Arthur. Speak. Speak. Speak. I know, I know, I wasn't always nice to you, I yelled when I shouldn't have yelled, I was often absent when I should have been present, I know, I know; and sometimes you bored the shit out of me, and I heard your stories too often, and I knew all your fucking little ways, man, and how you jived the people—but that's not really true, you didn't really jive the people, you sang, you sang, and if there was any jiving done, the people jived you, my brother, because they didn't know that they were the song and the price of the song and the glory of the song: you sang. . . . Oh, my God my God my God my God, forsake me if you will and I don't give a shit but give me back my brother, my God my God my God my God my God my God.

ARTHUR

Arthur relates his first homosexual encounter, and the feelings of shame it engendered.

Every time I pass that corner, next to the Renaissance, I remember this man who was standing on the corner one day when I came by, and he asked me to go to the store for him. I was about thirteen. He was about thirty or forty, a very rough-looking dude, tall and thin, he wore a hat. He said we had to go to his house to get the money.

He looked like he might give me a nickel or a dime. . . .

He said I was a cute boy—something like that—and he touched me on the face, and I just stood there, looking at him. And, while I was looking at him, his eyes got darker, like the sky, you know? and he didn't seem to be looking at me, just like the sky. And it was silent on those stairs, like you could hear silence just growing, like it was going to explode!

He took out *his* cock, and I just stared at that thing pointing at me, and man, you know how we were raised, I did not know *who* to scream for, and then he put his hand on *my* cock and my cock jumped and then I couldn't move at all. I just stood there, waiting, paralyzed, and he opened my pants and took it out, and it got big and I had never seen it that way, it was the first time and so it meant that I must be just like this man, and then he knelt down and took it in his mouth. I thought he was going to bite it off. But, all the time, it kept getting bigger, and I started to cry.

A door slammed somewhere over our heads, and he stood up, and he put some money in my hand, and he hurried down the steps. I got my pants closed best as I could and I ran home. I mean, I ran all the way. I locked myself in the bathroom, and I looked at the money; it was a quarter and two dimes. I threw them out the window.

HALL 2

*With bitter humor, the character describes the advantage of being black in
a store at Christmastime.*

There can be a great many advantages to being black; for example,
in those years anyway, when you walked into a store downtown everybody dropped whatever they were doing and hustled over to serve you
at once. If you had any sense, you didn't give them a lecture on how
you knew they'd come rushing over to you because they knew you
were a penniless thief. No, you smiled, and you smiled at the house
dick, idly buffing his fingernails next to the panic button, and let
them try to guess where you carried your wallet, if you had one. You
took your time, looking intelligent and mightily bored, and, with the
humility of the aristocrat, indicated that you'd like to *see*—? With
what was not quite a smile, you watched the salesperson nearly strangle
on his or her tongue, which had been, most unwisely, about to warn
you of the price. With the grace bequeathed you by your ancestors,
you pretend not to have noticed how narrowly the salesperson has
averted disaster: it is as though you understand how panic can make
a person fart, and you indicate that you know the smell won't linger.
Well, says he, or she, smiling, as taut as a wire, wishing to God the
smell of the fart would go away, *we have*—and produces, blindly, a
cascade of scarves. You know exactly what you want, but you finger
the scarves carefully, doing your best to conceal what is either contempt or despair: you know that this person, who is now anxiously
giving you the pedigree of the merchandise, merely works here—you
indicate, with a resigned shrug of the shoulder, that you, too, know
how hard life can be. And, unable to bear the other's misery a moment
longer, you finally say, like a good fellow, *I'll take this one*. Relief floods
the face, like sun breaking through the clouds—followed, however,
by a swift look at the man who has ceased buffing his nails and who
is now intently studying a rack of neckties. . . . The salesperson lin-
gers, slightly out of orbit; elaborately, you find your wallet, and count
out the money. You get your receipt, and your gift-wrapped package.
Merry Christmas! cries the salesperson, and *A merry Christmas to you!*
you say, and you both stagger, in different directions, out of the arena.

HALL 3

Hall addresses the subject of racial hatred. He observed that it seems more virulent in the Southern white man, who is taught to detest the black man even as he is being nursed at the mammy's breast.

All the years that we spent in and out of the South, I always wanted to say to those poor white people, so busy turning themselves and their children into little monsters: Look. It's not *we* who can't forget. *You* can't forget. We don't *spend* all our waking and sleeping hours tormented by your presence. *We* have other things to do: don't *you* have anything else to do? But maybe you don't. Maybe you really don't. Maybe the difference between us is that I never raped your mother, or your sister, or if and when I did, it was out of rage, it was not my way of life. Sometimes I even loved your mother, or your sister, and sometimes they loved me: but I can say that to you. You can't say that to me, you don't know how. You can't remember it, and you can't forget it. You can't forget the black breasts that gave you milk: but you don't dare remember, either. Maybe the difference between us is that it might have been my mother's or my grandmother's breasts you sucked at, and she never taught me to hate you: who can hate a baby? But *you* can: that's why you call me Tar Baby. Maybe the difference between us is that I've never been afraid of the prick you, like all men, carry between their legs and I never arranged picnics so that I could cut it off of you before large, cheering crowds. By the way, what did you do with my prick once you'd cut the black thing off and held it in your hands? You couldn't have bleached it—could you? You couldn't have cut yours off and sewn mine on? Is it standing on your mantelpiece now, in a glass jar, or did you nail it to the wall? Or did you eat it? How did it taste? Was it nourishing? Ah. The cat seems to have your tongue, sir. Tell you one thing: that God you found is a very sick dude. I'd check him out again, if I was you. I think He's laughing at you—I tell you like a friend.

THE WOMEN'S ROOM

by Marilyn French

1979

1 MONOLOGUE
Mira

SETTING: contemporary America

The Women's Room is a powerful story of Mira, a woman whose life is shattered by divorce and who must now face the harsh reality of starting a new life in her middle years. This tale chronicles her painful voyage from Daddy's little girl to wife and mother, and finally to an independent woman. What follows is a complex accounting of Mira's life and the lives of her friends and lovers.

Deserted by her husband, Mira attends graduate school at Harvard to earn a degree in literature. Proud of her new degree and self-reliance, Mira still finds it difficult to find a good teaching position. She ends up with a mediocre job at a community college in Maine, where she struggles with the prejudices against older women in the workplace. She offers no platitudes or pat solutions to the difficult problems women face in our society.

MIRA

Throughout the novel, Mira speaks of herself in the third person, leaving her identity a mystery until the end of the book. Here, Mira sees her younger self, trapped and rendered invisible by her appearance. She believes women to be "the most scorned class in America."

As I walk along the beach, my memory keeps going back to Mira those first weeks in Cambridge, tottering around on her high heels (she always walked shakily in high heels, but she always wore them) in a three-piece wool knit suit, with her hair set and sprayed, looking almost in panic at the faces that passed her, desperate for a sharp glance and appraising smile that would assure her she existed. When I think of her, my belly twists a little with contempt. But how do I dare to feel that for her, for that woman so much like me, so much like my mother?

Do you? You know her: she's that blonded made-up matron, a little tipsy with her second manhattan, playing bridge at the country club. In the Moslem countries, they make their women wear jubbah and yashmak. This makes them invisible, white wraiths drifting through streets buying a bit of fish or some vegetables, turning into dark narrow alleys and entering doors that slam shut loudly, reverberating among the ancient stones. People don't see them, they are less differentiated than the dogs that run among the fruit carts. Only the forms are different here. You don't really see the woman standing at the glove or stocking counter, poking among cereal boxes, loading six steaks into her shopping cart. You see her clothes, her sprayed helmet of hair, and you stop taking her seriously. Her appearance proclaims her respectability, which is to say she's just like all other women who aren't whores. But maybe she is, you know. Distinction by dress isn't what it used to be. Women are capable of anything. It doesn't really matter. Wife or whore, women are the most scorned class in America. You may hate niggers and PRs and geeks, but you're a little frightened of them. Women don't even get the respect of fear.

SOPHIE'S CHOICE

by *William Styron*

1979

2 MONOLOGUES
Sophie
Stingo

SETTING: post–World War II Brooklyn

Sophie's Choice is narrated by Stingo, a young man from the South who has come to New York City to seek his fortune as a writer. In his Brooklyn rooming house, Stingo meets the fascinating couple who live upstairs, Nathan and Sophie. Nathan is a charismatic intellectual who suffers from a nervous disorder that progressively affects his judgment and ability to perceive reality. Sophie is a beautiful Polish woman with a mysterious past. She tells Stingo of her life in Poland at the outbreak of the war. Her father was a professor who spoke out against the Nazis, and Sophie was captured and placed in a concentration camp.

Stingo gradually falls in love with the enigmatic Sophie, wishing to protect her from Nathan's growing madness. Sophie confesses the darkest secrets from her past to Stingo: Her father was actually a pro-Nazi fascist, and in the concentration camp, she was forced to select one of her two children to send to the ovens in order to save the life of the other. Driven to despair by sentencing her own child to die, Sophie lives in a self-made hell of eternal guilt and remorse. Despite Stingo's efforts to save her, Sophie joins Nathan on his path to self-destruction in this epic tragedy of the human soul.

SOPHIE

In this monologue, Sophie recalls her desperate attempt to save her child from the Children's Camp. She tells Stingo of her degrading confrontation with Höss, the commandant with whom she has begun a tentative friendship, and of the lengths she went to beg for the life of her son.

Yes. I had a child. It was my little boy, Jan, that they have taken away from me on the day I came there. They have put him in the place they call the Children's Camp, he was only ten years old. I know it must be strange to you that all this time you've known me I have never told you about my child, but this is something I have never been able to tell anyone. It is too difficult—too much for me to ever think about. . . . I'm telling you only because you will not be able to understand about me and Höss unless you understood about Jan. And after this I will not talk any more about him, and you must never ask me any questions. No, never again . . .

Anyway, that afternoon when Höss was looking down from the window I spoke to him. . . . "*Herr Kommandant*, I know I can't ask much for myself and you must act according to the rules. But I beg of you to do one thing for me before you send me back. I have a young son in Camp D, where all the other boys are prisoners. His name is Jan Zawistowski, age ten. . . . I yearn to see him. I am afraid for his health, with winter coming. I beg of you to consider some way in which he might be released." . . . Höss didn't reply to me, just looked straight at me without blinking. . . .

Would it make sense to you, Stingo, if I said that I couldn't help myself and I threw myself against him, threw my arms around his waist and begged him again, saying, "Please" over and over? But I could tell from the way his muscles become stiff and this trembling that ran through him that he was finished with me. Even so I couldn't stop. . . . I fell on my knees in front of him and pressed my face against his boots. . . .

There has been so much talk about people in a place like Auschwitz and the way they acted there. . . . People acted very different in the

camp, some in a cowardly and selfish way, some bravely and beautifully—there was no rule. . . . But such a terrible place was this
Auschwitz, Stingo, terrible beyond all belief, that you really could not
say that this person *should* have done a certain thing in a fine or noble
fashion, as in the other world. . . .

. . . I surrounded Höss's boots with my arms. I pressed my cheek
up against those cold leather boots as if they was made of fur or something warm and comforting. And do you know? I think maybe I even
licked them with my tongue, licked those Nazi boots. And do you
know something else? If Höss had give me a knife or a gun and told
me to go kill somebody, a Jew, a Pole, it don't matter, I would have
done it without thinking, with joy even, if it mean seeing my little
boy for only a single minute and holding him in my arms.

STINGO

*A self-described "horny young bachelor," Stingo finds himself enchanted
with Sophie. As she is forbidden to him, he contents himself with a relationship with Mary Alice Grimbal, who has "the most gorgeous sweetheart
of an ass that ever sashayed its way north from Spartanburg." In a lighter
moment, Stingo describes the nights that he and Mary Alice spent together.*

Mary Alice was—something *worse* than a Cock Tease, a Whack-off
artist. . . . She is utterly prudish (like so many Southern girls) in the
realm of language. When, for instance, an hour or so into our first
"lovemaking" session night before last I was carried away enough to
softly remark upon the marvelous ass I thought she had and, in my
excitement, made a vain attempt to reach around and lay a hand on
it, she drew away with a savage whisper ("I hate that word!" she said.
"Can't you say 'hips'?") and I realized then that any further indecencies
might prove fatal.

. . . But even though Mary Alice, like Leslie, will permit me to
lay not a finger on any of the more interesting crannies or recesses of
her incredibly desirable body, why is it that I am discomforted by the
bizarre fact that the *one* thing she *will* do, though in a pleasureless

and rather perfunctory way, is to whack me off hour after hour until I am a lifeless and juiceless stalk, exhausted and even humiliated by this dumb pursuit? At first it was wildly exciting, almost the first contact of its kind in my life, the feel of that little Baptist hand on my prodigiously straining shaft, and I capitulated immediately, drenching us both, which to my surprise (given her general squeamishness) she didn't seem to mind, blandly swabbing herself off with my proffered handkerchief. But after three nights and nine separate orgasms (three each night, counted methodically) I have become very close to being desensitized, and I realize that there is something nearly insane about this activity.

. . . I wonder why it has taken me these several nights to realize that my nearly suicidal despondency arises at least in part from the pathetic knowledge that the act which Mary Alice performs upon me with such sangfroid is something I could do much better myself, certainly with more affection.

PLAIN LISA

by Pamela White Hadas

1979

1 MONOLOGUE
Lisa

SETTING: Leonardo da Vinci's studio

From *Designing Women*, a book of poetry by Pamela White Hadas, "Plain Lisa" presents a new look at the model whose face is perhaps the most famous in human history.

LISA

If Mona Lisa had kept a diary, what would she have had to say about Signore da Vinci? What was it like to pose for him? Here, Lisa speaks about her employer and his studio.

PLAIN LISA

Leonardo's studio! who wouldn't smile to be a jot
in all that litter? Four corners are not enough;
one couldn't see its corners for the world.
Each time it takes a while for my eyes
to settle—so much to see—the planned obscurity
widening the pupil to take in the giant wing-frames
on the wall and tubes to spy on the sky or magnify
the joints of flies and the split human head
tabled with its tongue-loll and all

the pretty boys, lutanists, tame doe,
jesters, caged doves and fountain-fall.
Luckily Francesco
doesn't object to the rainy afternoons or evenings
Leonardo chooses to have me pose,
and I don't mind getting out of the house.

By now I'm used to the dissections
in mid-sitting when he throws down the brush, takes up the knife
and opens some ear or elbow, slices with such care to bare
bone past mauve muscles, fingers a taut white
tendon, exposes a connection.
Or, back to the eyes, one of the boys under instruction
spreads the dead lids to insert his fingers as if
pinching a plum from a tart and slowly pulls the soft ball out,
spits to glisten it, slowly rolls it
in the candlelight while the Master stares
and stares to get his reflections right.
The focus must be everywhere. Some say
he's a little crazy. I don't know.

I wonder—he has such a way
with fog and rain comes naturally to him
as to a father—I wonder:
did he invent just his forecaster or the very weather?
Anyway, he made up a formula
for proofing our capes against it.
He hasn't got it right yet and I still get soaked
attending the days he opts for—but no matter—
it's the thought that counts.
I have to smile.

THE LAST ENCHANTMENT

by Mary Stewart

1979

3 MONOLOGUES
Arthur 1
Arthur 2
Nimuë

SETTING: Ancient Britain of the legendary King Arthur

The Last Enchantment is the final book in a trilogy about the greatest of all sorcerers, Merlin the Enchanter. The story covers the time when Merlin was confidant and advisor to King Arthur.

According to legend, Merlin raised Arthur from infancy, fashioning the sword embedded in the stone that his ward would someday remove to prove his worthiness to be king. In Stewart's trilogy, Arthur marries two Guineveres. The first, spelled Guenever, dies tragically just as they were learning to love one another. The second, Guinevere, is the queen most familiar as the lover of Lancelot, who is called Bedwyr in this version of the legend.

In this story, Merlin foresees his own destruction at the hands of the beautiful Nimuë.

ARTHUR 1

After losing his first wife, Guenever, Arthur confides his grief to Merlin. The young king is also relieved that Merlin, whom he had feared dead, still lives.

You once said to me that life divided itself into light and dark, just as time does into day and night. It's true. One misfortune seems to breed another, and so it was with me. That was a time of darkness— the first I had suffered. When I came to you I was half-broken with weariness, and with the weight of losses coming one on the other, as if the world had turned sour, and my luck was dead. The loss of my mother, by itself, could be no great grief to me; you know my heart about that, and to tell you the truth, I would grieve more over Drusilla's death, or Ector's. But the death of my Queen, little Guenever . . . It could have been a good marriage, Merlin. We could, I believe, have come to love. What made that grief so bitter was the loss of the child, and the waste of her young life in pain, and with it, besides, the fear that she had been murdered, and by my enemies. Added to that—and I can admit this to you—was the weary prospect of having to start all over again to look for a suitable match, and going once more through all the ritual of mating, when so much else lies waiting for me to do.

ARTHUR 2

The king divulges his knowledge of Bedwyr's and Guinevere's love for one another. He realizes that he must not confront them, for he still loves and trusts them both.

You have just been telling me that love cannot be ruled or stopped. If you are prepared to accept love, knowing that it may well bring you to your death, then how much more should I accept this, knowing that it cannot destroy friendship or faith?

. . . Everything else you have ever told me has been true. Think back now over your prophecies about my marriage, the "white shadow" that you saw when Bedwyr and I were boys, the *guenhwyvar* that touched us both. You said then that it would not blur or destroy the faith we had in one another.

. . . Now we have seen 'the shadow. And now we see it falling across Bedwyr's life and mine. But if it is not to destroy our faith in one another, what would you have me do? I must give Bedwyr the trust and freedom to which he is entitled. Am I a cottager, with nothing in my life but a woman and a bed I am to be jealous of, like a cock on his dunghill? I am a king, and my life is a king's; she is a queen, and childless, so her life must be less than a woman's. Is she to wait year by year in an empty bed? To walk, to ride, to take her meals with an empty place beside her? she is young, and she has a girl's needs, of companionship and of love. By your god or any god, Merlin, if, during the years of days that my work takes me from court, she is ever to take a man to her bed, should I not be thankful it is Bedwyr? And what would you have me do, or say? Anything I say to Bedwyr would eat at the root of the very trust we have, and it would avail nothing against what has already happened. Love, you tell me, cannot be gainsaid. So I keep silent, and so will you, and by that token will faith and friendship stay unbroken. And we can count her barrenness a mercy. So the god works for us both in twisted ways, does he not?

NIMUË

Merlin and Nimuë are reunited after her attempt to strip him of his magic. Despite her lust for power, she loves him still.

Magic, it's magic, stronger than any I could ever know. And you told me you had given it all to me. I should have known, I should have known. Ah, Merlin, Merlin . . .

It's you. It's really you. You've come back. It is magic. You must still be the greatest enchanter in all the world.

. . . You had told me to learn all that you had to tell me. You had said that I must build on every detail of your life; that after your death I must be Merlin . . . And you were leaving me, slipping from me in sleep . . . I had to do it, hadn't I? Force the last of your power from you, even though with it I took the last of your strength? I did it by every means I knew—cajoled, stormed, threatened, gave you cordials and brought you back to answer me again and again—when what I should have done, had you been any other man, was to let you sleep, and go in peace. And because you were Merlin, and no other man, you roused yourself in pain and answered me, and gave me all you had. So minute by minute I weakened you, when it seems to me now that I might have saved you. . . .

Do you remember it, when I hung about you and tormented you to your death, like a spider sucking the life from a honey-bee? . . .

. . . But then, even all the power and knowledge you gave me could not show me that we had buried you living, and send me back to get you out. Merlin, I should have known, I should have known!

THE HITCHHIKER'S GUIDE TO THE GALAXY

by Douglas Adams

1979

1 MONOLOGUE
Zaphod Beeblebrox

SETTING: many points of interest in the Milky Way

"Don't Panic" is perhaps the best advice ever given to the hapless Arthur Dent in this outrageous comedy by Douglas Adams. Dent begins what will become the last and worst Thursday of his life with a terrible hangover. Dent's friend of fifteen years, Ford Prefect, soon arrives at his house and takes him to the local pub, where he reveals that he isn't from Guilford but from a planet in the vicinity of distant Betelgeuse, and that Earth is about to be destroyed. It seems that the Galactic Hyperspace Planning Council is designing a new express route and that Earth is in the way. In the two minutes left before Earth's demolition, Ford manages to save himself and Arthur by using his "Thumb"—a device that allows the owner to hitchhike a ride on the nearest space vessel.

So begins the greatest adventure of Arthur's life as he and Ford begin their tour of the Milky Way. Armed with their "Thumb" and their indispensable copy of "The Hitchhiker's Guide to the Galaxy," Ford and Arthur soon meet up with the irrepressible Zaphod Beeblebrox, president of the Imperial Galactic Government and cosmic bon vivant who welcomes them aboard his ship, the *Heart of Gold*. After a few misadventures in the vicinity of the Horsehead Nebula, the gang eventually heads off for a bite to eat at the Restaurant at the End of the Universe.

ZAPHOD BEEBLEBROX

Two-headed Zaphod suspects that someone has been tampering with his brain to prevent him from having good ideas. Here, he describes finding evidence to support his theory. It seems someone has cauterized crucial synapses in both brains and left his initials as well. The initials? Z.B.!

I don't know what I'm looking for. . . .

. . . I only know as much about myself as my mind can work out under its current conditions. And its current conditions are not good. . . .

No, wait . . . I'll tell you something. I freewheel a lot. I get an idea to do something, and, hey, why not, I do it. I reckon I'll become President of the Galaxy, and it just happens, it's easy. I decide to steal this ship. I decide to look for Magrathea, and it all just happens. Yeah, I work out how it can best be done, right, but it always works out. It's like having a Galacticredit card which keeps on working though you never send off the checks. And then whenever I stop and think—why did I want to do something?—how did I work out how to do it?—I get a very strong desire just to stop thinking about it. Like I have now. It's a big effort to talk about it.

. . . Last night I was worrying about this again. About the fact that part of my mind just didn't seem to work properly. Then it occurred to me that the way it seemed was that someone else was using my mind to have good ideas with, without telling me about it. I put the two ideas together and decided that maybe that somebody had locked off part of my mind for that purpose, which was why I couldn't use it. I wondered if there was a way I could check.

I went to the ship's medical bay and plugged myself into the encephalographic screen. I went through every major screening test on both my heads—all the tests I had to go through under Government medical officers before my nomination for presidency could be properly ratified. They showed up nothing. Nothing unexpected at least. They showed that I was clever, imaginative, irresponsible, untrustworthy, extrovert, nothing you couldn't have guessed. And no other anomalies. So I started inventing further tests, completely at random. Nothing. Then I tried superimposing the results from one head on top of the results from the other head. Still nothing. Finally I got silly, because I'd given it all up as nothing more than an attack of paranoia. Last thing I did before I packed it in was take the superimposed picture and look at it through a green filter. You remember I was always superstitious about the color green when I was a kid? I always wanted to be a pilot on one of the trading scouts?

And there it was, clear as day. A whole section in the middle of both brains that related only to each other and not to anything else around them. Some bastard had cauterized all the synapses and electronically traumatized those two lumps of cerebellum. . . .

Why? I can only guess. But I do know who the bastard was.

Because they left their initials burned into the cauterized synapses. They left them there for me to see. . . .

Z.B.

I'll tell you about it later.

THE COMPANY OF WOMEN

by Mary Gordon

1980

2 MONOLOGUES
Robert
Felicitas

SETTING: New York, 1980s

The Company of Women is the story of five women united by their devotion to Father Cyprian, a priest who serves as their mentor and friend. One of the women has a daughter, Felicitas, who becomes the focus of their lives. We follow Felicitas from her sheltered childhood to eventual motherhood. When Felicitas has a child out of wedlock, she leaves the city with her mother and aunts, seeking a haven with Father Cyprian in upstate New York. As the child grows, Felicitas feels the need to give her a normal life. She doesn't want her daughter to be reared as she was, with only a group of women and a priest as companions. This prompts her to marry Leo, an ordinary but good-hearted man.

ROBERT

A spoiled, wealthy, ersatz scholar, Robert has seduced the naive Felicitas. Here, he bemoans his privileged upbringing.

Let's just say that I was thirty-five goddamn years old before I did one thing I wanted to do. Privilege. God, how I hate it. My whole life stank of privilege. Exeter. Amherst. Harvard. God almighty, all those

Easter holidays in Nassau, all those summers on the Vineyard. What did they ever get me but more privilege? What did they ever make me but unbending and scared shitless of anything I couldn't control? I fucked my wife once a week from duty. Christ, in the prime of my life, I fucked as if I were paying a debt. . . .

I mean, I didn't know what women wanted because I was completely out of touch with the feminine side of myself. Now I wish I had been born a woman. A black woman. You know who I wish I had been born? Billie Holiday. There was a woman who knew things. . . . God, how I wish I'd been born Third World.

FELICITAS

In this monologue, Felicitas confesses her neglect of Linda, her daughter.

There are some neglectful acts for which there can be no forgiveness: the damage is too great. I neglected Linda; I neglected her shamefully, but she is all right. I have read that a mother's rejection can cause autism and schizophrenia, can create a child of violent rages who commits small acts of cruelty, which later, when the child's physical strength is greater, grow into assassinations, anonymous murders, sex crimes of such monstrosity that we forget the details. Now, of course, I think of the mothers of these criminals with understanding. I think of mothers who leave their babies in shopping bags in the post office, like any other parcel wrongly sent. I understand mothers who starve their children, who beat them, who allow them to live in their own filth. It is life they want to starve, to torture, to abandon. Life that was once their life. . . .

. . . That Linda is alive is a miracle, but not of instinct. Not of my instinct, in any case. She was kept alive by my mother and her friends, people who had rigorously worked to banish instinct from their lives. They circled her, they warmed her with their breath when I couldn't bear the touch of her skin. They said, as if they knew, "Later you will want her. Later it will be all right."

As if they knew the terrible hunger of love that overcomes me now at the sight of her, even of the top of her head, which I see from the second-story window where I sit, the panes reflecting the blue bowl of apples, reflecting the late summer roses I have picked for the green vase, and touch the glass that lets through the clear image of my little girl.

THE CITIES OF THE PLAIN

by Mona Van Duyn

1982

1 MONOLOGUE
Lot's Wife

SETTING: Biblical times

"The Cities of the Plain," a poem from the collection entitled *Merciful Disguises*, tells of the fall of Sodom and Gomorrah as seen by Lot's wife.

LOT'S WIFE

In this version of the tale, Lot is less than virtuous and is observed as such by his doomed wife.

> Their sex life was their own business,
> I thought, and took some of the pressure off women,
> who were treated, most of the time, as merely
> a man's way of producing another man.
> And there were plenty of the other kind—
> the two older girls got married when they wanted to.
> The riot in front of our house that evening,
> when a gang of young queers, all drunk and horny,
> threatened to break in, yelling
> for the two strangers, our guests, handsome
> as angels, to come out and have some fun,

was not intelligently handled by my husband,
to say the least. An uptight man,
he got so frightened he opened the door
and offered to send out our youngest girls
if they'd quiet down and leave us alone.
"Two little virgins," he told them. "Now, fellows,
wouldn't that be nicer, and more fun?"
That made them wild, and they would have dragged
him out and mounted him in the street
if our guests hadn't managed to get the door shut.

The two strangers, it turned out, were Inspectors.
Don't ask me why, for the sake of a Perfect
Idea, of Love or of Human Community,
all the innocent-eyed, babies and beasts
and birds, all growth, both food and flower,
two whole cities, their fabulous bouquets
of persons, frivolous, severe, rollicking,
wry, witty, plain, lusty,
provident, every single miracle of life
on the whole plain should be exploded
to ashes, I looked back, and that's what I saw.

Nobody knows my name. My husband
and our two adolescents kept their faces
turned to the future, fled to the future.
Sarah everyone knows, whose life,
past menopause, into the withered nineties
was one long, obsessed attempt to get pregnant,
to establish the future. As for me, I lost
all sense of human possibility
when the cloud rose up like a blossom over all that
death. I stood for nameless women
whose sense of loss is not statistical,
stood for a while, then vanished. Men
are always being turned to stone by something,

and loom through the ages in some stony
sense of things they were shocked into.
I was not easily shocked, but that punishment
was blasphemous, impiety
to the world as it is, things as they are.
I turned to pure mourning, which ends the personal
life, then quietly comes to its own end.
Each time the clouds came and it rained,
salt tears flowed from my whole being,
and when that testimony was over
grass began to grow on the plain.

TO MAKE A DRAGON MOVE: FROM THE DIARY OF AN ANOREXIC

by Pamela White Hadas

1983

1 MONOLOGUE
Anorexic Woman

SETTING: contemporary America

Hadas writes about a variety of famous, infamous, and anonymous women in her superlative collection of dramatic monologues, *Beside Herself* which describes the experience of American women from Pocahontas to Patty Hearst. "To Make a Dragon Move" is a poem about a young woman who becomes anorexic in order to take control of the only thing in her life she can—her body.

ANOREXIC WOMAN

This is the confession of a woman who has befriended hunger—the beast that lives within her. She will control the beast or die trying.

I have rules and plenty. Some things I don't touch.
I'm king of my body now. Who needs a mother—
a food machine, those miles and miles of guts?
Once upon a time, I confess, I was fat—
gross. Gross belly, gross ass, no bones

227

showing at all. Now I say, "No, thank you," a person
in my own right, and no poor loser. I smile
at her plate of brownies. "Make it disappear,"
she used to say, "Join the clean plate club."
. . . .
I guess that's what I want: to disappear.
That's pretty much what the doctor said, touching
me with his icy stethoscope, prying apart my smile
with that dry popsicle stick, and he said it to Mother.
And now all she says is "What kind of crazy person
would starve herself to death?" There I am, my gut
flipflopping at the smell of hot bread, my bone
marrow turning to hot mud as she eases the fat

glistening duck out of the microwave, the fat
swimming with sweet orange. I wish it would disappear;
that I . . . If I could just let myself suck a bone—
do bones have calories?—I wouldn't need to touch
a bite of anything else. I am so empty. My gut
must be loopy thin as spaghetti. I start to chew my smile.
Is lip-skin fattening? I know Hunger as a person
inside me, half toad, half dwarf. I try to mother

him; I rock and rock and rock him to sleep like a mother
by doing sit-ups. He leans his gargoyle head against the fat
pillow of my heart. But awake he raves, a crazy person,
turned on by my perpetual motion, by the disappearing
tricks of my body; his shaken fist tickles drool to my smile.
He nibbles my vagus nerve for attention. Behind the bone
cage of my chest, he is bad enough. He's worse in my gut
where his stamped foot means binge and puke. Don't touch

me, Hunger, Mother . . . Don't you gut my brain.
Bones are my sovereigns now, I can touch them here and here.
I am a pure person, magic, revealed as I disappear
into my final fat-free smile, where there is no pain.

ROSAMUND'S VISION

by Stuart Mitchner

1983

4 MONOLOGUES
François
C. C. Muldane
Ruby Jones
Konstantine

SETTING: contemporary New Bristol, New Jersey

Rosamund Coleridge, freelance editor and descendant of the great poet, Samuel Taylor Coleridge, is a stranger in a strange land: New Jersey. The down-to-earth young woman has fallen in love with C. C. (Charlie Chaplin) Muldane, a radio talk show host from the Garden State, where she moves to be with him. Rosamund's journey from Bristol, England, to New Bristol, New Jersey, crosses a cultural gap wider than the Atlantic, and she finds herself immersed in a wonderfully strange new world of economic depression and colorful characters. Rosamund takes great delight in dwelling in New Bristol's melting pot, and her observations of the eccentric and eclectic little city highlight this novel.

FRANÇOIS

A friend of Rosamund's describes C. C. Muldane as a zany clown, much like his namesake.

Like all American men of his type, he will be a *boy* forever, afraid to grow up, afraid to face reality! I can tell you, I have seen it. Last night, outside the hotel—listen, you will not believe this. . . . Last night he comes up to me outside the hotel and begins talking about Paris. He tells me he is a student of Paris, that he knows Paris as Balzac knew Paris—this person from *New Jersey*! Oh, yes, and soon he is telling me he is named for Charlie Chaplin, and it's no wonder, all he needs is the little mustache and the cane and *voilà*, you have a bad dream of Charlot, though he's too tall, of course, but listen, next thing I know he has his arm around my shoulder as if we are old comrades and he's being very serious, very confidential because I have told him I live near Buttes-Chaumont in the nineteenth arrondisse-ment. "You've got to watch out up there," he tells me, whispering very loudly, very theatrically. "You can't trust the streets up there, François!" "Oh really, *vraiment?*" I say, to humor him, you know. "And why is that?" "Because the streets up there are sinking," he whispers—such a melodrama this whispering! "Sinking," he tells me. "Caving in, sucking innocent people down into the earth." And now words are not enough, now he must begin his little pantomime, acting out this idiotic tragedy of someone on a promenade raising one hand to greet a friend when the pavement begins to crack and shift under his feet so he is losing his balance, like so, going first this way, then that way, like a drunkard on a treadmill, slipping, sliding, waving his arms, *help, help!* By now it's almost funny, truly like something out of Charlot, you can almost see him going under. "To be safe, always listen for the cough," he tells me. "Because always there is first a sound of coughing from below the street." Like a warning, you see. Cough! a lamppost goes under! Cough! a whole pissoir disappears! Cough! down goes the organ grinder and his monkey! He makes the street cough, no—he *is* the street, he has become the street. Imagine it, my God, a man pretending to be a street. "Balzac would love it!" he tells me. "The streets of Buttes-Chaumont coughing as they swallow their prey!" And when I dare to suggest I have not been taken in in the least by his foolishness! When I turn my back on him and begin to walk away! Then, *then*, in public view, by the riverside, by the— I have forgotten which one, the Tigris or the Euphrates—without a word of warning, he, how shall I tell you, he . . . he—kicked me.

C. C. MULDANE

In this monologue, C. C. defends New Bristol to Rosamund, describing its history and old sites in romantic terms. He particularly delights in the creaky gargoyle-laden Poe Bridge.

You wouldn't believe how many people are afraid of this bridge. They won't admit what really scares 'em though. They'll tell you it's 'cause the foundations are rotten. "Structurally unsafe," they say. It sways and shifts around too much! It's ugly, it's creepy, sneaky, craven, abject—an architectural leper! It smells, it babbles, it sleeps with its mouth open, and if you don't watch out, it'll knife you in the back, folks! But look at it! . . . The poetry of decay, dammit! . . .

. . . Listen: Poe. The name of the bridge. If it was called Long-fellow Bridge or Lincoln Bridge or even Hawthorne Bridge, do you think people would be afraid of it? If it'd been named after Emily Dickinson, would people always be whispering to you about what hap-pened to all the other bridges built on this spot: two burned down, and another done in by the great flood of 1901? But this is Poe Bridge. Just say the name and what does it conjure up? Ravens. Black cats. Men buried alive. Women stuffed up chimneys by orangoutans! . . .

. . . But wait, the joke, the beauty of it is: this bridge wasn't named for Poe. Not the poet, anyway. It was named for a cousin of his, an upstanding fellow, solid citizen, Princeton man, patron of the arts and merchant prince who lived here around the turn of the century. Helped endow the college. A deacon in the church. Also, from what I've heard, a priggish, self-righteous old fart who deserved his fate, which is that nobody crossing this bridge ever thinks of *him*, but of the other one—the black sheep, the drunkard, the morbid buffoon, the sublime Edgar! It's his bridge now. The poet wins, the merchant bites the dust!

RUBY JONES

The wife of the bookstore owner fears for her husband's health. Here, she expresses her concern that he has been "swallowed up" by the carnivorous city of Newark.

He's never been this late before! . . . Did you see the state he was in when he staggered outta here? His eyes were glassy, he couldn't hardly see where he was going. It's bad enough the way he gets whenever he's running off after books, but to go scrounging off to *Newark*, for God's sake, sloshed out of his mind . . . You got any idea what they do to old guys like Jonah when they come scrounging into Newark on a Saturday night in the middle of summer? They eat scroungers like him alive, that's what they do! They see him coming down some crummy street with that scroungy gleam in his eye, they think, "Hey, that old whitey's loaded," and *wham!* that's it, it's all over! I know, I know, I been there. Listen, if you ever saw Newark, honey, you'd think this place was paradise! I mean going to Newark is like committing suicide—it's death! Jesus! Why does he do it? I knew when he left, I tried to tell him, he knows about my dreams, he knows all the times I been right. . . .

Most people, you listen to their hearts, you hear something in there, right? . . . You listen to Jonah, you hear a tick-tick-tick. Jonah's got a heart like a wind-up toy, or like one of those little Baby Ben–type alarm clocks. Some guy hits him or jumps out at him with a knife, it's all over! That's what I see the doctors lookin' at in my dream, they're all like passing around Jonah's toy heart and wondering how that little thing possibly kept him alive all these years.

KONSTANTINE

Rosamund's recalcitrant Greek landlord goes on a rampage and tells her why he can't make the improvements on her apartment that she has requested.

Missus, you got brains . . . . I see you are a very smart lady. You think good. . . . I think good, too. I got brains. My people at home can tell you. They stay in Greece till they die. Not Konstantine. I get out. I come here with only a little bit money. I save. I think. I save more. I think more. Pretty soon I got enough to put down money, buy this place. One day maybe I sell, make back twice my money. Buy another place, two places, maybe a whole street and one day in Greece they hear I am a rich man. Because I *think*.

HEARTBURN

by Nora Ephron

1983

4 MONOLOGUES
Rachel 1
Rachel 2
Rachel 3
Arthur

SETTING: America, 1980s

Heartburn tells the story of Rachel Samstat, a cookbook author whose life is collapsing around her. Rachel describes her life in hilarious detail. She tells us about her analyst, her husband's analyst, her husband's mistress's analyst, her group therapy, her pregnancies, her frustrations, and her heartbreaks. Rachel's story is as touching as it is funny—and chock-full of great recipes, too.

RACHEL 1

This monologue is titled "Rachel Samstat's Jewish Prince Routine" and is a perfect tongue-in-cheek description of her errant husband, Mark.

You know what a Jewish prince is, don't you?
   (*Cocks her eyebrow*)
   If you don't, there's an easy way to recognize one. A simple sentence. "Where's the butter?"
   (*A long pause here because the laugh starts slowly and builds*)
   Okay. We all know where the butter is, don't we?

233

(*A little smile*)
The butter is in the refrigerator.
(*Beat*)
The butter is in the refrigerator in the little compartment in the door marked "Butter."
(*Beat*)
But the Jewish prince doesn't mean "Where's the butter?" He means "Get me the butter." He's too clever to say "Get me" so he says "Where's."
(*Beat*)
And if you say to him—
(*Shouting*)
"in the refrigerator"—
(*Resume normal voice*)
and he goes to look an interesting thing happens, a medical phenomenon that has not been sufficiently remarked upon.
(*Beat*)
The effect of the refrigerator light on the male cornea.
(*Beat*)
Blindness.
(*A long beat*)
"I don't see it anywhere."
(*Pause*)
"Where's the butter" is only one of the ways the Jewish prince reveals himself. Sometimes he puts it a different way. He says, "Is there any butter?"
(*Beat*)
We all know whose fault it is if there isn't, don't we?
(*Beat*)
When he's being really ingenious, he puts it in a way that's meant to sound as if what he needs most of all from you is your incredible wisdom and judgment and creativity. He says, "How do you think the butter would taste with this?"
(*Beat*)
He's usually referring to dry toast.
(*Beat*)

I've always believed that the concept of the Jewish princess was invented by a Jewish prince who couldn't get his wife to fetch him the butter.

RACHEL 2

Our heroine describes the misery of being lumpily pregnant and depressed.

If pregnancy were a book they would cut the last two chapters. The beginning is glorious, especially if you're lucky enough not to have morning sickness and if, like me, you've had small breasts all your life. Suddenly they begin to grow, and you've got them, you've really got them, breasts, darling breasts, and when you walk down the street they bounce, truly they do, they bounce bounce bounce. You find yourself staring in the mirror for long stretches of time, playing with them, cupping them in your hands, pushing them this way and that, making cleavage, making cleavage vanish, standing sideways, leaning over, sticking them out as far as they'll go, breasts, fantastic tender apricot breasts, then charming plucky firm tangerines, and then, just as you were on the verge of peaches, oranges, grapefruit, cantaloupes, God knows what other blue-ribbon county-fair specimens, your stomach starts to grow, and the other fruits are suddenly irrelevant because they're outdistanced by an honest-to-God watermelon. You look more idiotically out of proportion than ever in your life. You feel such nostalgia for the scrawny, imperfect body you left behind; and the commonsense knowledge that you will eventually end up shaped approximately the way you began is all but obliterated by the discomfort of not being able to sleep on your stomach and of peeing ever so slightly every time you cough and of leaking droplets from your breasts onto your good silk blouses and of suddenly finding yourself expert in mysteries you hadn't expected to comprehend until middle age, mysteries like swollen feet, varicose veins, neuritis, neuralgia, acid indigestion and heartburn.

RACHEL 3

In this monologue, Rachel sums up "sensitive" men.

There has been a lot written in recent years about the fact that men don't cry enough. Crying is thought to be a desirable thing, a sign of a mature male sensibility, and it is generally believed that when little boys are taught that it is unmanly to cry, they grow up unable to deal with pain and grief and disappointment and feelings in general. I would like to say two things about this. The first is that I have always believed that crying is a highly overrated activity: women do entirely too much of it, and the last thing we ought to want is for it to become a universal excess. The second thing that I want to say is this: beware of men who cry. It's true that men who cry are sensitive to and in touch with feelings, but the only feelings they tend to be sensitive to and in touch with are their own.

ARTHUR

In this short and funny monologue, Rachel's friend describes to Mark why men cheat.

You know how old you have to be before you stop wanting to fuck strangers? . . . Dead, that's how old. It doesn't stop. It doesn't go away. You put all this energy into suppressing it and telling yourself it's worth it because of what you get in exchange, and then one day someone brushes up against you and you're fourteen years old again and all you want to do is go to a drive-in movie and fuck her brains out in the back seat. But you don't do it because you're not going to be that kind of person, so you go home, and there's your wife, and she wears socks to bed.

THE OLD GRINGO

by Carlos Fuentes

1985

5 MONOLOGUES
Arroyo 1
Old Gringo
Arroyo 2
La Luna
Arroyo 3

SETTING: Mexico, 1914

Carlos Fuentes, Mexico's premier novelist, has long been fascinated with the American journalist Ambrose Bierce, who vanished without a trace in Mexico in 1914. In *The Old Gringo*, Fuentes offers his own account of Bierce's fate.

This is a powerfully mythic tale of three people who are drawn together during Pancho Villa's revolution in Mexico. "To be a gringo in Mexico . . . ah, that is euthanasia." These are the words of the nameless old man who has come to Mexico to die. The gringo appears mysteriously and asks to join Pancho Villa's army, where he meets the young general Tomás Arroyo, a man full of pride and rage. He travels with Arroyo's men to the estate of the Miranda family, where Arroyo was born a servant. Here they encounter Harriet Winslow, an American woman hired by the Mirandas to tutor their children. Since the family fled before the revolution, Harriet has no choice but to accept Arroyo's protection, and eventually, his passion. The enigmatic gringo confides some of his past to Harriet. His son's suicide, his daughter's rejection, and his disillusionment with America have combined to send him to Mexico, where he desires to be shot by Pancho Villa himself. Harriet's own father has deserted both the United States Army and her family, and she is struck by the similarities between the two men.

Arroyo is the keeper of ancient papers signed by the king of Spain which state that the land of Mexico belongs to the people. To hasten his death, perhaps, the old gringo burns the papers, and an enraged Arroyo shoots him. The gringo's body is taken to Pancho Villa, who orders that it be ceremoniously executed. Villa then shoots Arroyo. Harriet returns to the U.S. bearing the body of the old gringo and a lifetime of memories.

ARROYO 1

The young general angrily defends himself to Harriet when she questions his authority over the Miranda estate.

They got bored: the masters of the hacienda came here from time to time, only as a vacation. An overseer administered everything for them. These were no longer the times of the resident landowner who kept a close eye on the cattle and weighed every quintal of grain. When these owners came, they got bored and drank cognac. They fought the young bulls. They also went galloping through the tilled fields, terrifying the peons bent over their humble Chihuahua crops, beans, wild lettuce, spindly wheat; they beat the backs of the weakest men with the flat of a machete, and they lassoed the weakest women and then raped them in the hacienda stables while the mothers of the young gentlemen pretended not to hear the screams of our mothers and the fathers of the young gentlemen drank cognac in the library and said, They're young, this is the age for sowing their wild oats, better now than later. They'll settle down. We did the same. . . .

I am the son of some man's wild oats, the son of chance and misfortune, señorita. No one protected my mother. She was a young girl. She had no husband, no one to defend her. I was born to defend

her. Look, miss. No one defended anyone here. Not even the bulls.
Castrating bulls, yes, that was more exciting than fucking the local
girls. I saw their eyes shine as they cut off their balls, shouting, Ox,
ox, sexless cows!

. . . Who named me general? I tell you who. Misfortune named
me general. Silence named me general, having to hold my tongue.
Here they killed you if you made any noise in bed. If a man and a
woman moaned while they were in bed together, they were whipped.
That was lack of respect for the Mirandas. They were decent people.
We made love and we gave birth without a sound, señorita. Instead
of a voice, I have a paper. Ask your friend the old man. Is he taking
good care of you?

OLD GRINGO

*The mysterious old man confides some of his unhappy past to Harriet. He
is consumed with bitterness and regret.*

Old Bitters. A contemptible, muckraking reporter at the service of a
baron of the press as corrupt as any I denounced in his name. But I
was pure, Miss Harriet, do you believe me? Pure, but bitter. I attacked
the honor and dishonor of all men, without distinction. In my time,
I was feared and hated. Here, have another, and don't look at me like
that. You asked me to be frank. I am going to be. Being frank is what
I do best. . . .

. . . My name was synonymous with coldness, with anti-senti-
mentality. I was the devil's disciple, except that I wouldn't have accepted even the devil as master. Much less God, whom I defamed
with something worse than blasphemy: a curse on everything He had
wrought.

. . . Adore no images save those the coinage of the country shows;
Kill not, for death liberates your foe from persecution's constant woe;
To steal were folly, for 'tis plain, in cheating there is greater gain;
Honor thy parents, and perchance their wills thy fortune may advance.

So I invented myself a new family, the family of my imagination, through my Club of Parenticides, the target of destruction. Good God. Why, I detected signs of cannibalism even at my mother's breast, and I urged lovers to bite one another when they kissed, yes, nip, bite, animals, devour another, bite and . . . ha! . . .

Oh, I had my moment of glory. . . . I became so much a nemesis for California's great corruptor and defaulter that finally he invited me to visit him in his office, and tried to bribe me. "Oh, no," I said, "you can't corrupt me." He laughed, Miss Winslow, as I am laughing now, and said, "Every man has his price." I answered, "You're right. Write me a check for seventy-five million dollars." "In your name or made out to the bearer?" asked Leland Stanford, checkbook open and pen in hand, mocking me with something worse than mockery, the complicity in his mouse-gray eyes. "No," I said, "in the name of the Treasury of the United States, and for the exact amount of the public lands you stole!" Miss Winslow, you never saw a face like Stanford's when I told him that. Ha! . . .

I saw myself as a kind of avenging angel, you see. I was the bitter and sardonic disciple of the devil because I was trying to be as sanctimonious as the people I scorned. You surely understand, you a Methodist, I a Calvinist; each of us trying to be more virtuous than the next, to win the race to see who is the most puritanical, but, in the process, offending whoever is closest to us—for you will see, Miss Harriet, that in fact the only power I had was over my wife and children, not my readers, they were as smug as I, or Hearst; they were every one firmly on the side of morality and rectitude and indignation; each of them said: I'm not the person you're denouncing, no, that's my despicable brother, that other reader. No, I had no power over the targets of my journalistic rage and even less over the men who manipulated my humor and my anger to their own ends. Long live democracy!

ARROYO 2

Tomas tells of an experience in his childhood when he held the keys to the entire Miranda estate in his hand.

I was the witness of the hacienda. Because I was the bastard in the servants' quarters, I was forced to imagine what *they* took for granted. I grew up smelling, breathing, hearing every single room, every single corner of this house. . . . I could breathe with the place and see what each one was doing in his own bedroom, in his bathroom, in the dining room, there was nothing either secret or public for me the little witness, Harriet, I who saw them all, heard them all, imagined and smelled them all by simply breathing with the rhythm they didn't possess because they didn't need it, they took it all for granted, I had to breathe in the hacienda, fill my lungs with its smallest flake of paint, and be the absent witness to every single copulation, hurried or languorous, imaginative or boring, whining or proud, tender or cold, to every single defecation, thick or watery, green or red, smooth or caked with undigested corn, I heard every fart, do you hear, every belch, every spit fall, every pee run, and I saw the scrawny turkeys having their necks twisted, the oxen emasculated, the goats eviscerated and put on the spit . . . and the fevers running high in death and childbirth and children's diseases, I could touch the red velvets and creamy organdies and green taffetas of the hoopskirts and bonnets of the ladies, their long lace nightgowns with the Sacred Heart of Jesus embroidered in front of their cunts: the quivering, humble devotion to the votive lamps quietly sweating away their orange-colored wax as if caught up in a perpetual holy orgasm; contrasting, gringa, with the chandeliers of the vast mansion of stylish, expensive wooden floors and heavy draperies and golden tassels and grandfather clocks and wingtip chairs and rickety dining-room chairs bathed in golden paint—I saw it all, and then one day my old friend, the most ancient man in the hacienda, a man maybe as old as the hacienda itself . . . Graciano with his white stubble on head and chin was the old man charged with winding the clocks every evening, and one night he took me with him.

. . . He just took me by the hand and when we reached the clock in the sitting room where they were all having coffee and brandy after dinner, Graciano gave me the keys to the house. . . .

Gringa: I held these keys in my hand for one instant. They were hot and cold, as if the keys, too, spoke of the life and death of the rooms they opened.

I tried to imagine the rooms the hot keys would open; and which, the cold keys.

It was just an instant.

I clutched the keys as though clutching the whole house. The house was in my power during that instant. They were all in my power. They must have sensed it, because (I am sure) for the first time in anyone's life they stopped their chatter and their drinking and smoking and looked toward the old man winding the clock, and a beautiful lady in green saw me and came up to me, knelt in front of me, and said: "How cute!"

The young lady's appreciation of my nine-year-old cuteness was not shared by the rest of the company. . . .

Then the man who was my father barked: "Graciano, take those keys from the brat."

The old man held out his hand, asking for his gift back.

I understood don Graciano. I gave him the keys, letting him know that now that I had had them in my hands, now I understood that he had made me this wonderful gift for some reason unknown. When I gave back the keys, they were hot, but my hand was cold.

LA LUNA

Arroyo's beautiful Mexican lover tells Harriet a horrific tale of her loveless marriage and the humiliation she suffered at the hands of her abusive husband.

You know, Miss Winslow, we speak in terrible circumlocutions here, we were taught as girls never to say *legs*, but that's what I walk on, never *buttocks*, but that's what I sit on; . . . the body of a man who was God, the body of a man who shared his Godliness with two other men. . . . The church thus became a specter, as did my own home, as did my destiny; we were all specters wandering around in shifts— breakfast, then lessons, in what was known as home economy, then

lunch, then cake making, then prayers, then dinner, then a little
piano, then to undress in the dark and go to bed: like a child, and
you'll say it wasn't bad. But when the life of a man was yoked unto
the life of a child bride, Miss Harriet, then that life became dark,
repetitive, as things are when they come to a standstill and do not
blossom forth from what they were before, before the man, the father,
the husband, was there to see to it that you remained a child bride,
that marriage was a ceremony of fear: fear that you might be punished
for not being a little girl anymore; yet this man takes you, señorita,
and punishes you with his sex for not being a little girl anymore, for
betraying him with your sexual blood and your sexual hair, and I who
soon proved barren was for that reason worse—there was no justifi-
cation for my ugly hairy mound, my fierce hairy armpits, my abundant,
sewer-like menstruations, my irritated, inflated, blooming but milkless
nipples. He draped me in long coarse thick nightgowns with a slit in
front of my cunt and the Sacred Heart of Jesus embroidered there in
thick, red, silvery thread, a frozen emblem of my dirty womanhood,
holy now in this blind encounter with his own untouchable sex: a
quick thrust, a heavy sigh, a few seconds; I knew that he masturbated
many times so as to avoid me, and when his imagination dried up or
he needed me to prove his manliness to himself, even then he would
play with himself first, so as to be instantly ready to thrust it in, let
it come and swiftly withdraw it. I was not to have any pleasure, and
I refused to, with him or without him.

ARROYO 3

*The general has all but destroyed the Miranda estate. Here he addresses his
people and points out that he has saved the mirrored ballroom for them, as
a reminder of the brutal oppression they suffered.*

Look, look what I saved for you, the ballroom, the special places that
used to be only for them. I didn't touch that, I burned all the rest,
the image of your servitude, their store where our children's children
would still owe the shirt off their backs, I burned that, the stables

where the horses ate better than we did, the barracks where the Federal soldiers watched us all day, picking their teeth and sharpening their bayonets, you remember all that? the dining rooms where they stuffed themselves, the bedrooms filled with their fucking and their snoring, the polluted water, the stinking communal latrines, the mad dogs I see and fear in my dreams, my God, I destroyed it all for you, except for this building that, if we survive, will belong to you. A ballroom of mirrors.

I spent my childhood spying. No one knew me. From my hiding places I knew them all. All because one day I discovered the ballroom of mirrors and I discovered I had a face and a body. I could see myself. Tomás Arroyo. For you, Rosario, Remedios, Jesús, Benjamin, José, Colonel García, Chencho Mansalvo, even you La Garduña, in the name of the fleas and the straw sleeping mats, in the name of . . .

I'm no better than any of you, my children. But I am the one who safeguards the papers. Someone has to do it. The papers are the only proof we have that these lands are ours. They are the testament of our ancestors. Without the papers, we're like orphans. I fight, you fight, every one of us fights so that these papers will be respected. Our lives . . . our souls . . .

LESS THAN ZERO

by Bret Easton Ellis

1985

3 MONOLOGUES
Clay 1
Clay 2
Clay 3

SETTING: Los Angeles, 1980s

Less Than Zero is a searing novel of life in L.A.'s fast lane. As narrated by Clay, the privileged son of a film mogul, the story takes the reader on a gut-wrenching roller coaster ride through the clubs, mansions, parties, and restaurants that are the watering holes for Hollywood's extended Brat Pack. Sex 'n' drugs 'n' rock 'n' roll are the only binding elements in Clay's world, and he indulges in all three to excess.

Clay returns to Los Angeles for Christmas from his Eastern college and finds that nothing much has changed since he left. His friends are coke-addicted, desensitized rich kids who have little to no regard for anything beyond their immediate experience. The present is all that matters—that and where to get the best cocaine. Sex is rarely indulged in for love or even for pleasure, but rather to punctuate drug deals.

This nightmare vision of a world of decadence and debauchery is unforgettable, and Clay is a tragic hero in the classical tradition—a modern Odysseus searching in vain for a home that may no longer exist.

CLAY 1

*As he rides home from LAX with Blair, his girlfriend, Clay reveals his
introspective nature as he muses on the concept of merging.*

People are afraid to merge on freeways in Los Angeles. This is the
first thing I hear when I come back to the city. Blair picks me up
from LAX and mutters this under her breath as her car drives up the
onramp. She says, "People are afraid to merge on freeways in Los
Angeles." Though that sentence shouldn't bother me, it stays in my
mind for an uncomfortably long time. Nothing else seems to matter.
Not the fact that I'm eighteen and it's December and the ride on the
plane had been rough and the couple from Santa Barbara, who were
sitting across from me in first class, had gotten pretty drunk. Not the
mud that had splattered the legs of my jeans, which felt kind of cold
and loose, earlier that day in an airport in New Hampshire. Not the
stain on the arm of the wrinkled, damp shirt I wear, a shirt which
had looked fresh and clean this morning. Not the tear on the neck
of my gray argyle vest, which seems vaguely more eastern than before,
especially next to Blair's clean tight jeans and her pale-blue T-shirt.
All of this seems irrelevant next to that one sentence. It seems easier
to hear that people are afraid to merge rather than "I'm pretty sure
Muriel is anorexic" or the singer on the radio crying out about mag-
netic waves. Nothing else seems to matter to me but those ten words.
Not the warm winds, which seem to propel the car down the empty
asphalt freeway, or the faded smell of marijuana which still faintly
permeates Blair's car. All it comes down to is that I'm a boy coming
home for a month and meeting someone whom I haven't seen for four
months and people are afraid to merge.

CLAY 2

*It's Christmas, and Clay relates the events of the day, creating a sad image
of a family suffering from irreparable alienation.*

It's Christmas morning and I'm high on coke, and one of my sisters has given me this pretty expensive leather-bound datebook, the pages are big and white and the dates elegantly printed on top of them, in gold and silver lettering. I thank her and kiss her and all that and she smiles and pours herself another glass of champagne. I tried to keep a datebook one summer, but it didn't work out. I'd get confused and write down things just to write them down and I came to this realization that I didn't do enough things to keep a datebook. I know that I won't use this one and I'll probably take it back to New Hampshire with me and it'll just lie on my desk for three or four months, unused, blank. My mother watches us, sitting on the edge of the couch in the living room, sipping champagne. My sisters open their gifts casually, indifferent. My father looks neat and hard and is writing out checks for my sisters and me and I wonder why he couldn't have written them out before, but I forget about it and look out the window; at the hot wind blowing through the yard. The water in the pool ripples.

CLAY 3

While reading the paper at poolside, Clay watches his younger sisters at play.

While reading the paper at twilight by the pool, I see a story about how a local man tried to bury himself alive in his backyard because it was "so hot, too hot." I read the article a second time and then put the paper down and watch my sisters. They're still wearing their bikinis and sunglasses and they lie beneath the darkening sky and play a game in which they pretend to be dead. They ask me to judge which one of them can look dead the longest; the one who wins gets to push the other into the pool. I watch them and listen to the tape that's playing on the Walkman I'm wearing. The Go-Go's are singing "*I wanna be worlds away! I know things will be okay when I get worlds away.*" Whoever made the tape then let the record skip and I close my eyes and hear them start to sing "Vacation" and when I open my eyes, my sisters are floating face down in the pool, wondering who can look drowned the longest.

THE HANDMAID'S TALE

by Margaret Atwood

1985

5 MONOLOGUES
Offred 1
Offred 2
Offred 3
Offred 4
Moira

SETTING: the Republic of Gilead, the near future

Margaret Atwood's novel depicts a chilling vision of a future in which fundamental religious organizations are able to unite and overthrow the American government. This is the story of Offred, a Handmaid to the Commander's household. Forced into sexual servitude by the fanatic new government of Gilead, Offred has surrendered her identity to the state, where women who have committed the sins of divorce, abortion, or having had a career have become the childbearers for the sterile wives of the Commanders. Women are no longer permitted to read, work, or walk the streets without a specific reason to do so. Handmaids must be covered from head to toe in stifling red robes.

Denied any aspect of humanity, Offred is left alone with her memories of her former life, when she and her husband, Luke, and daughter lived happily together. Certain that Luke has been executed, Offred wonders what has become of her little girl. Offred's only chance for survival in this harsh new world is to become pregnant with the Commander's child. She and the Commander strike up a tentative friendship, which leads to a forbidden excursion to a brothel. There she discovers the fate of Moira, her friend from the Center, the training place for Handmaids. The former journalist has been given the choice of becoming a state prostitute or being sent to the Colonies to work on the body-burning detail in areas of radiation spills.

Offred finally manages to escape via the "Underground Femailroad." Her taped journals are discovered by future anthropologists, who present them as a lesson in history. Her actual fate will never be known.

OFFRED 1

As she bathes, Offred tries desperately to remember her daughter and wonders what the little girl has been told about her.

Cora has run the bath. It steams like a bowl of soup. I take off the rest of the clothes, the overdress, the white shift and petticoat, the red stockings, the loose cotton pantaloons. Pantyhose gives you crotch rot, Moira used to say. Aunt Lydia would never have used an expression like *crotch rot. Unhygienic* was hers. She wanted everything to be very hygienic.

My nakedness is strange to me already. My body seems outdated. Did I really wear bathing suits, at the beach? I did, without thought, among men, without caring that my legs, my arms, my thighs and back were on display, could be seen. *Shameful, immodest.* I avoid looking down at my body, not so much because it's shameful or immodest but because I don't want to see it. I don't want to look at something that determines me so completely.

I step into the water, lie down, let it hold me. The water is soft as hands. I close my eyes, and she's there with me, suddenly, without warning, it must be the smell of the soap. I put my face against the soft hair at the back of her neck and breathe her in, baby powder and child's washed flesh and shampoo, with an undertone, the faint scent of urine. This is the age she is when I'm in the bath. She comes back to me at different ages. This is how I know she's not really a ghost. If she were a ghost she would be the same age always. . . .

She fades, I can't keep her here with me, she's gone now. Maybe

I do think of her as a ghost, the ghost of a dead girl, a little girl who died when she was five. I remember the pictures of us I once had, me holding her, standard poses, mother and baby, locked in a frame, for safety. Behind my closed eyes I can see myself as I am now, sitting beside an open drawer, or a trunk, in the cellar, where the baby clothes are folded away, a lock of hair, cut when she was two, in an envelope, white-blond. It got darker later.

I don't have those things anymore, the clothes and hair. I wonder what happened to all our things. Looted, dumped out, carried away. Confiscated. . . .

I lie, lapped by the water, beside an open drawer that does not exist, and think about a girl who did not die when she was five; who still does exist, I hope, though not for me. Do I exist for her? Am I a picture somewhere, in the dark at the back of her mind?

OFFRED 2

Reduced to stealing pats of butter from the Commander's kitchen to use as a moisturizer, Offred applies the messy stuff with grim resolve.

This is what I do when I'm back in my room:
I take off my clothes and put on my nightgown.

I look for the pat of butter, in the toe of my right shoe, where I hid it after dinner. The cupboard was too warm, the butter is semi-liquid. . . .

I rub the butter over my face, work it into the skin of my hands. There's no longer any hand lotion or face cream, not for us. Such things are considered vanities. We are containers, it's only the insides of our bodies that are important. The outside can become hard and wrinkled, for all they care, like the shell of a nut. . . .

As long as we do this, butter our skin to keep it soft, we can believe that we will some day get out, that we will be touched again, in love or desire. We have ceremonies of our own, private ones.

The butter is greasy and it will go rancid and I will smell like old cheese; but at least it's organic, as they used to say.

To such devices have we descended.

Buttered, I lie on my single bed, flat, like a piece of toast. I can't sleep. In the semidark I stare up at the blind plaster eye in the middle of the ceiling, which stares back down at me, even though it can't see. . . .

I want Luke here so badly. I want to be held and told my name. I want to be valued, in ways that I am not; I want to be more than valuable. I repeat my former name, remind myself of what I once could do, how others saw me.

I want to steal something.

OFFRED 3

The Handmaid remembers watching a television documentary when she was a little girl. It told the story of a woman married to a Nazi who stood by her husband until her death.

I remember a television program I once saw; a rerun, made years before. I must have been seven or eight, too young to understand it. . . . I thought someone had made it up. I suppose all children think that, about any history before their own. If it's only a story, it becomes less frightening.

The program was a documentary, about one of those wars. . . . I don't remember much about it, but I remember the quality of the pictures, the way everything in them seemed to be coated with a mixture of sunlight and dust, and how dark the shadows were under people's eyebrows and along their cheekbones.

The interviews with people still alive then were in color. The one I remember best was with a woman who had been the mistress of a man who had supervised one of the camps where they put the Jews, before they killed them. In ovens, my mother said; but there weren't any pictures of the ovens, so I got some confused notion that these deaths had taken place in kitchens. There is something especially terrifying to a child in that idea. Ovens mean cooking, and cooking comes before eating. I thought these people had been eaten. Which in a way I suppose they had been.

From what they said, the man had been cruel and brutal . . . the mistress had once been very beautiful. There was a black-and-white shot of her and another woman, in the two-piece bathing suits and platform shoes and picture hats of the time; they were wearing cat's-eye sunglasses and sitting in deck chairs by a swimming pool. The swimming pool was beside their house, which was near the camp with the ovens. The woman said she didn't notice much that she found unusual. She denied knowing about the ovens.

. . . She was carefully made up, heavy mascara on her eyelashes, rouge on the bones of her cheeks, over which the skin was stretched like a rubber glove pulled tight. She was wearing pearls.

He was not a monster, she said. People say he was a monster, but he was not one.

What could she have been thinking about? Not much, I guess; not back then, not at the time. She was thinking about how not to think. The times were abnormal. . . . He was not a monster, to her. Probably he had some endearing trait: he whistled, offkey, in the shower, he had a yen for truffles, he called his dog Liebchen and made it sit up for little pieces of raw steak. How easy it is to invent a humanity, for anyone at all. . . . All this she would have believed, because otherwise how could she have kept on living? She was very ordinary, under that beauty. She believed in decency, she was nice to the Jewish maid, or nice enough, nicer than she needed to be.

Several days after this interview with her was filmed, she killed herself. It said that, right on television.

Nobody asked her whether or not she had loved him.

What I remember now, most of all, is the make-up.

OFFRED 4

Here the Handmaid asks the Commander for some proper hand lotion.
Although he agrees to her request, his ignorance of her living conditions
infuriates her.

On the third night I asked him for some hand lotion. I didn't want to sound begging, but I wanted what I could get.

Some what? he said, courteous as ever. . . . He didn't touch me much, except for the one obligatory kiss. No pawing, no heavy breathing, none of that; it would have been out of place, somehow, for him as well as for me.

Hand lotion, I said. Or face lotion. Our skin gets very dry. For some reason I said *our* instead of *my*. I would have liked to ask also for some bath oil, in those little colored globules you used to be able to get, that were so much like magic to me when they existed in the round glass bowl in my mother's bathroom at home. But I thought he wouldn't know what they were. Anyway, they probably weren't made anymore.

Dry? the Commander said, as if he'd never thought about that before. What do you do about it?

We use butter, I said. When we can get it. Or margarine. A lot of the time it's margarine.

Butter, he said, musing. That's very clever. Butter. He laughed.

I could have slapped him.

I think I could get some of that, he said, as if indulging a child's wish for bubble gum. But she might smell it on you. I wondered if this fear of his came from past experience. . . .

I'd be careful, I said. Besides, she's never that close to me. . . .

On the fourth evening he gave me the hand lotion, in an unlabeled plastic bottle. It wasn't very good quality; it smelled faintly of vegetable oil. No Lily of the Valley for me. It may have been something they made up for use in hospitals, on bedsores. But I thanked him anyway.

The trouble is, I said, I don't have anywhere to keep it.

In your room, he said, as if it were obvious.

They'd find it, I said. Someone would find it.

Why? he asked, as if he really didn't know. . . .

They look, I said. They look in all our rooms.

What for? he said.

I think I lost control then, a little. Razor blades, I said. Books, writing, black-market stuff. All the things we aren't supposed to have.

Jesus Christ, you ought to know. My voice was angrier than I'd in-
tended, but he didn't even wince.

Then you'll have to keep it here, he said.

So that's what I did.

He watched me smoothing it over my hands and then my face
with that same air of looking in through the bars. I wanted to turn
my back on him—it was as if he were in the bathroom with me—
but I didn't dare.

For him, I must remember, I am only a whim.

MOIRA

Offred's friend and ally from the Center tells her the story of her escape,
capture, and decision to become a prostitute for the state.

I left that old hag Aunt Elizabeth tied up like a Christmas turkey
behind the furnace. I wanted to kill her, I really felt like it, but now
I'm just as glad I didn't or things would be a lot worse for me. I couldn't
believe how easy it was to get out of the Center. . . .

I kept my shoulders back and chin up and marched along, trying
to think of what to do next. When they busted the press they'd picked
up a lot of the women I knew, and I thought they'd most likely have
the rest by now. I was sure they had a list. We were dumb to think
we could keep it going the way we did, even underground, even when
we'd moved everything out of the office and into people's cellars and
back rooms. So I knew better than to try any of those houses. . . .

They'd set up more checkpoints while we were inside the Center,
they were all over the place. The first one scared the shit out of me.
I came on it suddenly around a corner. I knew it wouldn't look right
if I turned around in full view and went back, so I bluffed it through,
the same as I had at the gate. . . .

By this time I'd hit Mass. Ave. and I knew where I was. And I
knew where they were too. . . . But I had to try it anyway, it was my
only chance. I figured they weren't likely to shoot me. It was about
five o'clock by this time. I was tired of walking, especially that Aunt's

way like a goddamn soldier, poker up the ass, and I hadn't had anything to eat since breakfast. . . .

So these people let me in right away. It was the woman who came to the door. I told her I was doing a questionnaire. I did that so she wouldn't look surprised, in case anyone was watching. But as soon as I was inside the door, I took off the headgear and told them who I was. . . . They didn't like having me there, that much was clear, it made them very nervous. They had two little kids, both under seven. I could see their point. . . .

I was underground it must have been eight or nine months. I was taken from one safe house to another, there were more of those then. They weren't all Quakers, some of them weren't even religious. They were just people who didn't like the way things were going.

I almost made it out. They got me up as far as Salem, then in a truck full of chickens to Maine. I almost puked from the smell; you ever thought what it would be like to be shat on by a truckload of chickens, all of them carsick? They were planning to get me across the border there; not by car or truck, that was already too difficult, but by boat, up the coast. I didn't know that until the actual night, they never told you the next step until right before it was happening. They were careful that way.

So I don't know what happened. . . . Whatever it was, they picked us up just as we were coming out the back door to go down to the dock. . . .

I thought it might be the end, for me. Or back to the Center and the attentions of Aunt Lydia and her steel cable. She enjoyed that, you know. . . .

We didn't end up at the Center though, we went somewhere else. I won't go into what happened after that. I'd rather not talk about it. All I can say is they didn't leave any marks.

When that was over they showed me a movie. Know what it was about? It was about life in the Colonies. In the Colonies, they spend their time cleaning up. They're very clean-minded these days. Sometimes it's just bodies, after a battle. The ones in city ghettos are the worst, they're left around longer, they get rottener. This bunch doesn't like dead bodies lying around, they're afraid of a plague or something.

So the women in the Colonies there do the burning. The other Colonies are worse, though, the toxic dumps and the radiation spills. They figure you've got three years maximum, at those, before your nose falls off and your skin pulls away like rubber gloves. They don't bother to feed you much, or give you protective clothing or anything, it's cheaper not to. . . .

So after that, they said I was too dangerous to be allowed the privilege of returning to the Red Center. They said I would be a corrupting influence. I had my choice, they said, this or the Colonies. Well, shit, nobody but a nun would pick the Colonies. I mean, I'm not a martyr.

ONE MORE SUNDAY

by John D. MacDonald

1985

4 MONOLOGUES
John Tinker Meadows
Glinda Lopez
Carolyn Pennymark
Preacher

SETTING: contemporary America

Roy Owen's wife, Lindy, a journalist, disappears while investigating the Eternal Church of the Believer, an organization so large that it has its own city, schools, offices, banks, and stores. At the heart of this holy conglomerate is its new CEO, John Tinker Meadows. This multi-million-dollar organization is run by state-of-the-art computers and boasts an impressive security system. Written before the televangelist scandals, this is an exceedingly perceptive study of mass media ministries.

JOHN TINKER MEADOWS

This is a sermon given by the head of the Eternal Church. Filled with hellfire and plenty of brimstone, Meadows lashes out against pornography, pollution, immigrants, and the education system.

O MIGHTY GOD, WHY HAVE YOU TURNED YOUR BACK ON THIS GOOD EARTH AND ON YOUR PEOPLE? . . .

What do we see around us?

We see a sickness, a cancer, a corruption on every side.

Through the same wondrous technology which allows us to send this service to the satellite and back to the cable stations and into your homes, filth is being broadcast across the land. Squalid garbage, rated with X's, showing exposed genitalia, scenes of rape and incest and torture. Any child who can reach the dials on the television set can be immersed in this soul-stunting dirt. . . .

Once upon a time our nation was great. Now we sag into despair. The climate changes, the acid rains fall, the great floods and droughts impoverish millions, taking the savings of those who thought they could be provident in these times. . . .

We see rapists and murderers and armed robbers turned loose after a short exposure to that prison environment which gratifies all their hungers and teaches them new criminal arts. . . .

We see the abortionists slaying the children of the future. . . .

Rich men get richer in businesses which produce nothing tangible or useful—only bits of paper. Documents. Bonds and warrants and options and money management accounts. Mergers and spinoffs and liquidations. . . .

We do not really live out there amid all that garbage. We live in the great peaceful country of the spirit. We live in the love of God and His only begotten son, and we live in the confidence that beyond that transition we call death there is eternal life for us who BELIEVE! . . .

. . . Come down now! . . . To be saved means to be safe. When a drowning man is saved, he is brought to the shore, safe from the wild waters. . . . Don't tell yourself you'll think about it, and maybe try it next time. Will there be a next time? Will you have another chance? This is your chance. Now! Come on along. Move down the aisles to me, to us.

GLINDA LOPEZ

A convert whose job it is to solicit contributions from delinquent church members, Glinda feels somewhat guilty about the deceitful role she must play. Here she tells a coworker how she came to the Eternal Church of the Believer.

It was kind of the end of the world for me. . . . I converted when I married Lopez. The priest couldn't seem to get hold of how desperate I felt. I loved Lopez, and for God's sake they had him in diapers, saying "Gooo." How do you rebuild your life? Then one evening I had the television on, it was a cable broadcast, and the Reverend Doctor John Tinker Meadows was sitting behing a desk. . . . He looked right into my eyes and he said very gently, "You are sick at heart, aren't you?" And I answered him! What kind of a nut talks to a television set? The tears busted right out of my eyes and ran down my face and I said, "Yes, yes I am!" . . . I wrote for the literature. I joined the Church. I took Bible lessons. I tithed ten percent. . . . I quit my job and came down here. . . . It isn't perfect. What is? . . . The sun isn't exactly shining yet, but maybe it will. . . . I pray a lot. I believe. I really believe that God is love, bless His holy name.

CAROLYN PENNYMARK

A writer from the same magazine as the missing Lindy Owen, Carolyn tells Roy her opinions about fundamental Christian organizations.

I was listening to some of the sermons that get broadcast from satellites before I came down here. They are strong and they contain a lot of nonsense. Right to life. Abortion is murder. I got over any chance I ever had to fall for that syrup when I did a story on the way little kids have to be warehoused in the big cities. Unwanted and unloved. They're brought into the world and there are not enough people to hold them, walk them, talk to them, bounce them up and down. That's the way babies learn, you know? So what happens? Those kids don't learn to talk until they are between two and three. . . . They are warehoused in cribs where all the attendants can do is work from one end of the huge rooms to the other feeding and changing them and ignoring them. Know what I would like to do if I was queen of the world? I would take a couple of platoons of those big elegant steely-eyed broads who think babies are too dandy to be aborted, and make them work the warehouses for a year, telling them that their job would be to turn those infants into human beings, people who would not have stunted minds and stunted emotions, and who would not go out on the streets like animals to rob and kill the helpless.

. . . Hey, I'm sorry. It made a big impression on me, and I keep on unloading every chance I get. Aside from that, the electronic preachers have a lot of other brands of shit. Amurrica for Amurri-cans. . . . Let's drop the big one on the dirty red Commie menace. Keep that Jap junk off our highways. Help our poor hardworking mil-lionaire farmers. Let's stop the press from destroying Amurrica by shak-ing the people's faith in their institutions. They don't miss a chance. They say the things they know will feed ignorance and hate and su-perstition because the listeners express their approval in money, and money buys more air time.

PREACHER

In this monologue, a rawboned, gifted preacher mesmerizes his audience.

I know what you've been doing in your dumb, sorry lives. . . . Ever' one of you. No exceptions. You and you way over there in the pink necktie. You've been having sick, rotten little thoughts. . . .

. . . You're ashamed of yourself and you're so glad nobody can see into your head. . . . *God can!* . . . In every black heart there's a little voice asking questions. They gone catch me? They gone find out? . . . Some of you got kids worthless as crabgrass, prowling the streets, stealing and fighting and fornicatin' in parked cars with other kids as worthless as they are. What's gone become of my kids? you ask. . . . I got more than I can carry. I'm all bent over double and stupid from the load of sweat and worry and hate and guilt and all the anxieties I got to carry around every living minute of every day, giving me the bad dreams and the bad sweats at night. . . . Running my heart out and not gaining one simple inch. Is that all there is? . . .

And you been *doin'* things! You been grunting away at it in dark places, sweatin' and gaspin'. . . . Grabbing flesh and grabbing money while your soul leaks out of you like spit down a drain. . . . Maybe there's a devil and a hell and eternal fire and all that. But nobody has ever proved it, have they? Nobody has ever come back to tell us all about the weird wild crazy sound of ten billion souls in an agony that never ends, all of them sizzling and screaming at once, screaming for all the rest of eternity, their throats wide open, the eyes starting out of their heads.

I'M HERE TO TELL YOU ABOUT IT! BECAUSE I CAN HEAR THE SCREAMIN'!!

GRYPHON

by Charles Baxter

1985

1 MONOLOGUE
Miss Ferenczi

SETTING: contemporary America

"Gryphon," from the collection *Through the Safety Net*, tells of a young boy's experience with a very unusual substitute teacher. Miss Ferenczi is whimsical, a little off-center, and most definitely controversial. Middle-aged with a gray bun, she is a fascinating character to an imaginative young boy, especially when she breaks free of the lesson plan to talk about Egyptian dead souls or gryphons—mythological creatures with the heads of eagles and the bodies of lions.

MISS FERENCZI

In this monologue, Miss Ferenczi makes her first impression on the class. She is not a run-of-the-mill substitute teacher!

Little boys, why are you bent over together like that? . . . Are you tormenting an animal? Put it back. Please sit down at your desks. I want no cabals this time of day. . . . I asked you to sit down. . . .

This room needs a tree. . . . A large, leafy, shady, deciduous . . . oak. . . .

. . . You may stare at me . . . for a few more seconds, until the bell rings. Then I will permit no more staring. Looking I will permit.

Staring, no. It is impolite to stare, and a sign of bad breeding. You cannot make a social effort while staring. . . .

. . . Good morning, I am Miss Ferenczi, your teacher for the day. I am fairly new to your community, and I don't believe any of you know me. I will therefore start by telling you a story about myself.

. . . For reasons that I shall not go into, my family's fortunes took us to Detroit, then north to dreadful Saginaw, and now here I am in Five Oaks, as your substitute teacher, for today, Thursday, October the eleventh. I believe it will be a good day: All the forecasts coincide. We shall start with your reading lesson. Take out your reading book. I believe it is called *Broad Horizons*, or something along those lines. . . .

. . . No allegiance pledging on the premises today, by my reckoning. Not with so much sunlight coming into the room. A pledge does not suit my mood. . . . Time *is* flying. Take out *Broad Horizons*.

THE FINISHING SCHOOL

by Gail Godwin

1985

3 MONOLOGUES
Justin
Ursula 1
Ursula 2

SETTING: contemporary America

Justin Stokes is a successful actress in her forties. One night she has a dream that prompts her to begin a reminiscence of the momentous summer of her fourteenth year. Justin's recently widowed mother had moved the small family from their home in Virginia to a town in upstate New York, where they are to live with Justin's Aunt Mona. Unhappy and lonely, Justin blames her mother for her newfound misery. She then meets Ursula DeVane, a middle-aged woman who lives with her pianist brother, Julian. Ursula is a vibrant and charismatic woman who becomes Justin's source of inspiration. Like most idols, Ursula soon topples from her pedestal, leaving Justin feeling betrayed.

Now, as an adult, Justin is finally prepared to confront the memory of that summer and see things as they really happened.

JUSTIN

The actress remembers playing Nina in The Sea Gull *in college. Her director has just told her to do a scene in the play as someone enchanted by Trigorin. The actor playing Trigorin is too young, and Justin retreats*

to her dorm room in an effort to summon the proper feelings of enchantment
necessary to play the part.

In college, I played Nina in *The Sea Gull*. I was having trouble with
the scene in which Trigorin is about to leave the Sorin estate and
Nina rushes in to tell him she has decided to run away to Moscow
and become an actress and she will meet him there. The director told
me I acted more thrilled by the prospect of going on stage than I was
by Trigorin. "Be enchanted!" he ordered. "Don't you know what it's
like to be enchanted?" I knew he was right. Part of the problem was
that the actor playing Trigorin was too young. I could not imagine
him as the seasoned literary man, the ironic, pleasure-seeking Trigorin; I could not imagine myself being enchanted by him. But I knew
that if I were going to do the part well, I would have to find a way
to feel enchanted by *Trigorin*, by the essence of enchantment a character named Trigorin personifies. I remember walking slowly back to
my dormitory room, determined to evoke in myself the necessary state
of enchantment. I waited until dusk, until my roommate had gone to
the library; then I opened the windows to the raw spring air. "This
is summer air on a country estate in Russia," I told myself, "and I am
an ambitious, impressionable young girl whose dreams and feelings are
getting too large for her quiet environment. She craves change, she
craves romance, she craves danger—the kind of danger that leads to
transformation. Then, enter suddenly this magnificent older man who
has not only seen and done the things she longs to do, but who seems
bored and sarcastic and even sad about it. She is enchanted by him
not only for the great world he represents, a world she wants to be a
part of, but because, when he looks at her and talks to her, he appears
to know something about her that she longs to know about herself.
She feels somehow that if she can know and possess him . . . if she
allows him to know and possess her . . . that the longed-for, mysterious world will be revealed and she will finally possess herself."

Having reasoned this out, speaking it aloud in my room, I felt
closer to Nina. Now, to imagine the scene.

But here my imagination balked. Perversely, it flashed images of

the face of the too-young actor playing Trigorin in our production;
not the face of the enchanter.

"Be *enchanted*," I ordered myself. "Imagine a convincing enchanter
and the rest will follow."

I tried turning my back on the enchanter. I closed my eyes and
inhaled the chilly spring air. Let the enchanter approach me from
behind. I would not try to picture his features, any features at all. I
would simply permit the essence of enchantment—what it would
mean to me, how it would make me feel—to enter this room.

After I stood there for a while, breathing deeply and getting very
cold, I did feel in the presence of something. I kept my eyes tightly
closed. What was approaching? I was slightly afraid. What if I had
invoked something?

It seemed I had.

Purposely breaking the spell I had invoked, I spun around and
faced an empty room.

But I knew, with a coward's knowledge, that by turning around
when I had, I had limited the Nina a braver me could have portrayed.
Yet, I couldn't do it. I was afraid to confront whatever had been in
the room with me.

URSULA 1

*The older woman relates to Justin her poignant memory of rehearsing in
front of the great George Bernard Shaw.*

I had planned to go to the Royal Academy of Dramatic Art in London,
and I was determined to go. I had waited for years, postponing it again
and again because of my father's long illness. I was twenty-six when
I finally sailed for Europe on the *Normandie*, having buried my father
and completely organized Julie's recital at Carnegie Hall after his grad-
uation from Juilliard. When I got on that ship, I said to myself, "Ursula, now it's your turn." First I wanted to see where my ancestors
had come from, and then I wanted to study acting: those were my
goals. One must never confuse goals with destiny, although one often

leads to the other. In my case, I *was* an actress—when I took the entrance exam at the Royal Academy, the principal, Sir Kenneth Barnes himself, told me I had an innate instinct for acting—but, as it turned out, my destiny was not to make my living by acting. And yet I have the comfort of knowing I was good, the one year I was in London. You've heard of George Bernard Shaw, I hope? . . .

. . . He was very old then, but he looked like a lean, cantankerous prophet, and he said the most wonderful things. One day, when I had been rehearsing for *St. Joan*—the part I had to abandon in order to rush back to America—he came up to me afterward stroking his long white beard, and said, "You'll make a very good Joan, Ursula, if you can remember that in the third scene you do not know you are going to be burned to death in the sixth." . . .

. . . Although my destiny has pointed me in another direction than acting, it gives me pleasure to remember that day: Shaw himself telling me I was going to make a good Joan. How many living actresses have a memory to compare to that?

URSULA 2

Justin's mentor urges her not to fear aging and death, saying that the only things in life to be feared are rigidity and complacency.

You know, I had a *memento mori* while you were in the bathroom, but it turned out to be rather wonderful. . . .

It's a reminder of your mortality. From the Latin: "Remember you must die." I was standing in the lobby, waiting for you, when this old man and his nurse came in from the porch. I suppose I must have stared, something I don't usually do, but he was so very old and white and frail, he was practically transparent with age, and I was impressed by the sheer phenomenon of someone that ancient, standing perfectly erect beside his nurse who was carrying a folded blanket. . . . And I knew he was thinking: One day you will be this old, and one day not

long after that you will die, but it's not horrifying as you think. It was
as if he were trying to tell me: "You are much more afraid of death
and age than I am." And I *smiled* at him. The smile just came out all
by itself. He acknowledged it with a slight bow, and then their elevator
came.

THE ACCIDENTAL TOURIST

by Anne Tyler

1985

3 MONOLOGUES
Muriel 1
Muriel 2
Muriel 3

SETTING: contemporary America

Macon Leary is a man who likes an orderly life. The author of a series of travel books for the businessman who, like himself, hates to travel, he writes for the person who wants to know exactly where to find a McDonald's in London or where to order a good steak in Tokyo.

Macon's well-ordered life is destroyed when his only son is murdered and his wife leaves him. He and Edward, a Welsh Corgi given to biting, begin a new, lonely existence. Then Macon trips over Edward and breaks his leg, forcing him to move back to the home of his eccentric brothers and sister while he recuperates. He meets the wonderfully wacky Muriel when he brings Edward to the boarding kennel where she works, and hires her to give Edward obedience training. Macon soon falls in love with Muriel and bids a fond farewell to his orderly life.

MURIEL 1

This uninhibited and exuberant woman is the divorced mother of a sickly son. She engages the reserved Macon in conversation, telling him how suddenly—overnight—she stopped looking like a movie star.

I guess you're wondering why I'd want a permanent when this hair of mine is so frizzy. Old mop! But I'll be honest, this is not natural. My natural hair is real straight and lanky. Times I've just despaired of it. It was blond when I was a baby, can you believe that? Blond as a fairy-tale princess. People told my mother I'd look like Shirley Temple if she would just curl my hair, and so she did, she rolled my hair on orange juice tins. I had blue eyes, too, and they stayed that way for a long long time, a whole lot longer than most babies' do. People thought I'd look that way forever and they talked about me going into the movies. Seriously! My mother arranged for tap-dance school when I wasn't much more than a toddler. No one ever dreamed my hair would turn on me.

. . . Think what it must feel like, waking up one morning and finding you've gone dark. It near about killed my mother, I can tell you. . . .

. . . So anyway. The reason it's so frizzy is, I got this thing called a body perm. You ever hear of those? They're supposed to just add body but something went wrong. You think *this* is bad! If I was to take a brush to it, my hair would spring straight out from my head. I mean absolutely straight out. Kind of like a fright wig, isn't that what you call it? So I can't even brush it. I get up in the morning and there I am, ready to go. . . .

MURIEL 2

Still chattering to the reticent Macon, Muriel discusses school, boys, her sister, and her frizzy hair.

I've got this little sister? Claire? *Her* hair never turned. She's blond as an angel. Here's what's funny, though: she couldn't care less. Braids her hair back any old how to keep it out of her eyes. Wears raggy jeans and forgets to shave her legs. Doesn't it always work that way? My folks believe she's wonderful. She's the good one and I'm the bad one. It's not her fault, though; I don't blame Claire. People just get fixed in these certain frames of other people's opinions, don't you find that's true? Claire was always Mary in the Nativity Scene at Christmas. Boys in her grade school were always proposing, but there I was in high school and no one proposed to *me*, I can tell you. Aren't high school boys just so frustrating? I mean they'd invite me out and all, like to drive-in movies and things, and they'd act so tense and secret, sneaking one arm around my shoulder inch by inch like they thought I wouldn't notice and then dropping a hand down, you know how they do, lower and lower while all the time staring straight ahead at the movie like it was the most fascinating spectacle they'd ever seen in their lives. You just had to feel sorry for them. But then Monday morning there they were like nothing had taken place, real boisterous and horsing around with their friends and nudging each other when I walked past but not so much as saying hello to me. You think that didn't hurt my feelings? Not one boy in all that time treated me like a steady girlfriend. They'd ask me out on Saturday night and expect me to be so nice to them, but you think they ever ate lunch with me next Monday in the school cafeteria, or walked me from class to class?

MURIEL 3

In this monologue, Muriel confides in Macon about her own failed marriage.

Everybody always asks me, "What is *your* dog like? I bet he's a model of good behavior," they tell me. But you want to hear something funny? I don't own a dog. In fact, the one time I had one around, he ran off. That was Norman's dog, Spook. My ex-husband's. First night we were married, Spook ran off to Norman's mom's. I think he hated me.

We were awful young to get married. I can see that now. I was seventeen. He was eighteen—an only child. His mother's pet. Widowed mother. He had this fresh pink face like a girl's and the shortest hair of any boy in my school and he buttoned his shirt collars all the way to the neck. . . . He made me feel like I had powers. There he was following me around the halls with his arms full of books and I'd say, "Norman? You want to eat lunch with me?" and he'd blush and

say, "Oh, why, uh, you serious?" . . . Got married the fall of senior
year, he was just dying to marry me so what could I say? and at the
wedding my daddy goes to Norman's mom, "Why, I believe I sold you
a car not long ago," but she was too busy crying to take much notice.
That woman carried on like marriage was a fate worse than death.
Then when Spook runs off to her house she tells us, "I suppose I'd
best keep him, it's clear as day he don't like it there with you-all."
With *me* is what she meant. She held it against me I took her son
away.

THE PRIEST'S CONFESSION

by Ai

1986

1 MONOLOGUE
Priest

SETTING: contemporary America

From *Sin*, a collection of poetry by Ai, comes "The Priest's Confession," in which a young man of the cloth struggles with his powerful sexual attraction to a young girl.

PRIEST

From the church's bell tower, a young priest observes the orphan Rosamund and is captivated by her. His fantasies both challenge and strengthen his faith.

I didn't say mass this morning.
I stood in the bell tower
and watched Rosamund, the orphan,
chase butterflies, her laughter
rising, slamming into me,
while the almond scent of her body
wrapped around my neck like a noose.
Let me go, I told her once,
you'll have to let me go,
but she held on.

She was twelve.
She annoyed me,
lying in her little bed—
Tell me a story, Father.
Father, I can't sleep. I miss my mother.
Can I sleep with you?
I carried her into my room—
the crucifix, the bare white walls.
While she slept,
she threw the covers back.
Her cotton gown was wedged above her thighs.
I nearly touched her.
I prayed for deliverance, but none came.
Later, I broke my rosary.
The huge, black wooden beads
clattered to the floor
like ovoid marbles,
and I in my black robe,
a bead on God's own broken rosary,
also rolled there on the floor
in a kind of ecstasy.
I remembered how when I was six
Lizabeta, the witch, blessed me,
rocking in her ladder-back chair,
while I drank pig's blood
and ate it smeared across a slice of bread.
She said, *Eat, Emilio, eat.*
Hell is only as far as your next breath
and heaven unimaginably distant.
Gate after gate stands between you and God,
so why not meet the devil instead?
He at least has time for people.
When she died, the villagers
burned her house.

PRESUMED INNOCENT

by Scott Turow

1987

3 MONOLOGUES
Rusty Sabich 1
Rusty Sabich 2
Rusty Sabich 3

SETTING: contemporary America

A riveting courtroom thriller, *Presumed Innocent* takes its hero, Rusty Sabich, an assistant prosecuting attorney, from an investigation of a murder case with personal implications to an indictment against himself for the same murder. Sabich tells his own story; a compelling account of passionate desire, political intrigue, and homicide. Accused of a vicious and cold-blooded crime, Sabich is totally unable to accept what is happening to him. He seesaws from professional objectivity to a state of crippling emotional turmoil.

RUSTY SABICH 1

How does a man who has been a prosecuting attorney for twelve years feel about politics, the courts, the police? Sabich has a realistic though somewhat cynical view.

God, I think politics is dirty. And the police department is dirtier. The Medici did not live in a world fuller of intrigue. Every secret allegiance in the community comes to bear there. To the alderman and your bookie and your girlfriend. To in-laws, your no-account brother, the guy from the hardware store who has always cut you a deal on screws. To the rookie you have to look out for, the junkie whose base sincerity gets to you, or the snitch you've got to watch. To the licensing inspector who helped out your uncle, or to the lieutenant who you figure has got an in with Bolcarro and is going to make captain soon and maybe more. Your lodge brother, your neighbor, the guy on the beat who's just a plain good sod. Every one of them needs a break. And you give it. In a big city police department . . . there is no such thing as playing by the book. The book got trashed many years ago. Instead, all two thousand guys in blue play it for their own team. . . .

RUSTY SABICH 2

Here, Sabich reveals his desperation, fear, and rage, and the numbness that helps him to cope.

And mostly I am like this, floating and remote. Of course, a great deal of the time is also spent wondering why this has occurred. But I find that at some point along the way my ability to assay ceases. My speculation seems to lead to a dark and frightening periphery, the edge of a black vortex of paranoia and rage from which, thus far, I have instantly withdrawn. I know that on some levels I cannot take much more, and I simply do not. I worry instead about when it will be over, and what the result will be. I want, with a desperation whose size cannot be encompassed by a metaphor, I want all of this never to have taken place; I want things to be as they were before, before I allowed my life to be ransacked by Carolyn and everything that followed. And then there is my consuming anxiety for Nat: What will happen to him? How can he be sheltered? How can I protect him from shame? How can I have brought him to the brink of being, for all purposes, half an orphan? These are in some ways my worst moments: this raging, lashing frustration, this sense of incompetence, these tears. And then, once or twice, in the last weeks, an extraordinary feeling, lighter than air, more soothing than a breeze, a hope that seems to settle in without accounting, and which leaves me with the sense that I have mounted some high rampart and have the courage to simply look ahead.

RUSTY SABICH 3

In this monologue, Sabich loses his grip as he faces mounting terror.

I cannot make things connect. After all these weeks, after all of this, I feel that I am finally going to go to pieces, and I find, stunningly, that as I turn about in the street, I am praying, a habit of my childhood, when I would try to cover my bets with a God in whom I knew I did not much believe.

And now, dear God, I think, dear God in whom I do not believe, I pray to you to stop this, for I am deathly frightened. Dear God, I smell my fear, with an odor as distinct as ozone on the air after a lightning flash. I feel fear so palpably it has a color, an oozing fiery red, and I feel it pitifully in my bones, which ache. My pain is so extreme that I can barely move down this hot avenue, and for a moment cannot, as my backbone bows with fear, . . . and whatever I may have done to make you bring this down upon me, release me, please, I pray, release me. Release me. Dear God in whom I do not believe, dear God, let me go free.

A BIRTHDAY POEM FOR MY LITTLE SISTER

by Edward Field

1987

1 MONOLOGUE
Man

SETTING: contemporary America

In "A Birthday Poem for My Little Sister," a man laments that he and his sister have grown apart as she has grown up.

MAN

An older brother sits down to write a birthday poem for his sister. He remembers her as a child and the suddenness of her growing up.

Dear Barbara, when you had the ear operation
And your hair was cut short like a baby dike
I sat by your crib because I considered you mine
And read you stories of cluck-cluck and moo-moo:
They didn't have to make sense, just noises.

I tried to keep you from masturbating
According to instructions in Parents' Magazine
Which recommended the diversion method rather than threats or
    punishment.
It was no use, your hand preferred your little cunt to toys I offered

Like the ape in the zoo who was jerking off
And all the kids asked their mothers, "What's he doing, ma?"
So the keeper tried to divert him from his hard-on with an ice-cream
     cone
But he shifted the cone to the other hand and licked it while he went
     right on.

And then during the war we were both in uniform
You in the Brownies and I in the Air Force:
When I came home that time with silver wings on
You threw youself into my arms like a furry bundle;
That was your contribution to the war effort, a hug for a soldier
Not bombing the Germans as you were convinced the Brownies were
     going to do.
. . . .
And suddenly you grew up and went out with boys . . . strangers
And you spoke with them in a language like a code
I mean you became a woman, so I'll never have you again:
There must be some taboo against brothers.
Of course now I have someone of my own who reaches to me with
     sweet arms
But the heart is a tree of many seasons
And old loves grow forever deep inside.

The moon rules old loves in their branching
And today the great white magic ball in the sky
Has wound up my heart like on a line of wool
Today on your birthday I remember
How I ran up and down the block knocking on all the doors
To tell the neighbors you were born
(Bored looks, after all you were the sixth child):
I was really announcing that you were born for me and would be mine.

But you grew up and went away and got married
As little girls grow up into women
Leaving us gasping and desperate and hurt.

And we recover and forget, or half-forget
Until sitting down to write a birthday poem we remember every-
    thing—
A little girl on her potty hunched seriously to the business
Or holding all of you at once in my arms, colt, calf, and pussy-cat:
All I mean is, I miss you my little sister.

THE BONFIRE OF THE VANITIES

by Tom Wolfe

1987

3 MONOLOGUES
The Mayor
Reverend Bacon
Judy

SETTING: New York City, 1980s

This is the story of Sherman McCoy, a privileged bonds broker with a fabulous penthouse on Park Avenue. Sherman has it all—a successful wife, an adorable daughter, and a gorgeous mistress. A WASP with a distinguished brokerage firm, Sherman mingles in the world of the elite until one night, when he and Maria, his lover, get lost in the Bronx. Set upon by thugs, they jump in their car with Maria driving, and take off. Sherman hears a thump as Maria backs up and fears that she has hit one of the boys who had attacked them.

Fate is lying in wait for Sherman in the forms of an ambitious assistant DA, Lawrence Kramer, and an unscrupulous and power-hungry black evangelist, the Reverend Bacon. These elements work to bring about the downfall of Sherman McCoy. He is vilified and destroyed by those who would have power for themselves.

THE MAYOR

While attempting to address an unruly crowd at a public meeting in Harlem, the mayor realizes that his political career is finished.

You're not making *me* look bad! You're letting a handful of hustlers in this hall make all of Harlem look bad! You let a couple of loud-mouths call me Goldberg and Hymie, and you don't shout *them* down—you shout *me* down! It's unbelievable! Do you—you hard-working, respectable, God-fearing people of Harlem, you Mrs. Lang-horns, you civic-minded people—do you really think they're your *brothers*! Who have your friends been all these years? The Jews! And you let these hustlers call me a *Charlie*! They call me these things and you say *nothing*? . . .

It'll be on TV. The whole city will see it. They'll love it. Harlem rises up! What a show! Not the hustlers and the operators and the players rise up—but *Harlem* rises up! All of black New York rises up! He's only mayor for *some* of the people! He's the mayor of White New York! Set fire to the mutt! The Italians will watch this on TV, and they'll love it. And the Irish. Even the Wasps. They won't know what they're looking at. They'll sit in their co-ops on Park and Fifth and East Seventy-second Street and Sutton Place, and they'll shiver with the violence of it and enjoy the show. Cattle! Birdbrains! Rosebuds! *Goyim!* You don't even know, do you? Do you really think this is *your* city any longer? Open your eyes! The greatest city of the twentieth century! Do you think *money* will keep it yours?

Come down from your swell co-ops, you general partners and merger lawyers! It's the Third World down there! Puerto Ricans, West Indians, Haitians, Dominicans, Cubans, Colombians, Hondurans, Koreans, Chinese, Thais, Vietnamese, Ecuadorians, Panamanians, Filipinos, Albanians, Senegalese, and Afro-Americans! Go visit the frontiers, you gutless wonders! Morningside Heights, St. Nicholas Park, Washington Heights, Fort Tryon—*por qué pagar más!* The Bronx—the Bronx is finished for you! Riverdale is just a little freeport up there! Pelham Parkway—keep the corridor open to Westchester! Brooklyn—*your* Brooklyn is no more! Brooklyn Heights, Park Slope—little Hong Kongs, that's all! And Queens! Jackson Heights, Elmhurst, Hollis, Jamaica, Ozone Park—whose is it? Do you know? And where does that leave Ridgewood, Bayside, and Forest Hills? Have you ever thought about that! And Staten Island! Do you Saturday do-it-your-selfers really think you're snug in your little rug? You don't think the future knows how to cross a *bridge*? And you, you Wasp charity-ballers sitting on your mounds of inherited money up in your co-ops with the twelve-foot ceilings and the two wings, one for you and one for the help, do you really think you're impregnable? And you German-Jewish financiers who have finally made it into the same buildings, the better to insulate yourselves from the *shtetl* hordes, do you really think you're insulated from the *Third World*?

You poor fatties! You marshmallows! Hens! Cows!

REVEREND BACON

Confronted by two white Episcopal Church representatives, Reverend Bacon explains what has happened to the large sum of money they donated to him for a child care center.

If you people were that worried about the children, you would build the day-care center yourself and hire the best professional people to work in it, people with experience. You wouldn't even talk about hiring the people of the streets. What do the people of the streets know about running a day-care center? No, my friend, you're investing in something else. You're investing in steam control. And you're getting value for money. *Value for money.* . . .

Steam control. It's a capital investment. It's a very good one. You know what capital is? You think it's something you own, don't you. You think it's factories and machines and buildings and land and things you can sell and stocks and money and banks and corporations. You think it's something you own, because you always owned it. You owned all this land. . . . You owned all the land, and out there, out there in . . . Kansas . . . and Oklahoma . . . everybody just lined up, and they said, "On the mark, get set, go!" and a whole lot of white people started running, and there was all this land, and all they had to do was get to it and stand on it, and they owned it, and their white skin was their deed of property . . . see . . . The red man, he was in the way, and he was eliminated. The yellow man, he could lay rails across it, but then he was shut up in Chinatown. And the black man, he was in chains the whole time anyway. And so you owned it all, and you still own it, and so you think capital is owning things. But you are mistaken. Capital is controlling things. Controlling things. You want land in Kansas? You want to exercise your white deed of property? First you got to control Kansas . . . see . . . Controlling things. I don't suppose you ever worked in a boiler room. I worked in a boiler room. People *own* the boilers, but that don't do 'em a bit of good unless they know how to control the *steam* . . . see . . . If you can't *control* . . . the steam, then it's Powder Valley for you and your whole gang. If you ever see a steam boiler go out of control, then you see a whole lot of people running for their lives. And those people, they are not thinking about the return of the investment, they are not thinking about the escrow accounts and the audits and the prudent thing . . . see . . . They are saying, "Great God almighty, I lost control," and they are running for their lives.

JUDY

Sherman has confessed the hit-and-run accident to his estranged wife, Judy, who is hurt and embittered by his previous deception.

Oh, I don't know what you did with your Maria Ruskin, and I don't care. I just don't. That's the least of it, but I don't think you understand that. . . .

What you've done to me, and not just to me. To Campbell. . . .

To your family. We *are* a family. This thing, this thing affecting all of us, it happened two weeks ago, and you said nothing about it. You hid it from me. You sat right next to me, in this very room, and watched that news report, the demonstration, and you didn't say a word. Then the police came to our home—the *police!*—to *our home!*—I even asked you why you were in such a state, and you pretended it was a coincidence. And then—that *same night*—you sat next to your . . . your friend . . . your accomplice . . . your sidekick . . . you tell me what to call her . . . and you still said nothing. You let me think nothing was wrong. You let me go on having my foolish dreams, and you let Campbell go on having her childish dreams, of being a normal little girl in a normal family, playing with her little rabbits and turtles and penguins. The night *the world* was learning of *your escapade*, Campbell was showing you a rabbit she made out of clay. Do you remember that? Do you? And you just *looked* at it and said *all the right things!* And now you come home . . . at the end of the day and you tell me . . . you're . . . gonna . . . be . . . arrested . . . in . . . the . . . morning. . . .

. . . Just listen to what I'm telling you. . . . I'm going to try to help you, and I'm going to try to help Campbell, in any way I can. But I can't give you my love, and I can't give you tenderness. I'm not that good an actress.

SLAVES OF NEW YORK

by Tama Janowitz

1988

2 MONOLOGUES
Eleanor
Borali

SETTING: contemporary New York City

Slaves of New York is a series of witty short stories about life and love in the Big Apple. Some characters, like Eleanor and Stash, her artist boyfriend, reappear throughout the book. Eleanor is a slave to her New York lifestyle and to the city itself, as are all the protagonists in Janowitz's urban tales.

ELEANOR

Eleanor describes her life in New York and the inherent problems of city-dwelling.

So now I'm living in New York, the city, and what it is, it's the apartment situation. I had a little apartment in an old brownstone on the Upper West Side, but it was too expensive, and there were absolutely no inexpensive apartments to be found. Besides, things weren't going all that smoothly for me. I mean, I wasn't exactly earning any money. I thought I'd just move to New York and sell my jewelry— I worked in rubber, shellacked sea horses, plastic James Bond–doll earrings—but it turned out a lot of other girls had already beaten me to it. So it was during this period that I gave up and told Stashua I

was going home to live with my mother. Stash and I had been dating
for six months. That was when Stash said we could try living together.

I'm getting used to it. In the morning I clean up some, I walk his
Dalmatian, Andrew, then I come back and cook Stash two poached
eggs, raisin tea biscuits, coffee with three spoons sugar. . . . I watch
a few soap operas and have a second cup. . . . Well, I'm getting used
to it. He still complains a lot if I leave makeup on the back of the
toilet. . . . I forget what else bugs him. . . .

My friend Abby called me up from Boston. She was all hysterical.
It's like this. She's been living with this guy for a few years . . . but
he still doesn't want to marry her. Just at this time Abby's old flame
reappears. He wants her to move to New York and live with him. . . .

I said, "Abby, don't do it. In the old days, marriages were arranged
by the parents, and maybe you ended up with a jerk but at least you
had the security of marriage, no one could dump you out on the street.
In today's world, it's the slave system. If you live with this guy in New
York, you'll be the slave."

BORALI

*A well-traveled anthropologist regales guests at a dinner about the second
most disgusting meal he was ever served.*

You know, when I was in Singapore I was in a restaurant with a number
of businessmen, all Asian except myself. I was eating something called
rice birds. Actually, I was feeling quite proud of myself for being able
to eat them. Rice birds are tiny birds caught in the wild and deep
fried. They come on a plate beneath a silver cover, and you eat each
bird whole.

. . . The birds are very tiny, you just pop each one in your mouth.
Curiously without flavor, but a lot of crunch. . . . There was a big
cage of monkeys in the corner of the room, which wouldn't have been
allowed in this country, but in many Indonesian and Asian countries
they don't have any regulations about animals in restaurants, you
know, so I didn't think anything of it. But I did notice that in the

center of each table was a large round hole. After the businessmen had eaten their soup, the waiter took one of the monkeys out of the cage and brought it over to the table. All the men nodded and said that it was fine, as if the waiter had brought over a bottle of wine. I began to feel uneasy. The waiter placed the monkey in a sort of stool and strapped it in. The monkey began to scream in a way that was extraordinarily human. Then the waiter brought the monkey underneath the table and placed the chair holding the monkey beneath the hole so that the monkey's head was sticking up through the hole. . . .

The monkey stopped screaming and began to moan. As if in sympathy, the other monkeys in the cage hooted and rattled the bars. I felt very much as if I was witnessing an execution in the gas chamber, though I didn't know what they were going to do to the monkey; but the businessmen were so detached, they seemed like newspaper reporters, watching but not commenting. The waiter came back to the table carrying a large chef's knife. With one stroke he sliced off the top of the monkey's head. The monkey was still alive. Its eyes were moving. At least, I thought it was still alive. Each businessman picked up a spoon, leaned forward, and began to scoop out the brains of the monkey and eat it. . . .

. . . Well, it was all I could do to keep eating my rice birds. I don't like to watch my food die in front of me; I like my meat to be killed and cooked offstage before I eat it. . . .

POSTCARDS FROM THE EDGE

by Carrie Fisher

1988

5 MONOLOGUES
Suzanne 1
Suzanne 2
Producer 1
Suzanne 3
Producer 2

SETTING: Los Angeles, 1980s

This is a humorous and scary tale about love, obsession, drugs, and the total self-absorption of Tinsel Town. The story begins in a drug rehab center, where we are introduced to Suzanne Vale, a beautiful, funny, thirtyish actress who lives in Hollywood's fast lane, and various other Hollywood types. This novel offers firsthand knowledge of the drug-soaked neuroses of the decadent film community.

SUZANNE 1

In this monologue, Suzanne expresses a mix of shame and irony as she regrets giving her phone number to the man who pumped her stomach.

Maybe I shouldn't have given the guy who pumped my stomach my phone number, but who cares? My life is over anyway. Besides, what was I supposed to do? He came up to my room and gave me that dumb stuffed animal that looks like a thumb, and there I was lying in bed twelve hours after an overdose. I wasn't feeling most attractive. I'd thrown up scallops and Percodan on him the night before in the emergency room. I thought that it would be impolite to refuse to give him my number. He probably won't call, anyway. No one will ever call me again.

SUZANNE 2

Our heroine reveals her obsession with her looks and with food.

You know, growing up in L.A., there's such an emphasis on looks. I mean, even in school, I decided what I was gonna wear the next day before I did my homework. There was this girl in my class, Beth Ann Finnerman, whose knee socks always stayed up, and mine seemed to sort of rumple toward the ankles. And I really thought my life would be better if I could do things like have my knee socks stay up. . . .

I've recently found that to keep up my appearance, it has to be through health. I used to think this was corny, but I guess "healthy" equals "attractive" now, you know? . . .

. . . I realize I'm talking a lot, but I don't want you to think I'm nervous. Maybe I *am*, but I don't want you to *think* I am. I skipped lunch today, and whenever I do that I get really wanged out. Also, I should tell you that I'm on Pritikin. My cholesterol is way up. I could have steamed vegetables or a little protein, like chicken. I mean, I'm not like a fanatic, I'm just trying out this Pritikin thing. Anyway, I don't go totally over the edge with this, but I do like to know. To be educated in these things, so when I do choose to eat a refined sugar or an oil or an animal fat product, I at least know what I'm doing. That I'm turning my arteries to pizza. And no eggs, *ever*. . . .

Oh, and I haven't had any caffeine since I started meditating a week ago. . . .

Actually, I'm a failed anorexic. I have anorexic thinking, but I can't seem to muster the behavior. . . .

I could never be bulimic. I could *never* make myself throw up. . . .

. . . Listen, it's too complicated to order something special. We're at Pasta Hello, I'll just have the lasagna. . . .

And one Diet Coke.

PRODUCER 1

A vacuous filmmaker laments his inability to become intimate.

For years I went to hookers, because, let's face it, I'm a very successful producer and writer, and I'm thinking of directing—Columbia really wants me to do a picture for them and direct it, and I feel it's the right time. I mean, I'm certainly developing films I feel I could direct. There's this one about high school that—Anyway, I've been doing this for a while now, and people might like me for my money. So I figured, if someone's gonna like me for my money, it might as well be a hooker, who's gonna like me for my money anyway. There was this girl, though. I don't know that we were in a committed relationship, but we went out for a while. But, you know, I saw other people. It's hard for me to . . . I don't know why, I think . . . When you grow up the way I did, maybe . . .

It's not that I have an intimacy *problem.* I just don't *want* to be intimate. I don't see the point. I mean, I'm very involved in my career and . . . It's not *really* that I don't want to be intimate. I don't want to be *committed.* I don't know, I suppose that's finally just an excuse. My lawyer says I *am* afraid of any real involvement. He lives with a girl, and it just looks like, what's the point? I don't really know what the *point* is. I *love* sex, don't get me wrong. One could even go so far as to say I'm compulsive about sex. I mean, I hope you don't think I'm blunt—I'm sort of known for my bluntness—but, you know, I'd like to have sex with you. I mean, you seem like someone who'd be great to have sex with. . . .

. . . Anyway, I'd *like* to want a relationship, because everybody else does, and it looks nice.

SUZANNE 3

Suzanne examines her habit of finding fault with every man with whom she begins a relationship.

Sometimes I'm with a guy and I think, "I *love* this person. This is *it*." But who I love is who I am when I'm with him. . . . It's me having an excuse to just do myself one more time, proving once again I'm bright and I'm funny and I'm powerful and that I *can*. That I still know how to pour blood in their shark pools. . . .

What I do is, as soon as I know they're devoted, I start to find fault with them. It's not that *I* find fault with them, really. It's the Sleeping Giant in my system who wakes up with a "Fe Fi Fo Fum!" and says, "Yecch! Look at that *hair*." Or, "Oh my God, did you hear the *stupid* thing he said?" The Sleeping Giant who knows no pity is hungry for faults, he hunts them like Easter eggs. . . . There's something in me that wants to warn them, *"Please don't be stupid,"* like people can help it. And then the Giant says, "He's not good enough." And the thing is, I truly—the Sleeping Giant doesn't—but I *truly care* about people. . . .

PRODUCER 2

In this monologue, the producer reveals his shallow nature and despicable chauvinism to his shrink.

It's starting to get on my nerves that I have this reputation for being sexually compulsive. I like sex a lot, I admit it. But, you know, I like food a lot, too, and nobody calls me a foodaholic. I just don't like that people are always putting a label on you. Women *expect* you to come on to them. It's like, if I didn't, they'd think I was a fag or something. Impotent. Well, it's not like I couldn't handle it if somebody thought I was impotent, but I don't *like* the idea of people thinking that. . . .

. . . My dick wants what it wants, and then *I* want what it wants.

. . . You know what I'm talking about. I see a woman mailing a letter, and I see from the way her breast is curved under her sweater that there's no bra and I want to bend her over a car and have her. You know, you see these movies of prehistoric people who just bend people over and, *Bam!* I wish it was like that. It's an appetite men have as mammals, damn it. I've always meant to do some more reading on it.

MAMA DAY

by Gloria Naylor

1988

5 MONOLOGUES
Narrator
Cocoa 1
Cocoa 2
Cocoa 3
Cocoa 4

SETTING: New York City and Willow Springs Island, 1980s

Mama Day is the mythic tale of the Day family of Willow Springs Island, an area claimed by both Georgia and South Carolina and owing allegiance to neither. Miranda "Mama" Day is the co-matriarch of the island, a post she shares with Abigail, her sister. Mama Day is ancient and claims that she does not intend to die. Indeed, at the beginning of the story the world awaits the birth of the new millenium, Mama Day right along with it.

The Days are descended from the union of Bascombe Wade and Sapphira, the beautiful slave and conjuring woman he bought and eventually married. Seven sons and seven grandsons later, Miranda and Abigail are born.

Cocoa is Abigail's granddaughter and the first of the island clan to make her way to New York City, where she leads a happy if somewhat lonely life. Cocoa and George first see each other at a luncheonette, and something stirs in both their hearts. After a tempestuous courtship, they marry and eventually travel back to Willow Springs, where they become victims of old bad blood that runs between Mama Day and Ruby, another woman of the island. Cocoa falls gravely ill as a result of Ruby's witchcraft, and although George is desperate to save his wife, a tremendous storm has destroyed the only bridge leading to the mainland. As Mama Day uses the conjuring skills she inherited from Sapphira Wade to undo Ruby's treachery, George's weak heart bursts, and he dies holding Cocoa's hand.

Cocoa slowly heals and eventually remarries. Mama Day refuses to die, and life on the island of Willow Springs continues as it always has and probably always will.

NARRATOR

The story of Mama Day *is told from several different perspectives: Cocoa's, George's, and nameless ghostly narrators. Here a narrator tells the legend of Willow Springs and Sapphira Wade.*

Everybody knows but nobody talks about the legend of Sapphira Wade. A true conjure woman: satin black, biscuit cream, red as Georgia clay: depending upon which of us takes a mind to her. She could walk through a lightning storm without being touched; grab a bolt of lightning in the palm of her hand; use the heat of lightning to start the kindling going under her medicine pot: depending upon which of us takes a mind to her. She turned the moon into salve, the stars into a swaddling cloth, and healed the wounds of every creature walking up on two or down on four. It ain't about right or wrong, truth or lies; it's about a slave woman who brought a whole new meaning to both them words, soon as you cross over here from beyond the bridge. And somehow, some way, it happened in 1823: she smothered Bascombe Wade in his very bed and lived to tell the story for a thousand days. 1823: married Bascombe Wade, bore him seven sons in just a thousand days, to put a dagger through his kidney and escape the hangman's noose, laughing in a burst of flames. 1823: persuaded Bascombe Wade in a thousand days to deed all his slaves every inch of land in Willow Springs, poisoned him for his trouble, to go on and bear seven sons—by person or persons unknown. . . . The wild card in all this is the thousand days, and we guess if we put our heads together we'd come up with something—which ain't possible since Sapphira Wade don't live in the part of our memory we can use to form words. . . .

. . . We're sitting here in Willow Springs, and you're God-knows-where. It's August 1999—ain't but a slim chance it's the same season where you are. Uh, huh, listen. Really listen this time: the only voice is your own. But you done just heard about the legend of Sapphira Wade, though nobody here breathes her name. You done heard it the way we know it, sitting on our porches and shelling June peas, quieting the midnight cough of a baby, taking apart the engine of a car—you done heard it without a single living soul really saying a word.

COCOA 1

This is Cocoa's description of her first sighting of George in a small coffee shop in Manhattan.

You were picking your teeth with a plastic straw—I know, I know, it wasn't really a straw, it was a coffee stirrer. But, George, let's be fair, there are two little openings in those things that you could possibly suck liquid through if you were desperate enough, so I think I'm justified in calling it a straw since dumps like that Third Avenue coffee shop had no shame in calling it a coffee stirrer, when the stuff they poured into your cup certainly didn't qualify as coffee. . . .

While you finished your lunch and were trying to discreetly get the roast beef from between your teeth, I had twenty minutes before the next cattle call. I was to be in the herd slotted between one and three at the Andrews & Stein Engineering Company. And if my feet hadn't swollen because I'd slipped off my high heels under the table, I might have gone over and offered you one of the mint-flavored toothpicks I always carried around with me. I'd met quite a few guys in restaurants with my box of toothpicks: it was a foolproof way to start up a conversation once I'd checked out what they ordered and how they ate it. The way a man chews can tell you loads about the kind of lover he'll turn out to be. Don't laugh—meat is meat. And you had given those three slabs of roast beef a consideration they didn't deserve, so I actually played with the idea that you might be worth the pain of forcing on my shoes. . . .

But when you walked past me, I let you and the idea go. . . . That much this southern girl had learned: there was a definite relationship between where you met some guy in New York and where he asked you out.

COCOA 2

Cocoa recalls her disastrous first date with George.

Surely, he jests. I swear, that's the first thing that popped into my head when you asked me out again. I don't know where that phrase came from—had to be something from my high school Shakespeare and you had been going on and on about him earlier in the evening. Just proves that Shakespeare didn't have a bit of soul—I don't care if he did write about Othello, Cleopatra, and some slave on a Caribbean island. If he had been in touch with our culture, he would have written somewhere, "Nigger, are you out of your mind?"

. . . But you weren't joking and that only left the alternative that you were psychotic. A guy like you couldn't have been desperate for company. . . . A masochist—had to be that. You were laboring under some *extreme* inferiority complex, thinking yourself such a total piece of junk that you would only date women who wanted absolutely nothing to do with you. The end to all this was clear: a black-lacquered bedroom, hardwood floors, black semigloss walls, and an antique set of razor straps and silk handcuffs. I'd read all about your type in *Cosmo*: ambivalent about your mothers, distant and uncaring fathers, should really be gay but thought other men were too good for you. I kicked myself because I should have known—the yellow roses, the top-drawer restaurant, the open and sensitive attempts and conversation, the gentle manipulation so that I spilled my guts and actually felt good about it. Oh, God, I should have known.

COCOA 3

In this emotional scene, Cocoa relates how George revealed his tragic childhood to her.

It was a gray and cold morning when I came out of that building and saw you standing there across the Drive, leaning against the promenade wall, your trench coat buttoned to the neck with the collar up. It didn't matter how you got there. All those months I had wondered, and this is how it ends. I was too drained to feel anything—shame, fear—when you finally walked over. Your face was still unreadable. And your voice was matter of fact when you took your hand out of your pocket and slapped the living daylights out of me.

"My mother was a whore. And that's why I don't like being called the son of a bitch."

My eyes were still blurred. My bottom lip had been slammed against my teeth and was starting to bleed. Your fingers were like a vise when they gripped mine as you began dragging me up Riverside Drive to Harlem. We reached the pier at 125th Street. Still crushing my hand, you pointed to a brownstone across the way.

"I found out that's where I was born. She was fifteen years old. And she worked out of that house. My father was one of her customers." . . .

"The man who owned this place found me one morning, lying on a stack of newspapers. He called the shelter and they picked me up. I was three months old. . . .

"Later, her body washed up down there. I don't have all the pieces. But there are enough of them to lead me to believe that she was not a bitch." . . .

I don't know how long I closed my eyes, but when I opened them, I asked you to marry me. Next week, you said, if I didn't mind spending my honeymoon in New Orleans.

COCOA 4

George and Cocoa have their first big fight on Willow Springs. This is Cocoa's version.

Our worst fight ever. And it was all your fault. You knew how nervous I was about that night and not a bit of sympathy. That's because you never remembered anything important I told you. No one in Willow Springs thought that anyone would ever want to marry me and half of them were coming just to be sure that you were real. . . . Who could possibly want the leper? It was awful growing up, looking the way I did, on an island of soft brown girls, or burnished ebony girls with their flashing teeth against that deep satin skin. Girls who could summon all the beauty of midnight by standing, arms akimbo, in the full sun. It was torture competing with girls like that. . . .

I know my old school friends were shocked to find out that you were successful, so it meant that you probably drooled on your shirt front or had such a godawful personality that you couldn't get any other woman but me. I couldn't wait for them to meet you so I could gloat. And I was going to be dressed for the part. Eat your hearts out— and he's all mine. I couldn't believe that you would sit there and watch me get ready for a whole hour before deciding that you wanted to fool around. . . . And then to get back at me you refused to tell me what you knew I needed so desperately to hear. . . . I had to be perfect that evening and I was shattered. But it wasn't the time or place for an argument, I was going to ignore you until you made that snide remark about me looking like a Tootsie Pop. Loud—you practically shouted it all the way across the room. . . .

I swear to you, that vase materialized out of nowhere into my hand . . .

APPENDIX:
MONOLOGUES BY GENDER
AND AGE

WOMEN'S ROLES:
1. Girls—age 10 through middle teens
2. Young Women—late teens through twenties
3. Women—thirty to fifty
4. Older Women—fifty and older

MEN'S ROLES:
1. Boys—age 10 through middle teens
2. Young Men—late teens through twenties
3. Men—thirty to fifty
4. Older Men—fifty and older

TYPES OF ROLES:
1. Dramatic
2. Seriocomic
3. Comic

AGE RANGE:

Unless a character is given a specific age, a reasonable range of ages has been provided for each role.

PAGE:

Page on which the appropriate monologue appears.

Book/Story/Poem   *Setting*

BOYS

The Adventures of Huckleberry Finn   pre–Civil War America
Mark Twain
1884

Treasure Island   19th-century England and
Robert Louis Stevenson   the South Seas
1883

YOUNG MEN

Comedies and Satires   19th-century America
Edgar Allan Poe
"Loss of Breath"
1833

Less Than Zero   Los Angeles, 1980s
Bret Easton Ellis
1985

The Priest's Confession   contemporary America
Ai
1986

A Season in Hell   late 19th-century France
Arthur Rimbaud
1873

Character	Type of Role	Age Range	Page
Huck Finn a philosophical American youth (2 monologues)	Seriocomic	10–17	94–95
Jim Hawkins an adventuresome young Englishman	Dramatic	15–19	91–92
Breathless Man an arrogant and self- absorbed man	Comic	20–30	34–35
Clay the jaded son of a Hollywood mogul (3 monologues)	Dramatic	17–22	245–47
Priest a man of the cloth tempted by his love for a girl	Dramatic	20–30	273–74
The Poet a man tormented by his vision of life (3 monologues)	Dramatic	18–25	81–83

Book/Story/Poem	Setting
Things Fall Apart Chinua Achebe 1959	Colonial Nigeria
Crime and Punishment Fyodor Dostoevsky 1866	19th-century Russia
On The Road Jack Kerouac 1955	post–World War II America
Postcards from the Edge Carrie Fisher 1988	Los Angeles, 1980s
Emma Jane Austen 1816	early 19th-century rural England
Emma Jane Austen 1816	early 19th-century rural England
One More Sunday John D. MacDonald 1985	America, 1980s
Sophie's Choice William Styron 1979	post–World War II Brooklyn

Character	Type of Role	Age Range	Page
Obierika a Nigerian who has seen a white man for the first time	Dramatic	20–30	156–157
Raskolnikov a man driven by poverty and starvation to commit murder	Dramatic	20–30	71–72
Sal a WWII vet in search of his country and himself	Seriocomic	20–30	149–150
The Producer a narcissistic film producer (2 monologues)	Comic	20–30	291, 292
Frank Churchill a gentleman in search of a bride	Seriocomic	20–30	21–22
George Knightly a kind and honorable man (2 monologues)	Dramatic	25–35	22–24
Preacher a fire-and-brimstone sermonizer	Dramatic	20–30	260–61
Stingo an aspiring writer	Seriocomic	20s	210–11

Book/Story/Poem	Setting
New Orleans Sketches William Faulkner 1925	New Orleans, 1920s
Green Mansions W. H. Hudson 1916	a South American rain forest at the turn of the century
O Captain! My Captain! Walt Whitman 1865	Civil War America
Rose in Bloom Louisa May Alcott 1876	19th-century Philadelphia
For Whom the Bell Tolls Ernest Hemingway 1940	Spain, 1936

MEN

Behind a Mask Louisa May Alcott 1866	Mountain resort in Europe, 1850s
Don Quixote Miguel de Cervantes Part I 1605 Part II 1615	17th-century Spain

Character	Type of Role	Age Range	Page
Johnny a street tough in love with a beautiful girl	Dramatic	20–30	117–18
Abel an idealistic and passionate man	Dramatic	20–25	114
Young Sailor a man grieves at the death of his leader	Dramatic	20–30	69–70
Mac a considerate gentleman	Dramatic	20s	85–86
Robert Jordan a brave American fighting in the Spanish Civil War	Dramatic	25–35	129–30
Gilbert a passionate man	Dramatic	25–35	76–77
Sancho Panza loyal squire to the mad knight	Dramatic	30s–50s	8

Book/Story/Poem	Setting
Frankenstein Mary Shelley 1818	18th-century Europe
Frankenstein Mary Shelley 1818	18th-century Europe
The Last of the Mohicans James Fenimore Cooper 1826	the early American frontier
The Adventures of Huckleberry Finn Mark Twain 1884	pre–Civil War America
Rebecca of Sunnybrook Farm Kate Douglas Wiggin 1903	turn-of-the-century rural America
Ethan Brand Nathaniel Hawthorne 1837	early 19th-century New England
Treasure Island Robert Louis Stevenson 1883	19th-century England and the South Seas
Comedies and Satires Edgar Allen Poe "How to Write a *Blackwood* Article" 1838	19th-century Philadelphia

Character	Type of Role	Age Range	Page
Victor Frankenstein the infamous scientist, a man haunted by his creation	Dramatic	30s–40s	25–26
The Monster a pathetic creature desperate for love and acceptance (2 monologues)	Dramatic	30s–40s	26–27
Indian a Native American	Dramatic	30s–50s	32–33
Pap Huck's abusive and bigoted father	Seriocomic	40s–50s	95–96
Mr. Cobb a kindhearted man	Seriocomic	50s	101–2
Ethan Brand a man driven to discover the ultimate sin	Dramatic	30s–50s	40–41
Long John Silver a salty old sea dog (2 monologues)	Seriocomic	40s–50s	90–91, 92
Mr. Blackwood publisher of the celebrated *Blackwood Magazine*	Seriocomic	40s–50s	37–38

Book/Story/Poem	Setting
Comedies and Satires Edgar Allan Poe "The Business Man" 1840	19th-century America
Slaves of New York Tama Janowitz 1988 ˙	New York City, 1980s
Things Fall Apart Chinua Achebe 1959	Colonial Nigeria
Wuthering Heights Emily Brontë 1847	19th-century rural England
Jane Eyre Charlotte Brontë 1847	19th-century England
Jane Eyre Charlotte Brontë 1847	19th-century England
The Bonfire of the Vanities Tom Wolfe 1987	New York City, 1980s

Character	Type of Role	Age Range	Page
The Business Man a foolish and narrow-minded man	Seriocomic	30s–50s	38–39
Borali a well-traveled anthropologist	Seriocomic	30s–40s	287–88
Okika a man determined to fight the rule of the whites in his homeland	Dramatic	30s–40s	157–58
Heathcliff a passionate man consumed by his need for revenge	Dramatic	30s–40s	52
Rochester lord of Thornfield, a brooding and arrogant man (2 monologues)	Dramatic	30s–50s	48–49
Mr. Brocklehurst the severe master of the Lowood School for orphans	Dramatic	50s	46
The Mayor an astute politician	Dramatic	40s–50s	281–83

Book/Story/Poem	Setting

The Bonfire of the Vanities
Tom Wolfe
1987

New York City, 1980s

Even Cowgirls Get the Blues
Tom Robbins
1976

America, 1970s

Even Cowgirls Get the Blues
Tom Robbins
1976

America, 1970s

Even Cowgirls Get the Blues
Tom Robbins
1976

America, 1970s

The Company of Women
Mary Gordon
1980

Upstate New York, 1980s

Les Liaisons Dangereuses
Pierre Choderlos de Laclos
1782

18th-century France

Heartburn
Nora Ephron
1983

America, 1980s

The Odyssey
Homer
c. 700 B.C.

ancient Greece

Character	Type of Role	Age Range	Page
Reverend Bacon an ambitious black leader	Dramatic	30s–50s	283–84
The Countess a flamboyant old queen (2 monologues)	Seriocomic	50s–60s	192, 193–94
Julian an American Indian living in New York City	Seriocomic	20s–30s	192–93
The Chink a self-proclaimed wise man	Seriocomic	40s–50s	195–96
Robert an annoyingly self-absorbed man	Seriocomic	30s–40s	221–22
Valmont a sinister nobleman whose greatest pleasure is breaking hearts (2 monologues)	Dramatic	30s–40s	16–17, 18–20
Arthur a man who understands his own nature	Comic	30s–40s	233–35
Odysseus king of Ithaca, a bold adventurer	Dramatic	30s–40s	4–5

Book/Story/Poem	Setting
The Odyssey Homer c. 700 B.C.	ancient Greece
The Old Gringo Carlos Fuentes 1985	Mexico, 1914
Madame Bovary Gustave Flaubert 1857	19th-century rural France
Madame Bovary Gustave Flaubert 1857	19th-century rural France
Rosamund's Vision Stuart Mitchner 1983	New Bristol, New Jersey, 1980s
Rosamund's Vision Stuart Mitchner 1983	New Bristol, New Jersey, 1980s
Rosamund's Vision Stuart Mitchner 1983	New Bristol, New Jersey, 1980s
Just Above My Head James Baldwin 1978	America and Europe, 1970s

Character	Type of Role	Age Range	Page
Agamemnon warrior of Troy, murdered by his wife	Dramatic	40s–50s	5–6
Arroyo a proud and passionate rebel general (3 monologues)	Dramatic	20s–40s	238–39, 240–42, 243–44
The Chemist an opinionated man	Dramatic	40s–50s	53–54
Rodolphe a self-centered despoiler of women	Seriocomic	30s–40s	54–55
François a Frenchman visiting the U.S.	Seriocomic	20s–40s	229–30
C. C. Muldane outrageous and outspoken radio talk show host	Seriocomic	30s–40s	231
Konstantine a philosophical Greek immigrant	Seriocomic	40s–50s	232
Hall a black man mourning the death of his brother (3 monologues)	Dramatic	30s–50s	201–2, 203–5

Book/Story/Poem	*Setting*
Just Above My Head James Baldwin 1978	America and Europe, 1970s
Anna Karenina Leo Tolstoy 1877	Imperial Russia
The Last Enchantment Mary Stewart 1979	Medieval Britain
One More Sunday John MacDonald 1985	America, 1980s
Slaughterhouse Five Kurt Vonnegut, Jr. 1969	post–World War II America
Presumed Innocent Scott Turow 1987	America, 1970s
A Tale of Two Cities Charles Dickens 1859	Paris, during the French Revolution
A Birthday Poem for My Little Sister Edward Field 1987	contemporary America

Character	Type of Role	Age Range	Page
Arthur a man recalling his first homosexual experience	Dramatic	30s–40s	203
Prince an aristocrat concerned for his daughter	Dramatic	40s–50s	87–88
Arthur mytho-poetic king of Britain (2 monologues)	Dramatic	30s–40s	214–16
John Tinker Meadows CEO of the Eternal Church of the Believer	Dramatic	30s–40s	257–58
Narrator a man haunted by his past (2 monologues)	Dramatic	40s–50s	162–64
Rusty Sabich assistant DA tormented by the past (3 monologues)	Dramatic	30s–40s	275–78
Sydney Carton a man redeemed by love	Dramatic	40s	62–63
Man the poet remembers his sister on her birthday	Seriocomic	30s–50s	278–80

Book/Story/Poem	Setting
The White Cliffs Alice Duer Miller 1940	England during World War II
A Tree Grows in Brooklyn Betty Smith 1943	turn-of-the-century Brooklyn
Selected Tales of Guy de Maupassant "Vain Beauty" 1890	late 19th-century France
Selected Tales of Guy de Maupassant "The Horla" 1887	late 19th-century France
Notes from Underground Fyodor Dostoevsky 1864	19th-century Russia
Fahrenheit 451 Ray Bradbury 1953	the future
New Orleans Sketches William Faulkner 1925	New Orleans, 1920s
The French Lieutenant's Woman John Fowles 1969	Victorian England

Character	Type of Role	Age Range	Page
Susan's Father a New England Yankee	Seriocomic	50s–60s	131–32
Johnny Francie's alcoholic father	Dramatic	40s–50s	140–41
Roger de Salnis a man disgusted by the base nature of life	Seriocomic	30s–40s	97–98
The Protagonist a man suffering from paranoid delusions	Dramatic	30s–50s	99
The Underground Man a bitter old misanthrope	Dramatic	50s–60s	67–68
Beatty a fire chief with a warped view of history and life (3 monologues)	Dramatic	30s–50s	145–48
The Cop a public servant reflects upon his life	Seriocomic	50s–60s	118–19
Charles a man obsessed with an enigmatic woman	Dramatic	30s–40s	167–68

Book/Story/Poem	Setting
QB VII Leon Uris 1970	England, 1970s
Portnoy's Complaint Philip Roth 1970	contemporary America
The Magus John Fowles 1977	Greece, 1970s
Candide Voltaire 1759	18th-century Europe, Turkey, and South America
Candide Voltaire 1759	18th-century Europe, Turkey, and South America
The Applicant Sylvia Plath 1961	contemporary America
The Hitchhiker's Guide to the Galaxy Douglas Adams 1979	the Milky Way Galaxy

Character	Type of Role	Age Range	Page
Dr. Adam Kelno a celebrated doctor accused of Nazi war crimes	Dramatic	50s–60s	174–75
Portnoy a man obsessed with his childhood and sex (4 monologues)	Seriocomic	30s–40s	176–81
Conchis a mysterious man haunted by his memory of war	Dramatic	50s–60s	197–99
Dr. Pangloss a man who believes this to be the best of all possible worlds	Seriocomic	50s–60s	10
Cacambo Candide's loyal and pragmatic valet	Seriocomic	20s–40s	13–14
Interviewer interviewing a potential mate	Seriocomic	20s–40s	159–61
Zaphod Beeblebrox two-headed President of the galaxy	Comic	20s–40s	218–20

Book/Story/Poem	Setting

Les Fleurs du Mal
Charles Baudelaire
1857

19th-century France

OLDER MEN

Lost Horizon
James Hilton
1933

Shangri-La: a secret
valley in the Himalayas

Don Quixote
Miguel de Cervantes
Part I 1605
Part II 1615

17th-century Spain

Silas Marner
George Eliot
1861

19th-century rural
England

Things Fall Apart
Chinua Achebe
1959

Colonial Nigeria

The Old Gringo
Carlos Fuentes
1985

Mexico, 1914

Green Mansions
W. H. Hudson
1916

a South American rain
forest at the turn of the
century

Character	Type of Role	Age Range	Page
The Poet the great French poet shares his vision (4 monologues)	Dramatic	30s–50s	57–60
High Lama the spiritual leader of Shangri-La	Dramatic	50s–70s	126–27
Don Quixote the infamous mad knight who insists upon seeing life as it ought to be	Seriocomic	50s–70s	7–8
Silas Marner a bitter man redeemed by the love of a child	Dramatic	50s–70s	66
Uchendu a wise tribal leader	Dramatic	60s–70s	155–56
Old Gringo a bitter man seeking his death in Mexico	Dramatic	60s	239–40
Nuflo a philosophical man living in the forbidden forest with Rima	Seriocomic	60s–70s	115–16

Book/Story/Poem   *Setting*

GIRLS

Through the Looking-Glass   Victorian England
Lewis Carroll
1871

Rebecca of Sunnybrook Farm   turn-of-the century rural
Kate Douglas Wiggin   Maine
1903

Rebecca of Sunnybrook Farm   turn-of-the-century rural
Kate Douglas Wiggin   Maine
1903

A Tree Grows in Brooklyn   early 20th-century
Betty Smith   Brooklyn
1943

Fahrenheit 451   the future
Ray Bradbury
1953

Jane Eyre   19th-century England
Charlotte Brontë
1847

YOUNG WOMEN

The Rainbow   England, 1920s
D. H. Lawrence
1915

Character	Type of Role	Age Range	Page
Alice a precocious English schoolgirl (2 monologues)	Seriocomic	10–16	78–80
Rebecca a lively young girl (2 monologues)	Seriocomic	10–16	101, 102–3
Huldah a vain schoolgirl	Comic	12–17	103–4
Francie a bright girl dreaming of love	Dramatic	15–18	142–43
Clarisse a young girl who questions authority	Dramatic	15–18	144–145
Helen Burns a spiritual-minded young woman	Dramatic	15–19	47
Ursula a passionate and independent woman (4 monologues)	Dramatic	18–25	109–12

Book/Story/Poem	Setting
Candide Voltaire 1759	18th-century Europe, Turkey, and South America
Rose in Bloom Louisa May Alcott 1876	19th-century America
Ivanhoe Sir Walter Scott 1820	England during the reign of Richard Lion-Heart
Green Mansions W. H. Hudson 1916	South American rain forest
Mandala Pearl S. Buck 1970	India, 1960s
The Last Enchantment Mary Stewart 1979	Medieval Britain
Postcards from the Edge Carrie Fisher 1988	Los Angeles, 1980s
Plain Lisa Pamela White Hadas 1979	the studio of Leonardo da Vinci

Character	*Type of Role*	*Age Range*	*Page*
Cunegonde a woman fallen on hard times	Seriocomic	20s	11–12
Rose a free-thinking woman	Dramatic	20s	84–85
Rebecca a beautiful young Jewess in love with Ivanhoe	Dramatic	18–25	28–29
Rima a beautiful native of the rain forest	Dramatic	18–25	114–15
Brooke a woman seeking love	Dramatic	20s	172–173
Nimuë a beautiful enchantress in love with Merlin	Dramatic	20–30	216–17
Suzanne an actress in therapy (3 monologues)	Seriocomic	20–30	289–90, 291–92
Lisa the famous model	Seriocomic	20–30	212–13

Book/Story/Poem	Setting
The Portable Dorothy Parker "Love Song" 1926	America, 1920s
The Portable Dorothy Parker "Symptom Recital" 1926	America, 1920s
The Portable Dorothy Parker "The Telephone Call" 1939	America, 1920s
The Gazebo Raymond Carver 1974	contemporary America
Even Cowgirls Get the Blues Tom Robbins 1976	America, 1970s
If Beale Street Could Talk James Baldwin 1974	New York City, 1970s
To Make a Dragon Move Pamela White Hadas 1983	contemporary America

Character	Type of Role	Age Range	Page
Woman in Love a woman evaluates her love	Seriocomic	20–30	121–22
Bitter Person a woman on the rebound	Comic	20–30	122–23
Waiting Woman a woman anxiously awaits a phone call	Seriocomic	20–30	123–24
Holly a married woman	Dramatic	20–30	182–83
Sissy a perky hitchhiker	Seriocomic	20–30	191–92
Tish a passionate unwed mother (3 monologues)	Dramatic	20s	184–87
Anorexic Woman a woman struggling to control her life	Dramatic	20s	227–28

Book/Story/Poem	Setting

Emma
Jane Austen
1816

early 19th-century
England

Wuthering Heights
Emily Brontë
1847

19th-century England

Patterns
Amy Lowell
1915

Victorian England

WOMEN

Oliver Twist
Charles Dickens
1838

19th-century London

Behind a Mask
Louisa May Alcott
1866

19th-century America

Behind a Mask
Louisa May Alcott
1866

19th-century America

For Whom the Bell Tolls
Ernest Hemingway
1940

Spain, 1936

Character	Type of Role	Age Range	Page
Emma a matchmaker	Seriocomic	20s	23
Catherine a passionate woman (2 monologues)	Dramatic	20s	51–52
Young Englishwoman a woman mourning the death of her love	Dramatic	20–30	105–8
Nancy a barmaid who befriends the poor orphan (2 monologues)	Dramatic	30s	42–44
Jean Muir a scheming actress	Dramatic	30s	74–75
Pauline a woman of great passion (2 monologues)	Dramatic	30s	75–76
Pilar a strong and determined woman married to a guerrilla fighter	Dramatic	30–40	128–29

Book/Story/Poem	Setting
A Tree Grows in Brooklyn Betty Smith 1943	early 20th-century Brooklyn
Selected Tales of Guy de Maupassant "Vain Beauty" 1890	late 19th-century France
New Orleans Sketches William Faulkner 1925	New Orleans, 1920s
The French Lieutenant's Woman John Fowles 1969	Victorian England
Bullet Park John Cheever 1969	suburban New York
The Magus John Fowles 1977	Greece, 1970s
The Women's Room Marilyn French 1979	New England, 1970s
Sophie's Choice William Styron 1979	post–World War II Brooklyn

Character	Type of Role	Age Range	Page
Katie hardworking wife and mother	Dramatic	40s–50s	141–42
The Countess a woman tired of having children	Seriocomic		98–99
Magdalen an aging courtesan	Dramatic	30s–50s	119–20
Sarah a mysterious and independent woman (2 monologues)	Dramatic	30s–40s	165–67
Mrs. Hammer a disgruntled wife	Dramatic	40s–50s	169–70
Alison an unhappy airline stewardess (2 monologues)	Dramatic	30s	199–200
Mira a struggling divorcée	Dramatic	40s–50s	206–7
Sophie a Polish refugee from Auschwitz	Dramatic	30s–40s	209–10

Book/Story/Poem	Setting
The Company of Women Mary Gordon 1980	Upstate New York, 1980s
The Portable Dorothy Parker "Diary of a New York Lady" 1939	New York City, 1930s
The Accidental Tourist Anne Tyler 1985	America, 1980s
The Finishing School Gail Godwin 1985	New York State, 1980s
The Finishing School Gail Godwin 1985	New York State, 1980s
Heartburn Nora Ephron 1983	America, 1980s
Anna Karenina Leo Tolstoy 1877	Imperial Russia
One More Sunday John MacDonald 1985	America, 1980s

Character	Type of Role	Age Range	Page
Felicitas a struggling mother	Dramatic	30s	222–23
New York City Lady a spoiled and vacuous socialite	Comic	30s–40s	124–25
Muriel a wacky dog trainer (3 monologues)	Seriocomic	30s	269–72
Ursula a retired actress (2 monologues)	Dramatic	50s	266–68
Justin a middle-aged actress	Dramatic	40s	264–66
Rachel a sassy cookbook author (3 monologues)	Comic	30s	233–36
Anna a passionate noblewoman destroyed by jealousy	Dramatic	30s–40s	88–89
Glinda Lopez a devoted church worker	Seriocomic	30–50	258–59

Book/Story/Poem	Setting
One More Sunday John D. MacDonald 1985	America, 1980s
Gryphon Charles Baxter 1985	the American Midwest
Even Cowgirls Get the Blues Tom Robbins 1976	America, 1970s
If Beale Street Could Talk James Baldwin 1974	New York City, 1970s
The Bonfire of the Vanities Tom Wolfe 1987	New York City, 1980s
The Cities of the Plain Mona Van Duyn 1982	Sodom and Gomorrah
Les Liaisons Dangereuses Pierre Choderlos de Laclos 1782	18th-century France
Slaves of New York Tama Janowitz 1988	New York City, 1980s

Character	Type of Role	Age Range	Page
Carolyn Pennymark a hard-nosed journalist	Dramatic	30s–40s	259–60
Miss Ferenczi an unusual substitute teacher	Seriocomic	30s–50s	262–63
Bonanza Jellybean a progressive cowgirl	Seriocomic	30s	194–95
Ernestine a protective older sister	Dramatic	30s–40s	187
Judy an estranged wife	Dramatic	30s–40s	284–85
Lot's Wife a pragmatic woman is turned into a pillar of salt	Dramatic	40s–50s	224–26
The Marquise a jaded aristocrat	Dramatic	40s	17–18
Eleanor a woman trying to make a life in New York	Seriocomic	30s	286–87

Book/Story/Poem	Setting

The Odyssey
Homer
c. 700 B.C.

ancient Greece

The Odyssey
Homer

ancient Greece

Madame Bovary
Gustave Flaubert
1857

19th-century rural France

The Old Gringo
Carlos Fuentes
1985

Mexico, 1914

Why I Live at the P.O.
Eudora Welty
1941

China Grove,
Mississippi, 1940s

Wuthering Heights
Emily Brontë
1847

19th-century England

Comedies and Satires
Edgar Allan Poe
"How to Write a *Blackwood* Article"
1838

19th-century Philadelphia

Jane Eyre
Charlotte Brontë
1847

19th-century England

Character	Type of Role	Age Range	Page
Calypso a beautiful sea nymph	Dramatic	30s	3–4
Penelope queen of Ithaca and wife of Odysseus	Dramatic	40s	6
Emma a woman with insatiable longings	Dramatic	30s–40s	55–56
La Luna a long-suffering woman	Dramatic	30s–40s	242–43
Sister a disgruntled family member (4 monologues)	Comic	30s–40s	135–39
Catherine a woman on her deathbed	Dramatic	30s–40s	51–52
Signora Psyche Zenobia a pompous society woman	Comic	30s–40s	36–37
Jane Eyre a strong and independent woman	Dramatic	30s	47–48

Book/Story/Poem	*Setting*
Silas Marner George Eliot 1861	19th-century England
Silas Marner George Eliot 1861	19th-century England
The Empress Catherine and the Princess Dashkof Walter Savage Landor 1824	Imperial Russia
The White Cliffs Alice Duer Miller 1940	England during World War II
The Applicant Sylvia Plath 1961	contemporary America
The Handmaid's Tale Margaret Atwood 1985	the near future
The Handmaid's Tale Margaret Atwood 1985	the near future

Character	Type of Role	Age Range	Page
Dolly Winthrop a kindhearted woman	Seriocomic	40s–50s	65
Pricilla Lammeter a down-to-earth housewife	Seriocomic	30s–40s	65–66
Empress Catherine a scheming woman	Seriocomic	30s–40s	30–31
Susan an American married to an Englishman (2 monologues)	Dramatic	30s	132–34
Interviewer interviewing a potential mate	Seriocomic	20s–30s	159–61
Offred a woman forced into sexual slavery by a fundamentalist state (4 monologues)	Dramatic	30s–40s	249–54
Moira a woman forced into prostitution	Dramatic	30s–40s	254–56

Book/Story/Poem	Setting
Atlas Shrugged Ayn Rand 1957	the near future
Atlas Shrugged Ayn Rand 1957	the near future
Mama Day Gloria Naylor 1988	Willow Springs Island and New York City
Mama Day Gloria Naylor 1988	Willow Springs Island and New York City

OLDER WOMEN

Candide Voltaire 1759	18th-century Europe, Turkey, and South America
Mandala Pearl S. Buck 1970	India, 1960s

Character	Type of Role	Age Range	Page
Dagny Taggart a powerful and passionate woman	Dramatic	30s	152–53
Lillian Reardon a spurned and embittered wife	Dramatic	40s–50s	152
Narrator an unidentified and somewhat ghostly voice of Willow Springs	Seriocomic	open	294–95
Cocoa a wry and passionate woman remembering her dead husband (4 monologues)	Seriocomic	30s–40s	295–98
Old Woman a woman who has known great suffering	Seriocomic	50s–70s	12–13
Grandmother a woman who has known much love	Dramatic	60s–70s	171–72

Book/Story/Poem	*Setting*
Rosamund's Vision Stuart Mitchner 1983	New Bristol, New Jersey, 1980s
The Boarding Denis Johnson 1974	contemporary America

Character	Type of Role	Age Range	Page
Ruby Jones an outspoken neighborhood woman	Seriocomic	50s–60s	231–32
Bag Lady a slow-moving street person	Seriocomic	50s–70s	188–89

BIBLIOGRAPHY

Achebe, Chinua. *Things Fall Apart*. New York: Astor-Honor Inc., 1959.

Paperback. New York: Fawcett Books, 1985.

Adams, Douglas. *The Hitchhiker's Guide to the Galaxy*. New York: Crown, 1979.

Paperback. New York: Pocket Books, 1984.

Ai. "The Priest's Confession," from *Sin*. New York: Houghton Mifflin, 1986.

Alcott, Louisa May. "Behind a Mask," "Pauline's Passion," from *Behind a Mask: The Unknown Thrillers of Louisa May Alcott*. New York: Quill, 1984. Originally published in 1866.

―――. *Rose in Bloom*. Boston: Little, Brown & Co. Originally published in 1876.

Atwood, Margaret. *The Handmaid's Tale*. New York: Houghton Mifflin, 1985.

Paperback. New York: Fawcett Books, 1987.

Austen, Jane. *Emma*. Introduction by Mark Schorer. New York: Dell Publishing Co., 1964. Originally published in 1816.

Baldwin, James. *If Beale Street Could Talk*. New York: Dial Press, 1974.

Paperback. New York: Dell, 1986.

―――. *Just Above My Head*. New York: Dial Press, 1978.

Paperback. New York: Dell, 1980.

Baudelaire, Charles. *Les Fleurs du Mal*. Translated by Richard Howard. Boston: David R. Godine, Publisher, Inc., 1983. Originally published in 1857.

Baxter, Charles. "Gryphon," from *Through the Safety Net*. New York: Viking Penguin, 1985.

Bradbury, Ray. *Fahrenheit 451*. New York: Ballantine Books, 1953.

Paperback. New York: Ballantine Books, 1987.

Brontë, Charlotte. *Jane Eyre*. New York: Bantam Books, 1981. Originally published in 1847, text of third edition Smith and Cornhill, 1848.

Brontë, Emily. *Wuthering Heights*. New York: Pocket Books, 1983. Originally published in 1847.

Buck, Pearl S. *Mandala*. New York: The John Day Company, 1970. Paperback. New York: Pocket Books, 1976.

Carroll, Lewis. *Through the Looking-Glass*. New York: Originally published in 1871. Paperback. New York: Bantam Books, 1981.

Carver, Raymond. *What We Talk About When We Talk About Love*. New York: Alfred A. Knopf, 1981. Paperback. New York: Vintage, 1982.

Cervantes, Miguel de. *Don Quixote*. Translated by Walter Starkie. New York: New American Library, 1964. Originally published in 1605 (part I), 1615 (part II).

Cheever, John. *Bullet Park*. New York: Alfred A. Knopf, 1969. Paperback. New York: Ballantine Books, 1980.

Cooper, James Fenimore. *The Last of the Mohicans*. New York: Viking Penguin, 1986. Originally published in 1826.

de Laclos, Pierre Choderlos. *Les Liaisons Dangereuses*. Translated by Lowell Blair. New York: Bantam Books, 1989. Originally published in 1782.

de Maupassant, Guy. *Selected Tales of Guy de Maupassant*. New York: Random House, 1950. "The Horla" originally published in 1887. "Vain Beauty" originally published in 1890.

Dickens, Charles. *Oliver Twist*. New York: Dodd, 1984. Originally published in 1846.

———. *A Tale of Two Cities*. New York: Oxford University Press, 1988. Originally published in 1859.

Dostoevsky, Fyodor. *Crime and Punishment*. Translated by Constance Garnett. New York: Random House, 1956. Originally published in 1866.

———. *Notes from Underground*. Translated by Constance Garnett. New York: Dial Press, 1945. Originally published in 1864.

Eliot, George. *The Mill on the Floss*. New York: Bantam Books, 1987. Originally published in 1860.

———. *Silas Marner*. New York: Bantam Books, 1986. Originally published in 1861.

Ellis, Bret Easton. *Less Than Zero*. New York: Simon & Schuster, 1985.

Paperback. New York: Viking Penguin, 1987.

Ephron, Nora. *Heartburn*. New York: Alfred A. Knopf, 1983.

Paperback. New York: Pocket Books, 1984.

Faulkner, William. *New Orleans Sketches*. New York: Random House, 1925.

Paperback. New York: Random House, 1968.

Field, Edward. "A Birthday Poem for My Little Sister," from *New and Selected Poems*. Riverdale-on-Hudson, N.Y.: Sheep Meadow Press, 1987.

Fisher, Carrie. *Postcards from the Edge*. New York: Simon & Schuster, 1988.

Paperback. New York: Pocket Books, 1988.

Fitzgerald, F. Scott. *The Great Gatsby*. New York: Charles Scribner & Sons, 1925.

Paperback. New York: Charles Scribner & Sons.

Flaubert, Gustave. *Madame Bovary*. Translated by Gerard Hopkins. New York: Oxford University Press, 1988. Originally published in 1856.

Fowles, John. *The French Lieutenant's Woman*. Boston: Little, Brown & Co., 1969.

Paperback. New York: NAL, 1981.

————. *The Magus*. Boston: Little, Brown & Co., 1977.

Paperback. New York: Dell, 1985.

French, Marilyn. *The Women's Room*. New York: Summit Books, 1977.

Paperback. New York: Ballantine Books, 1989.

Fuentes, Carlos. *The Old Gringo*. Translated by Margaret Sayers Penden and Carlos Fuentes. New York: Farrar, Straus & Giroux, 1985.

Paperback. New York: Harper & Row, 1986.

Gaines, Ernest. *The Autobiography of Miss Jane Pittman*. New York: G. K. Hall, 1971.

Paperback. New York: Bantam Books, 1982.

Godwin, Gail. *The Finishing School*. New York: Viking Penguin, 1985.

Paperback. New York: Avon, 1986.

Gordon, Mary. *The Company of Women*. New York: Random House, 1980.

Paperback. New York: Ballantine Books, 1986.

Hadas, Pamela White. "Plain Lisa," from *Designing Women*. New York: Alfred A. Knopf, 1979.

———. "To Make a Dragon Move," from *Beside Herself (Pocahontas to Patty Hearst)*. New York: Alfred A. Knopf, 1983.

Hawthorne, Nathaniel. "Ethan Brand," from *Twice-Told Tales*. Cleveland: Ohio State University Press, 1974. Originally published in 1837.

Hemingway, Ernest. *For Whom the Bell Tolls*. New York: Charles Scribner & Sons, 1940

Paperback. New York: Charles Scribner & Sons, 1988.

Hilton, James. *Lost Horizon*. New York: Pocket Books, 1933.

Paperback. New York: Pocket Books, 1984.

Homer. *The Odyssey*. Translated by Walter Shewring. New York: Oxford University Press, 1980.

Hudson, W. H. *Green Mansions*. New York: The Modern Library, 1916.

Johnson, Denis. "The Boarding," from *The Incognito Lounge*. New York: Random House, 1974.

Paperback. New York: Random House, 1982.

Kerouac, Jack. *On the Road*. New York: Viking Penguin, 1958.

Paperback. New York: Viking Penguin, 1976.

Landor, Walter Savage. "The Empress Catherine and Princess Dashkof," from *Imaginary Conversations*. Edited by Llewellyn Jones. Chicago: Geographical Publishing Co., 1936.

Lawrence, D. H. *The Rainbow*. New York: Modern Library, 1915.

Paperback. New York: Viking Penguin, 1982.

Lowell, Amy. "Patterns," from *The Oxford Book of American Verse*. New York: Oxford University Press. Originally published in 1915.

MacDonald, John D. *One More Sunday*. New York: Fawcett Books, 1985.

Miller, Alice Duer. *The White Cliffs*. New York: Coward McCann, Inc., 1940.

Mitchner, Stuart. *Rosamund's Vision*. Boston: Little, Brown & Co., 1983.

Naylor, Gloria. *Mama Day*. New York: Houghton Mifflin, 1988. Paperback. New York: Vintage, 1989.

Parker, Dorothy. "Love Song," "Symptom Recital," "The Telephone Call," "Diary of a New York Lady," from *The Portable Dorothy Parker*. New York: Viking Penguin, 1973.

Plath, Sylvia. "The Applicant," from *Ariel*. New York: Harper & Row, 1961. Paperback. New York: Harper & Row, 1981.

Poe, Edgar Allan. *Comedies and Satires*. New York: Viking Penguin, 1987. "Loss of Breath" originally published in 1831. "How to Write a *Blackwood* Article" originally published in 1838. "The Business Man" originally published in 1840.

Rimbaud, Arthur. *A Season in Hell*. Translated by Enid Rhodes. New York: Oxford University Press, 1973. Originally published in 1873.

Robbins, Tom. *Even Cowgirls Get the Blues*. New York: Houghton Mifflin, 1976. Paperback. New York: Bantam, 1984.

Roth, Philip. *Portnoy's Complaint*. New York: Bantam Books, 1970. Paperback. New York: Fawcett Books, 1984.

Scott, Sir Walter. *Ivanhoe*. New York: Bantam Books, 1988. Originally published in 1820.

Shelley, Mary. *Frankenstein*. New York: Bantam Books, 1981. Originally published in 1818.

Smith, Betty. *A Tree Grows in Brooklyn*. New York: Harper & Row, 1943. Paperback. New York: Harper & Row, 1968.

Stevenson, Robert Louis. *Treasure Island*. New York: Dodd, 1985. Originally published in 1883.

Stewart, Mary. *The Last Enchantment*. New York: William Morrow, 1979. Paperback. New York: Fawcett Books, 1984.

Styron, William. *Sophie's Choice*. New York: Random House, 1979. Paperback. New York: Bantam Books, 1982.

Tolstoy, Leo. *Anna Karenina*. Translated by David Magarshac. New York: New American Library, 1961. Originally published in 1877.

Turow, Scott. *Presumed Innocent*. New York: Farrar, Straus & Giroux, 1987.

Paperback. New York: Warner Books, 1988.

Twain, Mark. *The Adventures of Huckleberry Finn*. New York: Viking Penguin, 1986. Originally published in 1884.

Tyler, Anne. *The Accidental Tourist*. New York: Alfred A. Knopf, 1985.

Paperback. New York: Berkley, 1988.

Uris, Leon. *QB VII*. New York: Doubleday, 1970.

Paperback. New York: Bantam Books, 1972.

Van Duyn, Mona. "Cities of the Plain," from *Merciful Disguises*. New York: Atheneum, 1982.

Voltaire. *Candide*. Translated by Lowell Blair. New York: Bantam Books, 1988. Originally published in 1759.

Vonnegut, Kurt, Jr. *Slaughterhouse Five*. New York: Delacorte Press, 1964.

Paperback. New York: Dell, 1970.

Welty, Eudora. "Why I Live at the P.O.," from *A Curtain of Green and Other Stories*. New York: Harcourt Brace Jovanovich, 1968.

Paperback. New York: Harcourt, Brace, Jovanovich, 1982.

Whitman, Walt. "O Captain! My Captain!" from *Leaves of Grass*. New York: Bantam Books, 1983.

Wiggin, Kate Douglas. *Rebecca of Sunnybrook Farm*. New York: Harmony, 1981. Originally published in 1903.

Wolfe, Tom. *The Bonfire of the Vanities*. New York: Farrar, Straus, & Giroux, 1988.

Paperback. New York: Bantam Books, 1988.

P. Roberts, Esquire, G. D'Andelot Belin, Esquire and Houghton Mifflin Company. Reprinted by permission of Houghton Mifflin Company; excerpts from *Mama Day* by Gloria Naylor. Copyright © 1988 by Gloria Naylor. Reprinted by permission of Ticknor & Fields, a Houghton Mifflin Company.

ALFRED A. KNOPF, INC.: Excerpt from *What We Talk About When We Talk About Love* by Raymond Carver. Copyright © 1981 by Raymond Carver; excerpt from *Bedside Herself: Pocahontas to Patty Hearst* by Pamela White Hadas. Copyright © 1983 by Pamela White Hadas; excerpt from *Designing Women: Portraits and Poets* by Pamela White Hadas. Copyright © 1979 by Pamela White Hadas; excerpts from *Heartburn* by Nora Ephron. Copyright © 1983 by Nora Ephron; excerpts from *The Accidental Tourist* by Anne Tyler. Copyright © 1985 by Anne Tyler Modarressi; excerpts from *Bullet Park* by John Cheever. Copyright © 1969 by John Cheever; excerpts from *One More Sunday* by John D. MacDonald. Copyright © 1984 by John D. MacDonald Publishing, Inc. Reprinted by permission of Alfred A. Knopf, Inc.

LITTLE, BROWN AND COMPANY: Excerpts from *The Magus* by John Fowles. Copyright © 1977 by John Fowles Limited; excerpts from *The French Lieutenant's Woman* by John Fowles. Copyright © 1969 by John Fowles Limited. Reprinted by permission of Little, Brown and Company.

MACMILLAN PUBLISHING COMPANY: Excerpts from *Notes from the Underground* by Fyodor Dostoevsky, translated from the Russian by Constance Garnett (New York: Macmillan, 1923). Reprinted by permission of Macmillan Publishing Company.

MCCLELLAND AND STEWART AND HOUGHTON MIFFLIN COMPANY AND JONATHAN CAPE LIMITED: Excerpts from *The Handmaid's Tale* by Margaret Atwood. Copyright © 1985 by O. W. Toad, Ltd. Reprinted by permission of the Canadian Publishers, McClelland and Stewart, Toronto, Houghton Mifflin Company and Jonathan Cape Limited.

STUART MITCHNER: Excerpt from *Rosamund's Vision* by Stuart Mitchner. Copyright © 1983 by Stuart Mitchner. Reprinted by permission of the author.

WILLIAM MORROW & COMPANY, INC. AND HODDER & STOUGHTON LTD: Excerpts from *The Last Enchantment* by Mary Stewart. Copyright © 1983 by Mary Stewart. Reprinted by permission of William Morrow & Company, Inc. and Hodder & Stroughton Ltd.

WILLIAM MORROW & COMPANY, INC. AND JOHN FARQUHARSON LTD.: Excerpts from *Lost Horizon* by James Hilton. Copyright 1933, 1936 by James Hilton. Copyright renewed 1961 by Alice Hilton. Reprinted by permission of William Morrow & Company, Inc. and John Farquharson Ltd.

NEW AMERICAN LIBRARY: Excerpts from *Anna Karenina* by Leo Tolstoy and *Don Quixote* by Manuel Cervantes published by New American Library. Reprinted by permission of New American Library.

OXFORD UNIVERSITY PRESS: Excerpts froom *Madame Bovary* bu Gustav Flaubert, translated by Gerard Hopkins (1981); excerpts from *The Odyssey* by Homer, translated by Walter Shewring (1980). Copyright © 1980 by Walter Shewring; excerpts from *A Season in Hell: The Illuminations* by Arthur Rimbaud, a new translation by Enid Rhodes Peschel. Copyright © 1973 by Oxford University Press, Inc. Reprinted by permission of Oxford University Press. Permission to copy or record in any form or to perform, except within the classroom or an audition, must be cleared with Oxford University Press, Inc., 200 Madison Avenue, New York, NY 10016.

PUTNAM PUBLISHING GROUP: Excerpts from *The White Cliffs* by Alice Duer Miller. Copyright 1940, © 1967 by Denning Miller. Reprinted by permission of The Putnam Publishing Group.

RANDOM HOUSE, INC.: Excerpts from *New Orleans Sketches* by William Faulkner, edited by Carvel Collins. Copyright © 1958 by Carvel Collins; "The Boarding" from *The Incognito Lounge* by Denis Johnson. Copyright © 1982 by Denis Johnson; excerpt from *Final Payments* by Mary Gordon. Copyright © 1978 by Mary Gordon; excerpt from *The Company of Women* by Mary Gordon. Copyright © 1981 by Mary Gordon; excerpts from *Portnoy's Complaint* by Philip Roth. Copyright © 1967, 1968, 1969 by Philip Roth; excerpts from *The Best Stories of Guy de Maupassant*, selected by Saxe Commins. Copyright 1945 by Random House, Inc.; excerpts from *Sophie's Choice* by William Styron. Copyright © 1976, 1978, 1979 by William Styron. Reprinted by permission of Random House, Inc.

CHARLES SCRIBNER'S SONS: Excerpts from *For Whom the Bell Tolls* by Ernest Hemingway. Copyright 1940 by Ernest Hemingway. Copyright renewed 1968 by Mary Hemingway;

ABOUT THE EDITORS

Marisa Smith is President of Smith and Kraus Inc., literary agency. She has edited or packaged five other anthologies of monologues or scenes for actors. She lives in Newbury, Vermont.

Kristin Graham is a faculty member at Southern Connecticut State University where she teaches theater history and acting. She belongs to the Theatre Artists Workshop of Westport, Connecticut and lives in Stratford, Connecticut.